Home and

Harem

Post-Contemporary Interventions

Series Editors: Stanley Fish and

Fredric Jameson

*H*OME AND *H*AREM

Nation, Gender, Empire, and

the Cultures of Travel

Inderpal Grewal

Duke University Press

Durham and London

1996

© 1996 Duke University Press

All rights reserved

Printed in the United States of America on acid-free paper ∞

Typeset in Monotype Fournier by Keystone Typesetting, Inc.

Library of Congress Cataloging-in-Publication Data

Grewal, Inderpal.
Home and harem : nation, gender, empire, and the cultures of travel / Inderpal Grewal.
p.   cm.—(Post-Contemporary Interventions)
Includes bibliographical references and index.
ISBN 0-8223-1731-1 (cloth : alk. paper).—
ISBN 0-8223-1740-0 (pbk. : alk. paper)
1. Travelers' writings, English—History and criticism.   2. Literature and society—
Great Britain—History—19th century.   3. Literature and society—India—History—
19th century.   4. Culture conflict in literature.   5. Great Britain—Relations—India.
6. India—Relations—Great Britain.   7. Intercultural communication.   8. East and
West in literature.   9. Women—Books and reading.   10. Feminism and literature.
11. Sex role in literature.   12. Women—India—History.   13. Imperialism.   I. Title.
PR756.T72G74   1996
820.9'355—dc20   95-36396   CIP

For my mother, Tej Kaur Grewal, and her long interest in an

intellectual life— "Life is an experience . . ."

And my late father, Mehar Singh Grewal, whose encouragement

and faith in my abilities was tremendous

Contents

Acknowledgments

Since this project has taken far too many years, I am particularly grateful to all those who have been so encouraging over this long haul. In particular, Alfred Jessel, whose support, encouragement, and care enable me to enjoy and perform my work; Sukhminder Grewal and Paula Kavathas, who believed that I could be an academic; Kirin and Sonal, who give pleasure and enjoyment and so much love and keep me centered; friend and coauthor for so many projects, Caren Kaplan, whose help, understanding, and enthusiasm is never-failing; Cynthia and Walter Jessel, supportive and wonderful; Maninder and Harkiran and their families; Tejinder and Gurmit, whose hospitality enabled early research for this book; the Santa Cruz and Berkeley groups for the critical study of Colonial Discourse and Jim Clifford's seminars for early inspiration for this project; friends and fellow coalition workers in the Bay Area Asian American feminist community who make living in the United States possible: Deanna Jang, Jayne Lee, Leti Volpp, Beckie Masaki, Mimi Kim, Jacquiline Agtuca, Nina Kabir, Manuela Albuquerque, Lalita Prasad, Viji Sundaram, Chic Dabby; Amarpal Dhaliwal and Jasbir Puar, two special allies; Ken Wissoker, who has been unfailingly supportive and encouraging at Duke University Press; all the wonderful, special readers for this project who gave me so much encouragement; those who read various parts and versions of this book: Ella Shohat, Tani Barlow, Chinosole, Parama Roy, Lisa Bloom, Jenny Sharpe, Mary Layoun, Uma Chakravarty, Houston Baker Jr., Masao Miyoshi, D. A. Miller, Paul Rabinow, and Eric Smoodin; research assistants, Arti Kohli and Randall Williams; a community of scholars whose inspiration is so important: Norma Alarcón, Denise Albanese, Janaki Bakhle, Aditya Behl, Akhil Gupta, Devon Hodges, Abdul Jan Mohammed, Lydia Liu,

David Lloyd, Donald Lowe, Wahneema Lubiano, Lata Mani, Purnima Mankekar, Minoo Moallem, Chandra Mohanty, Roberto Rivera, Robert Stam, Susan Sung, Kamala Visweswaran. I am appreciative of my students at S. F. State who taught me so much and shared their enthusiasm in three years of seminars on colonialism, gender, and travel. My thanks also to San Francisco State University for an Affirmative Action grant that helped complete this book, and to the Humanities Center at U.C. Davis for a fellowship that enabled quite a bit of writing and research.

Introduction

In this book I trace the impact of the nineteenth-century European culture of travel on social divisions in England and India in order to show the cultural basis and effects of imperialism. Gaining power and prominence during that period, this culture is still visible in contemporary cultural productions of travel, mediated in various parts of the world through specific agendas inflected by the geopolitics of the tourist industry. Any cursory glance at travel brochures or of clothing catalogues such as Banana Republic or J. Peterman reveals the desire for the exotic, a disdain for "natives," a search for the "authentic" Other, and a need to merge with the "native" culture and not be seen as a visitor. Other travel narratives that see themselves as outside colonial frameworks often reveal similar imperial discourses; for example, the postmodernist mode of travel writing inscribes metropolitan desires of peripheralizing others within representational practices marked by inequalities.[1]

The rhetoric and discourse of European travel was an eighteenth-century construct that began with the Grand Tour that young men of the English aristocracy undertook as part of their education, a mode of travel that was central to class and gender formation.[2] By the nineteenth century, as John Urry suggests, travel changed from an opportunity for discourse to travel as "eyewitness observation," within which there was developed a visualization of experience and the development of the "gaze."[3] Narratives of exploration, science, discovery, and anthropology recoded such class and gender formations in new forms of authority during the nineteenth century. Romantic discourses of the Self, the "native," and the "savage" performed such recodings. The difference between "travel" and "tourism" contained important forms of English class and gender divisions that separated out the middle- and working-class "day-tripper" from the "traveler" and the "explorer."[4]

Many contemporary critics have maintained these distinctions in problematic ways that reinscribe constructs such as the polarity of "high culture" and "mass culture"; such a scholarship remains Arnoldian in its concept of "culture" as aesthetic education.[5] In her important book *Imperial Eyes*, Mary Louise Pratt describes this form of travel not in terms of an Arnoldian culture but as a Eurocentric form of " 'planetary' consciousness," as "bourgeois forms of authority" that are marked by the imperial metropolis's "need to present and re-present its peripheries and its others continually to itself."[6] Pratt examines the domestic subject of Euroimperialism, and no work on travel can exclude the important matter of subject formation, ideology, and imperialism. The many works that treat travel writing in terms of apolitical genre consideration or merely as descriptions of who went where reiterate imperial gestures of unreflexive objective, anthropological, and scientific representation.[7]

That this mode of travel became and is hegemonic to this day is revealed by the deployment of the term *travel* as a universal form of mobility. Such a use erases or conflates those mobilities that are not part of this Eurocentric, imperialist formation, while including some, like the trope of exile, that reinscribe European hegemonic aesthetic forms.[8] For instance, migration, immigration, deportation, indenture, and slavery are often erased by the universalizing of European travel. In resistance to such aestheticization, this book links scholarly traditions and modes of analysis that are often kept separate and is formulated through the scholarship on these other forms of mobility, even though it does not directly address them.

Gaining essential insights from the extensive work on colonization, slavery, and labor movements contained within ethnic American studies scholarship, this book engages with issues of race and colonization without which understandings of imperialism and travel are impossible.[9] Such studies have enabled me to see that the analysis of travel requires an awareness of the dark side of travel itself, that is, those movements and uprootings that colonization's violence demanded and within which racial formations are constructed.

Outside ethnic American studies scholarship and in the related fields of British imperialism and India, one work that had a formative influence on my project was Rozina Visram's *Ayahs, Lascars and Princes: The Story of Indians in Britain 1700–1947*. This book, which is not at present widely cited or read, examines the unequal relations of Indians in Britain in the eighteenth and nineteenth centuries, describing their presence in Britain as a continuous one for three centuries.[10] This text enabled me to question the erasures of Euroimperial travel and to combine the analysis of European travel with other notions of travel, such as pilgrimage in the context of India and Indian women. Consequently my discussion of two Indian widows' trips to England and America in the second part of this book demonstrates the limits of the discourse of European travel. I will argue that, while Toru Dutt as an upper-class, English-educated Bengali woman frames her narratives of her visit to England within this Euroimperial discourse, Pandita Ramabai's and Parvati Athavale's cannot be so contained.

Another area of study that has influenced this work is the examination of colonial diasporas and borders. Works as various as John Berger's representation of migrant workers in Europe, *A Seventh Man*, Homi Bhabha's essay, "DissemiNation: Time, Narrative, and the Margins of the Modern Nation," Gloria Anzaldua's *Borderlands/La Frontera*, and D. Emily Hicks's *Border Writing* problematize travel as a consolidation of stable unitary identities of nation, class, sexuality, or gender, and suggest forms of Selfhood that evade such consolidations.[11] Yet unlike some writers on "border" issues, my intent is not to represent border crossings or hybridity as embodying a celebratory transnationalism but to question notions of essentialism or authenticity that often are contained in works on this topic.

A third area that forms the background of this book is the scholarship on contemporary issues such as multinational corporations and the movements of capital, labor, objects, and information. Such work is essential to understanding forms of travel and mobility at the present time. In the area of feminist scholarship, work on free trade zones, sex tourism, development issues, labor movements, and women's labor has created an important tradition that illuminates the power relations between women and addresses questions of difference within feminisms and of feminist practices in a transnational world.[12] Within this area of scholarship, "globalization theories" enact new forms of imperial knowledge by privileging the "center" as the "West" and ignoring specific practices of mobility and consumption that are not recognizably "Western."[13]

More than a trope, travel is a metaphor that, I argue, became an ontological discourse central to the relations between Self and Other, between different forms of alterity, between nationalisms, women, races, and classes. It remains so to this day, through continuities and discontinuities. Whether travel is a metaphor of exile, mobility, difference, modernity, or hybridity, it suggests the particular ways in which knowledge of a Self, society, and nation was, and is, within European and North American culture, to be understood and obtained. To examine such uses I work on texts that utilize travel, traveling, and its culture in order to reveal the ways in which movement within space came to be ideologically inscribed in the nineteenth century in British culture, and then to examine how such ideologies were deployed by non-Europeans. Such movements were also crucial for class and gender formation in multiple and linked locations.

Unlike Mary Louise Pratt's important work, this book is not strictly about travel writing. Rather than looking at orientalist texts or the literature of colonialism or of the "contact zones," as Pratt designates the spaces in Asia, Africa, and the Americas that were seen as peripheries, I look at the effects of imperialism on cultural formations that seem to be unrelated to it. Thus, while I have interspersed all through the book many references to the narratives of travel, I also pay attention to cultural productions that are not strictly seen as travel narratives, such as museum guidebooks, essays by English suffragists, and eighteenth-century English landscape aesthetics. This methodology enables me to argue that what Pratt terms "contact zones," that is, the "space of colonial encounters," exist not just in the so-called peripheries, but in the colonial metropolis itself.[14] By tracing the discourses of travel in what I call the constructions of "home" and "harem," that is, the spatial constructions that metaphorically and metonymically construct home and away or empire and nation at various sites in the colonial period through gendered bodies, I argue that the "contact zones" are everywhere and are contained in particular discursive spaces that embody and control the narratives of encounters with difference.

To examine dissimilar deployments of travel, the book is divided into two parts. The first section concerns what colonial discourse called "home" or "England," seen as the domestic space of the English nation. I examine class and gender formation in the Victorian period and Englishwomen's differential relation to and insertion within the commodifications of imperial culture. The second part focuses on what colonial discourse called the "harem," and looks at the ways in which Indian women, inhabiters of these "harem" spaces, saw themselves rather within a contentious and uneven relation to nation articulated as "home." Both "home" and "harem" are, I argue, relational nationalist constructs that require the deployment of women and female bodies within the antagonistic and comparative framework of colonial epistemology.

The orientalist discourse of the "harem" has been critiqued by many scholars in recent years, by Edward Said, Ella Shohat, Malek Alloula, Mervat Hatem, and others, yet continues to be deployed in various forms.[15] While Said's landmark work *Orientalism* influenced this book and many others, scholars such as Gayatri Spivak, Ella Shohat, Tani Barlow, Mary Layoun, Lata Mani, Nupur Choudhury, Margaret Strobel, Uma Chakravarty, and others have pushed further to examine the various modalities in which such constructs existed and continue to do so at the present time;[16] Ella Shohat's work on the Hollywood cinema is an exemplary instance of such scholarship.[17] Spivak's work continues to teach and illuminate through her attention to subaltern subjects of colonial and nationalist agendas.

In this book I have used interchangeably the idea of the harem with those of South Asian related terms such as *zenana, purdah,* or *antahpur.* I have done so to suggest that in colonial discursive practices, all of these lose their specificities to mark a colonial "phantasm," as Malek Alloula calls it, of the incarcerated "Eastern" woman, lacking freedom and embodying submission and sexuality as well as an inaccessibility that colonial power hopes to penetrate.[18] Though the particularities of these colonial formations vary according to colonial rule in various regions, they function as a trope that enables subject formation in many places. My intention, therefore, is not to claim the similarities of forms of veiling or women's lives or locations within domestic spaces in the Middle East or India, but to reveal the utilization of female incarceration as a regulative psychobiography, in Gayatri Spivak's terms, within various patriarchal forms under British colonialism. This narrative operates powerfully within the Romantic discourse of "Othering" pervasive within modernist notions of travel, and enables imaginings of the nation as a community, serving as the "outside" that Geoffrey Bennington argues is necessary for the nation to narrate itself.[19]

"Home" is a crucial category within European travel because it is the space of return and of consolidation of the Self enabled by the encounter with the "Other." In his essay, "Notes on Travel and Theory," James Clifford reveals that in modernist literature the points of departure are clear as are the returns. Home, Clifford states in examining Paul Fussell's book, *Abroad: British Literary Travelling Between the Wars*, "is a stable place to tell one's story, show one's photos, get one's knighthood. . . . home and abroad are still clearly divided, self and other spatially distinct."[20] Clifford goes on to suggest that such a cartography is no longer possible since the "West" in the "postcolonial" moment is a site of "ongoing power and contestation, of centrality and dispersal."[21]

Caren Kaplan critiques Fussell as well, arguing that such modernist notions of travel are forms of imperialist nostalgia that construct both an idealized upper-class traveler and a proper native. Kaplan sees postmodern theories of displacement as problematic, arguing that within constructions of "postcolonial" hybridity there exists a form of periodization that denies the continuations of modernist forms of power relations within contemporary cultural productions of "theory" in the United States.[22] Clifford's notion of a center as a site of "ongoing power and contestation" would suggest that such contestations were not the case in the past, whereas it is rather the erasure of such contestations that marks the domination of European modernist modes of travel. Such attempts at erasure are obvious within the discourse of contemporary "culture wars" in the U.S. public sphere.

The work of Lata Mani, Uma Chakravarty, and Partha Chatterjee has contributed to our understanding of the place of gender in colonialism and anticolonial nationalism within India, especially in relation to consolidations of patriarchy.[23] Lata Mani has argued in her essay, "Contentious Traditions," that the discourse of sati in the nineteenth century reveals that women were the "grounds" for debate between colonizers and the reformists rather than the subjects.[24] Partha

Chatterjee, in the essay "The Nationalist Resolution of the Woman Question," argues that the male nationalists "resolved" the issue of the "woman question" by placing women in the space of home / spirituality in opposition to the male and material world of the marketplace.[25] Nineteenth-century European discourses of the female "domestic" space as a binary opposition to the public space of the market were recuperated within Indian nationalism, enabling the nationalist narrative of the "motherland" of India as independent nation. Though Chatterjee's analysis simplifies a complex phenomenon by focusing only on a few elite, male writers, the list of movies from Bombay cinema, novels, essays, and various cultural productions that use home as a metaphor for nation is endless. The concepts of "home" as nation, as feminized space of domesticity, and as spirituality that was to be kept pure and sacred therefore link up with modernist discourses of travel when they are deployed by Indian nationalists and reformers. Partha Chatterjee has stated that home is "not a complementary but rather the original site on which the hegemonic project of nationalism was launched."[26] While Chatterjee's aim is to recuperate "authentic, creative and plural development of social identities" that he argues were made possible through cultural nationalism, he does not suggest that one identity possible is that of feminist. My project, from a feminist viewpoint, presents home as a place mediated in the colonial discursive space through notions of the harem. I see home not only as the original site of nationalism but also of feminism, since it is here that women can resist nationalist formations by rearticulating them as a site of struggle rather than of resolution.[27]

In the first part of this book, which is devoted to British imperial culture, my goal is to show the effect of travel on an Arnoldian notion of national "culture." In chapters 1 and 2 I analyze in detail the confluence of gender, class, and imperial discourses within the culture of travel in nineteenth-century England. In chapter 3, I examine how the nexus of imperialism, masculinity, and consumerism works to become part of the aesthetic "habitus," as Pierre Bourdieu calls it, within which the education of the English working class and the formation of an English national culture become concerns.[28] Matthew Arnold's notion of himself as the representative aesthetic man, created from literary study that is both moral and political and creating a national culture that is universalist in its scope, indicates the framework of an English education that was orientalist and imperialist.[29]

As texts that reveal clearly the issue of the interpellation of imperial subjects in the nineteenth century, Matthew Arnold's writings show the hegemonic formation of a particular form of nationalist English culture in the nineteenth century. In *Culture and Anarchy*, Arnold suggests that to belong to national life, one had to belong to institutions such as the Anglican Church.[30] This unitary and moral notion of what it means to have "culture" attempts to erase differences in order to impose a hegemonic notion of culture from above. Since Arnold was the son of Thomas Arnold, one of the dominant influences on British education formulated as a classical education, and was responsible for the introduction of English literature as a subject in British schools,[31] the impact of these ideas cannot be underestimated. Few who were educated could escape interpellation as colonizing subjects; while some working-class radicals were profoundly suspicious of such education, many others absorbed it. Yet the notion of national culture was fractured by divisions of gender and class, and of practices that were, as Philip Dodd notes in an essay on Englishness and national culture, "within and against those offered to them from above."[32] My work suggests that imperialism, through imperial education, an emerging consumerism, and varied commodifications of classed and gendered bodies, attempts to suture these divisions.

I examine English culture in the nineteenth century through the lens of colonial discourses. This approach has been utilized in works such as Patrick Brantlinger's *Rule of Darkness*, Lisa Lowe's *Critical Terrains*, Sara Suleri's *The Rhetoric of English India*, Gauri Viswanathan's *Masks of Conquest*, and Jenny Sharpe's *Allegories of Empire*, which have followed in the footsteps of Edward Said's *Orientalism*.[33] My work in a related but different vein leaves aside the canon of English and colonial literature and pays attention to representations of subordinate groups as well. By looking at discourses internal to both colonizer and colonized, I suggest that all constructions of "home" during this period are implicated within colonial discourses. My work follows on the lines Robert Young suggests in *White Mythologies*:

Colonial discourse is placed in the unique position of being able to examine English culture, literature and indeed Englishness in its widest sense, from its determined position on the margins: not questing for the essence of Englishness but examining the representations it has produced for itself of its Other, against and through which it defines itself, together with the functions of such representations in a structure of power in which they are used instrumentally.[34]

To focus merely on what happens in the colony is thus to leave out a major factor in the discourse of colonization. As Svati Joshi says in her introduction to *Rethinking English*, "This is an important agenda . . . , of looking into the social history of England in the nineteenth century, asking how the demands of empire were inscribed into the evolving bourgeois ideologies in Britain, and what effects this development between colony and empire had on the British imagination."[35] While my project remains within this scope, it also suggests that the movements of discourses were not unidirectional, that is, that the "demands of empire" did not always change ideologies in Britain, and quite often the "demands of Britain" affected what went on in the colonies.

One discursive encounter that occurs in many locations is between European women and the women of countries colonized by the Europeans. This encounter is central to constructions of English nationalism, of feminist subjects, and of power relations between women and the formations of feminisms. In *The Rhetoric of English India*, Sara Suleri asks what lines can be drawn between the Anglo-Indian woman's "collusion with, and confinement in, the colonization of the subcontinent?"[36] With this question, Suleri raises an important issue that is being discussed within feminist studies of imperialism and its relation to European women. Rather than seeing it as an oppositional discourse or even as a "dialogue" that presumes coevalness, I take it as a given that various imperial, racist, and gendered narratives were part of the lives of all women who lived in England, and that these varied by class and nationalism. For instance, being Irish might have affected participation in Victorian imperial culture. Kamala Viswewaran points out, for instance, that it is not merely a coincidence that some of the British women working in India against imperialism, such as Margaret Cousins and Annie Besant, were Irish.[37] Even the use of the term *the Anglo-Indian woman* is problematic in that it suggests a monolithic category, whereas British women who went to India came from different classes; the duration of their stay in India varied considerably, so that it is unclear what qualified some women to be called "Anglo-Indian" as opposed to "English" women. Margaret Strobel's research reveals that the consolidation of this category needs to be questioned.[38]

How Englishwomen participated in these discourses of travel is another question to be considered, one that I take up in chapter 2. Recently there has been a spate of new publications on this question. From Helen Calloway's book on Englishwomen in Nigeria, *Gender and Colonialism*, to Dea Birkett's *Spinsters Abroad*, Strobel and Choudhury's *Western Women and Imperialism*, Laura Donaldson's *Decolonizing Feminism: Race, Gender and Empire-Building*, and Margaret Strobel's *European Women and the Second British Empire*, this issue has aroused a lot of interest among feminists in the United States and Europe who are working in the area of travel and empire.[39] While some of this interest comes from recent reissues by feminist presses of European and U.S. women's travel writing, some of it also comes from interest in feminist subjectivity and feminist struggle. Scholarship on colonial discourse as well as recent critiques of white bourgeois feminism within the United States as neglecting issues of race, colonialism, and cultural diversity[40] have also contributed to an interest in this area. U.S. feminists of color charge that certain forms of U.S. and European feminism have but one agenda that universalizes.[41] Such a universalizing neither accounts for power differentials among women nor for the ways in which the category "woman" is historically and culturally specific.[42]

Seeing feminist discourse not in its multifaceted resonance, or through its negotiations with discourses of state, nation, empire, and modernity that provide conditions of possibility, some analyses of Western women's travel literature suggest that Englishwomen who traveled, for instance, were subversive both to English patriarchy and to a masculine imperialism, and that, in fact, to be oppositional to the patriarchy in England was to be in opposition to imperialism.[43] Mary Kingsley and Lady Mary Montague are given as examples, whereas what is left out is their participation in European power and empire, differences in class between Englishwomen, and the ways in which feminism participated in discourses of nationalism. Both Lisa Lowe's analysis of Lady Mary Montague and Mary Louise Pratt's discussion of Mary Kingsley are a welcome change in their useful and measured understandings of the complex locations of Western women as they rewrite and participate in colonial discourses.[44] The desire to create feminism as a space outside these patriarchal formations is, of course, not specific to Euro-American feminists. Many forms of feminisms existed through participating in certain dominant discourses so that the issue, then, is not a search for a transparent or transcendent feminism but a need to examine the conditions of possibility of these feminisms. Consequently, this book suggests that feminisms everywhere must be historically contextualized. Rather than debate feminism's collusions or resistances, I argue that nationalism, imperialism, and colonial discourses shaped the contexts in which feminist subjects became possible in both England and India.

To that end, I focus on the way in which the space in which English feminism could resonate at the turn of the nineteenth century was that of nationalism and imperialism. Thus I examine how English feminists use the image of what they saw as victimized "sisters" in India, for instance, in order to position themselves as English citizens when the notion of the "citizen" was itself gendered. My emphasis is on examining specific formations in the period with a view to revealing that universalist feminist discourses that have seen themselves only in relation to men have, in fact, been articulated in relation to other women. This use of other women, as Spivak and women of color feminists in the United States such as bell hooks have suggested, has been part of the discourse of Western feminism in its utilization of the individual subject.[45] Thus while much feminism in the West saw itself only in relation to men, what was implicit and crucial within it were the relations between women of other classes and races. Much of feminist literary criticism on the nineteenth century in Europe leaves out imperialism and empire in its analysis of women's writing and of forms of female subjectivity. In fact, the extensive scholarship on Englishwomen in the nineteenth century excludes imperialism as a factor in feminist subject formation, and takes relations between Englishmen and Englishwomen as central to female subjectivity. Relations between different classes and races of women within a context of empire, a context that overpoweringly defined Victorian culture, English masculinity, and English nationalism, are often seen to be of no account.[46]

Rather than revealing whether Englishwomen were imperialist or not and whether feminism is anti-imperialist, feminists need to examine the ideologies and discourses that provided possibilities and problematics. Liberatory narratives of the movement from victimage to freedom are especially problematic at the present time because they collaborate with U.S. ideologies of democracy and freedom. For many Euro-American feminist critics the need to see Western feminism as anti-imperialist in the face of much evidence to the contrary comes out of the denial of such collaborations and the desire to see feminism as wholly oppositional and existing outside particular ideological formations. Some forms of "women of color" feminism are also implicated within certain hegemonic strategies in relation to women from other locations, suggesting the need to examine their negotiations. The construct called "Indian feminism" similarly, as my book reveals, must be historically contextualized to search for the discursive practices located between nation, emerging communities, and empire that makes such a formation possible.

This project is useful also to suggest the continuation of nineteenth-century practices in the present. For instance, a recent film by Pratibha Parmar and Alice Walker, entitled *Warrior Marks*, on the subject of clitoridectomy, replicates imperialist "global feminism" by suggesting that all women in sub-Saharan Africa have to undergo this pain, and, by showing village women and mud huts and frightened young girls, they position themselves as enlightened rescuers.[47] The subject positions that Parmar and Walker construct for themselves are of modern, free, enlightened women as opposed to the oppressed African women unable to rescue themselves. The history of plastic surgery and of medical surgeries such as mastectomies and hysterectomies that occur every day in the United States is forgotten in this discourse of primitivism and modernity. What is required is rather an examination of the ways in which women's bodies are surgically disciplined in specific locations if this north/south division is to be problematized. Thus, rather than look at feminisms as essentialized binaries between women of color and Western women, I focus on the multiplicity of discursive practices utilized by women.

My interest is thus not in imperial antagonisms nor in oppositions between the dominant and the dominated as monolithic groups. Writing as a South Asian feminist living in the United States, conscious of diasporas, migrancies, and complex constructions of "home," I find it impossible to use binaries such as dominant and dominated, colonizer and colonized, primitive and modern. Such a scholarship becomes either relativist or nationalist, or creates problematic categories of the "real" such as the "native" or the "indigenous."[48] Feminist work that attends to issues of class, caste, and sexuality interrupts such binarism, working against the hegemonic formations that occur within both sides. However, by paying rigorous attention to multileveled power relations created within such binaries, I want to dissipate any notion of a relativist approach in which all forms of domination are equated or nullified.

I include many social categories in my analysis to suggest that, for instance, in the case of British rule in India, imperialism continued because its discourses, programs, and strategies served multiple agents. Thus, rather than debating whether middle-class Englishwomen or working-class men and women in England were anti-imperialist or not, I suggest that part of the way they were interpellated as subjects was through colonial discourses. Thus I reject a methodology of "opposition," one that would equate "women" and the "colonized" and would suggest that opposition to imperialism could come from a coalition of Englishwomen or the English working class and colonized people. Through their relation to the culture of travel, I argue that the interests and the agendas of these groups in India and England were often contradictory.

Another problematic of essentialized binaries is that women are seen as victims rather than as complex agents interpellated by various discourses. This leads to a tendency to equate all oppressed groups as similar, to neglect the specific hegemonic formations and oppressions that create agency in various contexts, or to see agency in terms only of celebrations of "voices" of resistance. For instance, while Englishwomen positioned themselves in comparison to their Indian "sisters," a hegemonic comparison of English working classes to "savages" was also going on. However, these two comparative frameworks were quite distinct in their agendas, contexts, and participation in empire. In colonial India, on the other hand, the heterogeneity of English politics and classes was erased through colonial discourse that at the same time saw Indian women as victims or as grounds for debates on authenticity and culture of "natives," as Lata Mani's work on sati reveals.[49]

However, what is similar to gender and class discourses in England is the context of empire; the English working class, like bourgeois women, were being constructed as gendered consumers on the basis of their participation within the English nation and empire. Just as middle-class Englishwomen were interpellated as feminist through imperialist subject positions, working-class men and women saw themselves as a class vis-à-vis colonized people. Whereas E. P. Thompson suggests that "classes arise because men and women in determinate productive relations identify their antagonistic interests, and come to struggle, to think and to value in class ways, therefore the process of class formation is a process of self-making,"[50] I reveal in chapter 3 that the mediations in this process of class formation include imperial education. Class struggle, as Thompson describes it, explains some important aspects of British nineteenth-century culture; however, the impact of imperialism, as a powerful, defining discourse in that culture, on different classes and different genders, needs also to be explained.[51]

Comparisons between English factory workers and "savages" enabled the English working class to see themselves as similar in their exploitation but also to critique discourses of abolition because of what they ignored close to "home." Working-class concerns were at once ignored by the upper classes in the construction of English racial and civilizational superiority, and thus of nationalism as well, as I discuss in chapter 1. However, the education given to all classes was one of participation in imperialism and of the view of the world as consumable and colonizable, although the relation to this world was different according to class and gender, as I will show.

In the second part of this book, I address the issue of subject formation among the colonized. While the first part of the book concerns itself with the ways in which English men and women in the nineteenth century came to see themselves as English, my final chapters examine the circulation and impact of the culture of Euroimperial travel on non-Europeans. Travel as modernity, as Caren Kaplan points out, was part of Eurocentrism.[52] Yet modernity was also part of the disciplinary apparatus of colonialism, as so much of the recent historical work by feminists in South Asia and the Subaltern Studies group has revealed.[53] It remains so to this day to govern people's lives in almost all parts of the world through agencies such as the U.N. and the World Bank. It is also an intrinsic part of neocolonial and nationalist formations, and thus is an important issue for understanding the nineteenth and twentieth centuries. My concern is with the formation of colonial modernity through the discourse of Euroimperial travel as it becomes incorporated into the lives of colonized people. I take the specific case of India and of Indian women in order to examine how they travel and what subject positions are created out of their experiences of travel.

By focusing on issues of colonialism, nationalism, and the culture of travel, I examine the ways in which Indian women utilized the discourse of European travel and the politics that demanded how they utilize them. All of these practices led to the formation of a modernist feminism within India, which utilized colonial modernity and altered it through oppositions to nationalist and colonialist patriarchy. The nature of modernity under colonial conditions has engendered much debate, with various historians arguing whether notions of liberal reform were at all possible in such circumstances. South Asian historians have contributed variously to our understandings of the nature of Indians' negotiations and deployment of modernity. More recently, East Asian historians have contributed to the debate; for example, an issue of *positions* was devoted to this topic and the editor's introduction stated: "Asian modernities perform their own recodings of the discourses of modernity within a hegemonic capitalist world. Modernities in East Asia were undertaken in multiple, overlapping colonial dominations, and participated in the shaping of global forces under numerous local exigencies that it behooves us to fully understand."[54] The discourse of travel as it is utilized by Indian men and women, containing as it does the ontological and epistemological questions of "comparison" between "East" and "West," provides an excellent opportunity to understand colonial modernity in nineteenth-century India not as a universalized discourse but as a gendered one. This forms the subject of chapter 4. Indian men and women had vastly different opportunities for travel and utilized travel in specific ways according to their caste and class status. Their utilization of European travel along with more indigenous forms of mobility varied accordingly. Such heterogeneity led to dissimilarities and links in the feminist traditions that emerged at the time. Travel is a crucial factor in the emergence of Indian feminists and feminism in India, and chapter 5 examines this emergence.

I do not see the utilization of Western discourses of travel as a form of "colonial mimicry," as suggested by Homi Bhabha, a mimicry in which "the look of surveillance returns as the displacing gaze of the disciplined."[55] Bhabha's analysis remains within the binarism of colonized and colonizer, one that explains some aspects of a colonial dialectic but not the ways in which various forms of hegemony occur within the two sides of the binary and the relation of all these to colonial discourses. Furthermore, as Lydia Liu suggests, Bhabha assumes that any kind of colonial mimicry is subversive and threatening to the colonial order, an assertion that erases many forms of response to the colonial situation.[56] Roberto Schwartz's work on Brazil also offers important insights into the experience of inauthenticity, copying, lag, or provincialism that Bhabha has designated as mimicry. Questioning the notion of authenticity or origin of the colonial metropolis, Schwartz argues that it is not copying in general "but the copying of one class that constitutes the problem"[57] and the forms of inequality with which the dominant classes exploited the poor that lead to the feeling of alienation or artificiality. Though Schwartz uses the notion of patriotism to suggest an organic, unexploitative relation within a society, he does not address issues of boundary formation that lead to an experience of what comes to be demarcated as a culture or a society. Even so, his work provides a crucial understanding of the intersection of class, inauthenticity, and transnationalism that underlies colonial relations. My work, in its attention to class, examines such intersections to argue for analyzing the problem of colonial modernity as a classed and gendered one.

Many upper-class Indian women utilized the discourse of travel, but they utilized it according to the needs of their situations; furthermore, other discourses of travel were also influential in the ways in which Indian women constructed themselves as traveling subjects. Sometimes their actions were absorbed into dominant discourses (these are also many and diverse) in ways that had nothing to do with their needs; in some instances their actions reinforced colonial hegemony and in some instances it interrupted it. Thus mimicry is not always mimicry; rather than remaining caught within the psychoanalytic logic of its own ambivalence, it seems more useful to shift the focus of sociohistorical issues of reconstitution and recasting of patriarchy in relation to colonial culture. Such a focus that looks at changing relations between the many groups that come into contact with each other within asymmetrical power relations has been suggested by KumKum Sangari and Sudesh Vaid in their anthology, *Recasting Women*.

For Indian women, as for their English counterparts, all feminist practices need to be seen in their variety as in their multiplicity. Quoting Svati Joshi again, "the complex processes of mutual differentiation and affiliation between the colonial rulers and the dominant as well as emerging indigenous groups provided the larger discursive field within which culture formations came to be shaped."[58] For instance, Indian feminism's relation to Indian nationalism is now a topic of much interest; how and where Indian women could participate in the discourses of feminisms and nationalism becomes the issue.[59] While women writing and speaking out against different exploitations need to be seen as feminists, what also has to be examined are the locations from which they speak and the contradictions that marked these locations. The mediations in women's voices are my interest in seeing the reconstitutions of discourses of travel and modernity within Indian women's texts.

While postcolonial cultural studies is often mentioned as a field defined by scholars such as Stuart Hall, Gayatri Spivak, and Homi K. Bhabha, what is not often attended to are the new kinds of "transnational" methodology that it has enabled. In the introduction to *Scattered Hegemonies: Postmodernity and Transnational Feminist Practices*, Caren Kaplan and I have argued for a transnational mode of analysis rather than a comparative one, since the comparative approach does not include within it a notion of the geopolitical forces that are the condition of possibility for comparative analysis. Our understanding of transnational methodology is indebted to the work of critics such as Gayatri Spivak, for instance, who has done groundbreaking work in looking at the ways in which women in different locations speak to, across, and against each other; for instance, she has examined how French feminism resonates in different locations.[60] Rather than see my work as postcolonial cultural studies, I see it within an emerging field of transnational feminist cultural studies.[61] As an interdisciplinary, cross-national study of the culture of travel as it interpellates multiple, gendered-subject positions in the nineteenth century, this book is an example of a very different approach to cultural studies that looks at linkages between and specificities of cultures rather than at similarities. I examine discourses of class and gender within India and England as they intersect with a European culture of travel and mobility. By doing so I argue that, first, disciplinary discourses that form subjectivities in India and England are related and connected not only because India is often a place to experiment with new social technologies, but also because certain discourses such as those of the "harem" become nodal points around which groups within colonizing and colonized cultures can formulate different and related hegemonic relations and their own subject positions. This approach, formulated by Gayatri Spivak as the study of the "worlding" of the Third World, seems to me to be most productive in the way it accounts for the multiple and related representational practices that mark colonial hegemonies.[62]

A second area of comparative work has emerged from what Edward Said in *The World, the Text and the Critic* called "traveling theory."[63] In critiquing Said's account as one of "an all-too-familiar story of immigration and acculturation," James Clifford has called for a more complex understanding of "the ambivalent appropriations and resistances that characterize the travels of theories and theorists, between place in the 'First' and 'Third' worlds."[64] Here comparative analysis is directed at examining the ways in which concepts, such as the novel form,[65] nationalism,[66] and feminism,[67] travel and resonate in other contexts and locations, an approach that combines with what Adrienne Rich calls the "politics of location."[68] The journal *Public Culture* calls this methodology an examination of "transnational cultural flows" and the asymmetries that mark and map these flows. *Public Culture*'s inaugural statement brings out two agendas of my book, the ways in which much comparative focus on distant cultures ends up, first, "exceptionalizing the West through its absence on the discursive stage" and, second, homogenizing the "Third World."[69]

A third comparative approach works effectively as a deconstructive political strategy. That is, in teaching classes on international feminism theory, I find that I can effectively deconstruct colonial discourses by bringing them "home," as it were. For instance, in discussions of Islam and women, which inevitably in classrooms turn into attacks on Islam as a misogynist religion, I find that examinations of religious formations in the United States and commonalities and linkages between them become necessary. We look, for instance, at what in Islamic laws comes from British common law and how these "borrowings" or linkages took place under colonial recastings of patriarchies. From there we move on to discussions of feminist subject formations enabled through utilization of a "misogynist Islam" discourse and what is being misrecognized in the United States in the process. Quite recently, Gayatri Spivak illustrated this methodology in her essay "Scattered Speculations on the Question of Culture Studies," where she argues for examination of "transnational complicities" rather than the "comparative gesture."[70]

Of course this process also is complemented by presenting different ideas about Islam, about Islamic women revising fundamentalist history, and about the ways in which the rhetoric of "Westernization" within Islamic societies is a powerful counter-discourse against feminist practices. I do not wish to suggest that the transnational approach can take the place of examining, for instance, the violence of the colonial project on the colonized. However, it works also to show colonial discourse as a representational practice that catachrestically did not even apply to its own "home." Thus "civilizing" discourse was a colonial and class construction that worked at several levels in constructing both "home" and "harem" through violence to many Others. English nationalism can be seen as a formation that is created through imperialism and that enacts its own displacements and elisions.

Starting out as a project on the politics and aesthetics of European travel, this work had focused on the aesthetics of the sublime, the picturesque, and the beautiful as they were deployed within English travel literature. The books that were the impetus for that project, and have been for this one as well—Edward Said's *Orientalism* and Mary Louise Pratt's work on travel, now published as *Imperial Eyes*—enabled me to think about and change my project in ways that I hope have made it more interesting. First of all, I decided to look at Indian travel accounts and move away from English literature, leaving aside, in the second part of the book, strictly colonial discourse approaches, a change that became extremely important to the transnational methodology that I have outlined above. Starting out with participation in the Group for the Critical Study of Colonial Discourses at U.C. Santa Cruz and U.C. Berkeley in the early 1980s, and going through a period that included critiques of *Orientalism*, of Anglo-American feminism by Third World women, and developments in cultural studies work on colonialism, as well as the curriculum debates and the Reagan-Bush years, I had to move away from English contexts and cultural productions to Indian ones. The contributions of South Asian feminists and feminist historians and cultural critics have changed the field of colonial discourse studies to show both its strengths and limitations. This book marks that shift as well, leading to an engagement both with specifics of regional studies approaches as well as with the deconstructive critiques of colonial discourse methodology. Neither one by itself seems adequate to me.

PART I

English Imperial Culture

Chapter 1

Home and Harem:

Domesticity, Gender, and

Nationalism

She opened her curtains, and looked out towards the bit of road that lay in view, with fields beyond, outside the entrance-gates. On the road there was a man with a bundle on his back and a woman carrying her baby; in the field she could see figures moving—perhaps the shepherd with his dog. Far off in the bending sky was the pearly light; and she felt the largeness of the world and the manifold wakings of men to labour and endurance. She was a part of that involuntary, palpitating life, and could neither look out on it from her luxurious shelter as a mere spectator, nor hide her eyes in selfish complaining.[1]

In George Eliot's *Middlemarch*, Dorothea Casaubon experiences this transformative moment early one morning in the dawn light when, looking out of her bedroom window, she realizes the significance of the landscape she sees below her. It is the moment in which she reaches womanly maturity and understands her role in the community.

If, as Mary Pratt suggests, the "monarch of all I survey" is a trope within the nineteenth-century travel narratives in which a "rhetoric of presence" creates a "relation of domination between seer and seen," then Dorothea's location utilizes as well as departs from this masculinist mode.[2] While her position at the window suggests her domination of the landscape below, the description of her epiphany places her "within" rather than "above." This location "above" is a dislocation of women's proper place within English nineteenth-century culture, a departure from Tennyson's portrayal of "compulsive domesticity" in "The Lady of Shallot" (first published in 1833) when the Lady is forbidden to look out of her window and dies when she does. Eliot's narrative of Dorothea's epiphany reveals a transformation of a trope in order to suggest other forms of connection between women and the world.[3]

Middlemarch was published in 1871–1872 and Mary Kingsley's *Travels in West Africa* appeared in 1897. In those forty-some years between Tennyson's poem and Eliot's and Kingsley's narratives, Englishwomen had begun to travel in large numbers and Victoria had been queen for most of that time. Kingsley's narrative, Pratt suggests, does not include any "monarch of all I survey" scenes, and while imperial mastery is present in the narrative, there is also a denial of domination and a parody of power.[4] Yet this female participation and mastery, also available in Dorothea's narrative, combines to create a subject position for middle-class Englishwomen that is gendered through discourses of class and imperialism. Pratt's "contact zones" are here in the heart of the English landscape, interpellating gendered subjects that are nationalist as well, revealing what it means to be an Englishwoman, as well as what it means to be other classes of Englishwomen and other races of women. The position of a gendered imperial subject is negotiated, as the figures of Dorothea and Mary Kingsley suggest, within the conflict between imperial, masculinist ideology and female experience as constructed within class, race, and nation.[5] Such a conflict is visible in the comparisons between women and landscape and the ways in which the English notion of beauty as transparency is constructed through the discourses of women's work and leisure.

What Dorothea's epiphany illustrates is the way in which representations of the domestic landscape of England, by including certain features such as fields and cottages, working men and women, farm animals and children, taught its viewers what domesticity meant. The English landscape, as represented in Wordsworth's poetry and Constable's paintings, was didactic, teaching labor and endurance by portraying it, yet showing labor to be the lot of the working class, for the members of the bourgeoisie, such as Dorothea, merely consumed these scenes of landscape and labor without having to work themselves. Dorothea's epiphany does not mean that she would labor in the fields, but that she sees herself as being part of the community in which she will take her place as a middle-class, domesticated woman, not as the barren scholar she had mistakenly wanted to be with Mr.

Casaubon. The position of the scholar, which was becoming professionalized during this period, was clearly unavailable to women, leaving them keepers of the domestic space, a situation that suggested both an existence that denied the value of housework or child care, but which was valorized as fulfilling and necessary moral labor for women. While labor and work were valorized discourses of the Industrial Revolution, the eighteenth-century pastoral Arcadia of idle shepherds and shepherdesses portrayed values that the poor must not be taught, and was perceived, by the end of the eighteenth and nineteenth centuries, as either an "idealizing falsification" or an idea "dangerously radical."[6]

This discourse of "home," of domesticity, of beauty, however, played differently within the colonial context of India, especially in the second half of the nineteenth century, when colonial rule became more authoritarian and Indian nationalism was growing to become a powerful force. For instance, in India the English *memsahib* is seen as idle, useless, and too free in her associations with men; the Indian nationalists construct the Indian woman, a reconstruction of a middle-class Victorian woman, as the moral and spiritual opposite of the Englishwoman. Many Indians, especially those with an English education, used Victorian values to suggest Indian women as morally and spiritually superior and thus the proper symbol of "home." Consequently, "home" became a space that was deployed variously by multiple agents, though the usages were linked through colonial education. For the Indians, what colonial discourse termed the *harem*, a space of opacity, became then *home*, a reconstituted Victorian space that was transparent in its clear manifestation of moral virtues as symbolized by Indian middle-class women.

In England, it was because of a tension between a mythic harmony and working-class unrest, between the threat and the domination of the unknown, that transparency, as the visibility of what lay underneath, or the matching of surface with depth, became an important cause of beauty in the nineteenth century. Though obscurity and mystery were sought after, for instance, by travelers in search of the exotic, these did not constitute the aesthetic of beauty, for beauty was the result of clarity and the opposite of the opacity of the exotic. Jean Starobinski's account of the Rousseauist dream of the transparent society explains what Foucault reads as the fear of darkened spaces, of the pall of gloom that prevents the full visibility of things, which appeared in the aesthetic of the Gothic. Foucault sees the landscapes of Ann Radcliffe's novels, which were composed of mountains, forests, caves, ruined castles, and dark convents, as the "imaginary spaces [which] are like the negative of the transparency and visibility which it is aimed to establish."[7] The nationalist dream is the dream of transparency, one that English writers like Dickens and Wordsworth and landscape artists like John Constable represented in their works.

Gothic opacity, as the darkness of the prerevolutionary era, was both perceived in and sustained by travel and exploration, for it was recuperated in the representations by eighteenth- and nineteenth-century European travelers of regions and cultures of Asia, Africa, and the Americas. What became known as the "East," in particular, which mostly comprised Asia, was depicted as this area of darkness not only because it was unknown and perceived as mysterious, but also because it was believed that these lands were ruled by a despotism equivalent to that which had been removed in Europe, a darkness Foucault describes as that of the "unlit chambers where arbitrary political acts, monarchical caprice, religious superstitions, tyrannical and priestly plots, epidemics and illusions of ignorance were fomented."[8] The complement to this fear of opacity is Bentham's panopticon, this instrument that would enable society to become transparent. The panopticon was thus the reversal of the dungeon; it was the metaphoric opposite of the harem where the principle of visibility governed technologies of power.[9]

The Eighteenth Century in England: Gender, Physiognomy, and the Feminine Aesthetic

For writers of the late eighteenth and nineteenth century, what was beautiful was the Rousseauist dream of a transparent civil society with the perfect social contract, where homogeneity was the predominant trait ensuring knowledge, a single will, and a disciplined populace. Here democracy and equality were present only because everybody was like everybody else and people saw into each other's hearts.[10] In

England the fear of a revolution underwrote such a desire, taking shape as an upper-class attempt to see harmony in the land while maintaining class distinctions and upholding a patriarchal culture.

The desire for transparency was clearly visible in conceptualizations of women, in which the supposed opacity of female nature was to be understood. Writers such as Burke and Ruskin saw beauty only in the face of a woman. With the interest in physiognomy, the face became an indication of inner qualities. Within such an aesthetic, blackness as a racial category became associated with opacity, fear, and horror, and features could be read as analogous to moral characteristics. As Jeanne Fahnestock suggests, the face was believed to be an accurate mirror of the character, for the woman with irregular features was believed capable of irregular conduct.[11] Perfection of a feature became a sign of perfection of a quality. Thus in Trollope's *The Way We Live Now*, published in 1875, we are told of Hatty Carbury that "her face was a true index of her character."

With such knowledge, the fallen woman's degradation is visible on the face. Louis Enault, a French visitor to London, shows the influence of physiognomy when he says of the prostitutes in London: "their hideous features, objects of horror and disgust, bear the trace of their depravity and degradation."[12] The attempt to hide was therefore a sign of immorality. Artifice and makeup become the trademarks of the prostitute, who must hide the depravity written on her face. Makeup symbolized an opacity that was to be found only in the prostitutes and, in some nineteenth-century travel narratives, on oriental women. The "curled and painted" prostitute, so frequently written about in the literature of the London poor by writers such as Henry Mayhew and William Acton, was presented as a contrast to the visibly virtuous bourgeois woman.[13]

In all these aesthetic discourses, perfection of features was described often as "classical" and "regular," and perfection implied, as in Burke, that the moral virtues were visible on the face. Physiognomy, or the practice of seeing qualities of character on the face, indicated the knowledge and power of the viewer who could scan the inside from the outside and the alignment of inside with outside. It was thus a discourse of knowledge as power. Yet while emphasis remained on the moral virtues as a component of beauty and the insistence on transparency as the visibility of the virtues on the face, physiognomy also illustrated that all faces could be read: the virtuous and the imperfect. Nothing could remain hidden, for the science of physiognomy had provided the power to remove the darkness of mystery. Transparency no longer meant only the harmony of inside with outside, for it also implied what had been discovered and was open to knowledge. Implicitly, without this physiognomic discourse, the harmony of virtue and features could not be known. Consequently, in the nineteenth century, where the divisions of class remained along with the desire for harmony, the pursuit of knowledge of the female sex as well as classes and populations became predominant in the attempt to conceive of England as a unified community that comprised a nation.

In discourses of the aesthetic of the nation, the debate whether England could be described as beautiful or picturesque presented two different views of the condition of England. Whereas those claiming that the beautiful, which implied order and hierarchy, best represented England, those arguing for the picturesque believed that variety was necessary for a pleasing aesthetic. Such debates in the last two decades of the eighteenth century and the early part of the nineteenth were part of the upheaval caused in Europe by the events leading up to the French Revolution and its aftermath.[14]

The aesthetic of the beautiful was implicated in very many discourses, all of which were governed by the politics of transparency and opacity, of knowledge and darkness, that indicated a wish to establish a homogeneous populace in England and a known, unthreatening one in the colonies. Romantic and Victorian ideas of beauty owe much to Burke's *Philosophical Enquiry into the Origin of Our Ideas of the Sublime and the Beautiful*.[15] Burke's taxonomy, published in 1764, was the result of a felt need to bring an exactness to aesthetics, and to inscribe an aesthetic status quo that could teach taste and judgment to the upper classes. He saw the necessity for maintaining the superiority of the ruling classes before the "swinish multitude," which might wish for a revolution. Burke's *Enquiry* suggests the fashioning of an English social order that by a taxonomy of aesthetic responses resists any revolutionary upheavals. He saw the increasing poverty of the laboring poor by the end of the eighteenth century as a natural corollary to the industrial expansion of Britain.

As he remarked, "the laws of commerce are the laws of nature, and consequently the laws of God."[16] Poverty was thus naturalized and considered the proper order of things. Believing in the principle of free trade, Burke saw the hardships in the life of the poor as temporary and an exception and thought that it was not governmental interference but charity that could be of help.[17] He had what Eric Hobsbawm calls "a frankly irrationalist belief in the virtues of tradition, continuity and slow organic growth."[18] This anxiety about any upheaval was a result of working-class unrest and emerged from a desire for a continuation of the traditional hierarchies of class and gender.

His definition of the beautiful, consequently, stressed order and submission. Whereas the sublime feeling of terror could be caused by seeing a black woman, beauty, the qualities of which were smallness, smoothness, gradual variation, and fairness, caused the "social quality" of love and affection. Burke argued that the origin of what he saw as the universal love for beauty was the love of society which was intrinsic to all mankind. He suggested that all mankind was agreed on what constitutes beauty; those who did not had either "vitiated palates" or had acquired an "unnatural" relish opposed to what was "natural."[19] Here he naturalized both the taste for beauty as well as the term *society* as he had naturalized poverty, assuming that upper-class culture and taste were "natural" and universal and thereby normalizing them.

In this universal aesthetic, Burke saw beauty as a feminine quality, yet one that was racialized because it could not belong to a woman who was not white. He suggested that the beautiful was that which was small, "because we love what submits to us" (113). It came, he claimed, from the "softer virtues" (110). It was the weakness of women that Burke defined as beauty, saying that "Beauty in distress is much the most affecting beauty" (204), and "an air of robustness and strength is prejudicial to beauty" (218); thus those bodies that were "pleasant to the touch, are so by the slightness of the resistance they make" (229). Formulating a gendered opposition of the sublime and the beautiful, Burke pointed out that people admire "great" objects and submit to them, whereas they love "what submits to them" (212).[20] Beauty was a restful and "amiable" quality, marked by the "softer virtues such as easiness of temper, compassion, kindness and liberality" (205).

Smooth bodies, weak bodies, a smooth bed, fragile flowers, a dove: these were Burke's examples of beautiful objects. In Burke's taxonomy all these qualities of beauty were available in one object: a white woman. A black woman could not be beautiful because she could only arouse a feeling of terror and would therefore be in the category of the sublime. Burke cites the case of a boy who was cured of his blindness and was made uneasy by black objects and was "struck with great horror" at seeing a black woman.[21] Furthermore, a beautiful woman belonged to home and offered relaxation and not the exercise of lustful passion. Burke effectively showed beauty as a quality that could only belong to the upper classes, since no woman who worked in the fields, the factories, or in the domestic space could possibly have the softness and smoothness ascribed to beautiful women; it was only the aristocratic woman whose idle life enabled the cultivation of such qualities.

This feminized beauty was also moral. The eye that was termed beautiful in a woman should be, according to Burke, clear and transparent: like diamonds, clear water, glass. His analogies suggest that the inner moral qualities must match the externals. Using physiognomic discourse, Burke implied that a beautiful woman was one whose moral qualities, which promoted the love and preservation of society and which included submission, weakness, and dependence, appeared on her face. By using glass as an example of transparency and beauty, he insisted that the outer form would necessarily mirror the inner. A woman who lacked virtue would be ugly or deformed. Thus he said, "the face must be expressive of such gentle and amiable qualities, as correspond with the softness, smoothness and delicacy of the outer form" (118), and the eye "is expressive of some qualities of the mind" (225). And since the moral and the physical must be in harmony, beauty implied "union with neighboring parts" (118). The aesthetic of beauty, therefore, attempted to put the realm of Englishwomen in order, for it implied that no woman who was beautiful could be mysterious or deceitful or possess faults that she wanted to hide.

The need for conformity and order comes about because of Burke's ambivalence about the nature of women, for he shows a profound anxiety that this object could evade his ordering and his definition. Such anxiety is obvious in the following passage: "Observe that part of a beautiful woman where she is perhaps the most beautiful, about the neck and breasts; the smoothness; the softness; the easy and insensible swell; the variety of the surface, which is never for the smallest space the same; the deceitful maze, through which the unsteady eye flies giddily, without knowing where to fix, or whither it is carried" (216). The insistence on moral beauty occurs because there is a fear of an inherent deceitfulness in women. It is this suspicion of the physical aspect of women, of the body containing "the deceitful maze," that calls for his need to define and categorize in order to clarify and to know. It is the "deceitful maze" of the hidden parts of the female body that unsettles him; whereas he had earlier defined beauty as causing rest and comfort, the body of the woman instead leads to unsteadiness and giddiness in the eye. While Burke is comfortable with describing a face as beautiful with all its soothing attendant qualities, he cannot do so with the body of a woman.

In the eighteenth century, therefore, Burke's aesthetics effectively divide face and body, an opposition homologous to a realm familiar and knowable from one mysterious and uncontrolled. Transparency is opposed to deceit as is the face of a woman to her body. Submission, weakness, smallness are therefore clearly beautiful because they indicate a disciplined body. Such a body implies the harmony of a like-minded, homogeneous citizenry. Burke's aesthetic gendering is thus central to his political views, which reflect his concerns with the order and hierarchy of English society.

To read, therefore, Burke's aesthetic as evidence of the ambiguity and ambivalence of spectatorship, as Sara Suleri does in her book, *The Rhetoric of English India*, curiously depoliticizes this aesthetic, even as Suleri's topic is the long overdue one of Burke's attack on Warren Hastings's impeachment and his view of India. Seeing any readings of Burke's aesthetic gendering as "too simple," Suleri emphasizes his "anguish of spectatorship."[22] Yet what is also important is the class and gender location of this spectator, and not merely the instability of his categorizing. Burke's belief and commitment is to tradition and continuity, as Hobsbawm argues, rather than to India's difference, which for Suleri is the "object of Burke's passionate respect."[23] Burke's conservatism, apparent in all his writings, rather than a respect for "difference," is a more powerful argument both for his opposition to upheavals in India as well as to revolution in France.[24]

The Feminine Landscape from Wordsworth to Ruskin:
Nationalism and Gender

With Romanticism appeared an interest in rustic landscape and rustic life that was different from the pastoral arcadias of the eighteenth century. The aesthetics of the beautiful no longer connect beauty only to women. Beauty now belonged to both Englishwomen and the English landscape, which were seen as analogous and connected because the one could exist only in the other. Rural scenes were important because only in such scenes was domestic life believed to exist in harmony. The laboring poor from these areas were appreciated as part of nature; they belonged to the landscape and were merged with it. Every element of this landscape existed together in harmony. Such harmony was perceived as part of nature and thus a part of the beauty of nature. Like Burke, Wordsworth preferred not to think of the working class as a dissatisfied section of the populace, dispossessed of their land and their living by the increasing enclosures of wastes and fields, the loss of common rights to lands, and the movement from an agrarian to an industrial civilization.[25] Their poverty was naturalized, their houses swept clear of dirt and their faces of anger, and they were endowed with that pain of humanity which a middle-class Wordsworth shared. The Wordsworthian landscape of the Lake District, which valorized rural England as the norm of beauty, was not the nineteenth-century landscape of rapid industrialization; it did not reveal changes due to industrialization, just as Wordsworth's notions of "happy poverty" elided the real economic problems and the effects of harsh poverty on agricultural labor in early nineteenth-century England.

Wordsworth's attitude toward the English land and its people is clearly visible in his travel narrative, *A Guide Through the District of the Lakes*, the first version of which was published in 1810. In a section within the *Guide* which is entitled "Directions to the Tourist," Wordsworth includes his own verses in praise of the landscape of the Lake District.[26] While much of the *Guide* describes the picturesqueness of the Lake District,[27] there is concern to show its beauty as well, a beauty that comes from the known familiarity of the landscape. Even though Burke had stated that custom had no part in the effect of beauty, to Wordsworth the familiar causes love and brings comfort. While to Burke what was clearly seen to be under control could be beautiful even though it was novel, Wordsworth sees the familiar as beautiful for he naturalized and elevated the poor to reflect middle-class concerns with an abstract humanity. Whereas for Burke the working class was an unknown entity that needed to be controlled for fear they might follow the revolutionary path, Wordsworth, writing in the aftermath of the French Revolution and with disappointment in its promise, does not have such fears. He seems not to even see the misery of the poor as anything other than the endurance of a natural calamity that provides lessons for a universalized humanity. What is common to both is the notion of the domestic space as central to political constructions of Englishness.[28]

Transparency remains central for Wordsworth, though for reasons very different from Burke's. Wordsworth's landscape is beautiful because it provides "intercourse" between man and nature. A lake provides "in perfection the beauty of one of these days," for it reflects the sky and therefore creates a transcendent landscape: "the earth is mainly looked at, and thought of, through the medium of a purer element" (82). Wordsworth's beauty, caused by the transparency of the lake, is both domestic and divine for it aids the imagination in penetrating "into recesses of feeling otherwise impenetrable" (82). Such beauty is the highest perfection of nature and a sight that can satisfy, says Wordsworth, "the most intense cravings for the tranquil, the lovely, and the perfect, to which man, the noblest of her creatures, is subject" (83). A harmonious society is necessary for Wordsworth because it can provide the poet with the means to reach his highest Self.

Women, too, perform a similar function for Wordsworth; they are, as with Dorothy Wordsworth, Lucy, or the Solitary Reaper, the transparent medium through which the poet can reach a higher Self. Wordsworth's Lucy poems illustrate the use of the female as mediator between man and nature, helping man reach self-identity.[29] In Wordsworth's landscape, women are often identified with nature, and they belong to this natural landscape. Landscape and women are both fertile and nurturing and exist for the same purpose as the fields, lakes, and rivers: to lead Wordsworth to a higher and more civilized Self.

In contrast to the beauty of the Lake District, a beauty so tied to its familiarity, there is the alienation of the city. For Wordsworth, the polar opposite of the beauty of the rural landscape was the "mystery" of London. In the seventh book of *The Prelude* he writes:

> O Friend! one feeling was there which belonged
> To this great city, by exclusive right;
> How oft, amid those overflowing streets,
> Have I gone forward with the crowd, and said
> Unto myself, "The face of every one
> That passes by me is a mystery!" (VII, 595–598)[30]

Though in the 1850 version, Wordsworth sees in the urban crowd the unity of man,[31] yet the earlier section records a set of feelings that seemed to embody the alienation felt in the industrial, urban setting. Here where no one knows anyone else, where people walk by each other as strangers, we have the loss of Rousseau's transparent society. There is the lack of the common will and the common aim. Division and alienation exist in the city, and Wordsworth, overcome with anxiety during his sojourn in London, seems unable to cope with it. Here the beneficial effects of the countryside can be ruined; here he sees, instead of the incorruptible madonnas of rural England, the corrupt woman and the "overthrow / of her soul's beauty" (VII, 432–433):

> And for the first time in my life did hear
> The voice of woman utter blasphemy
> Saw woman as she is to open shame
> Abandoned, and the pride of public vice (VII, 417–420)

Thus country and city are shown to be in opposition; the familiarity of the country is contrasted with the mystery of the city, the beauty of the former with the crowds and corruption of the latter. In the rural scene, he could distance himself from the presence and effects of industrialization and commerce that are inescapable in the city. The problem of industrial capitalism is thus resolved in this aesthetic alienation from a native landscape.

Within an urban landscape of rapid industrialization, it is not surprising that the city produced such an ambivalent attitude. Yet what is remarkable is the kind of resolution offered by Wordsworth that becomes quite apolitical. Consequently, during the nineteenth century, Wordsworth's peaceful rural scenes have much in common with landscape art of the time. Dorothea Casaubon's view from her window shares the attributes of a Wordsworthian scene and a Constable painting: fields, road, shepherd, farm animal, working man, woman, and child. This was Wordsworth's patriarchal landscape, an ordered realm in harmony with patriarchal values that placed the working classes and the middle-class woman in service to the bourgeois male. The domesticity, fertility, and labor recuperates what John Barrell calls "the paternalistic fantasy of rural social harmony," which, in various combinations, was repeatedly represented in English landscape painting of the time.[32]

When Constable published a series of his views in mezzotint plates in 1830, his aim was, according to the introduction, to "increase the interest for, and promote the study of, the Rural Scenery of England, with all its endearing associations, its amenities, and even in its most simple localities; abounding as it does in grandeur, and every description of Pastoral Beauty. . . ."[33] In this description, Constable promotes the love of a rural scenery whose beauty includes many elements of Burke's model: it has the "endearing" quality that inspires love, it is domestic and bright with summer skies that have no hint of the Sublimity of gloomy scenes, even though it is grand. For Constable, this scenery was the model for rural English scenes. He calls it "home scenery," which is "taken from real places" and "meant particularly to characterize the scenery of England."[34]

Constable's peaceful rural scenes are, like so many of Wordsworth's, of a nostalgic past. His Suffolk views are those of his childhood where he grew up as the son of a prosperous miller. It is a landscape of reaction from the present that leads him into a rural idyll of the past, glorifying England and its countryside.[35] Such glorification was a predominant part of English landscape painting of the eighteenth and nineteenth centuries. Artists such as David Cox, Peter De Wint, and Samuel Palmer all valorized the English landscape; as one reviewer of Samuel Palmer commented, Palmer, like Cox, Crome, Constable, and De Wint, was a "painter of England, and England against the world."[36]

With the increase in travel as well as in the emigration of English men and women to the colonies, the representations of the English landscape continued to be idyllic for it was believed that such domestic beauty could not be found anywhere else. An example of such a work is a landscape by Richard Redgrave, who entitled his work *The Emigrants' Last Sight of Home*. This is a warmly glowing picture of gently rolling hills and woods at which the emigrants in the foreground, their backs to the viewer, are gazing sadly. Ruskin commented on its "beautiful distance," and the *Art Journal* remarked that Redgrave had painted the landscape with "a fervency of devotion rarely witnessed."[37]

For Redgrave, such landscapes and domesticity characterized British painting of the time.[38] Commenting on the contrast between the English and French paintings at the 1855 International Exhibition in Paris, he said: "To pass from the grand salons appropriated in the Palais des Beaux Arts to French and Continental works, into the long gallery of British pictures, was to pass at once from the midst of warfare and its incidents, from passion, strife, and bloodshed, from martyrdoms and suffering, to the peaceful scenes of home."[39] The English landscape here becomes a symbol of peace; home and peace were one in contrast with the strife and turmoil of postrevolutionary France. The Wordsworthian landscape of rural harmony had become a symbol of England, so that the aesthetic of beauty became imbued with nationalist connotations. This nationalism found continuation in Ruskin's definitions of beauty in *Modern Painters*, where the "law of nationality" had to operate in any representation of beauty.

Ruskin believed that only in representing the landscape or the women of his native land could the painter create beauty. In *Modern Painters*, he remarks, for example, that John Frederick Lewis's visit to Italy, Spain, and Egypt would not lead him to paint beautiful landscapes, since "English artists are ruined by residence in Italy."[40] Only by painting the British and the English landscape could English painters succeed in capturing beauty. For Ruskin "whatever is to be truly great and affecting must have on it the strong stamp of the native land," so that "if we are to do anything great, good, awful, religious, it must be got out of our own little island, and out of these very times, railroads and all; if a British painter, I say this in earnest seriousness, cannot make historical characters out of the British House of Peers, he cannot paint history; and if he cannot make a Madonna of a British girl of the nineteenth century, he cannot paint one at all."[41] With the madonna figure as the ideal, it is not surprising that, for Ruskin, the most important characteristic of beauty was virtue. In *Modern Paint-*

ers, he proclaims: "I wholly deny that the impressions of beauty are in any way sensual; they are neither sensual nor intellectual, but moral. . . ."[42] Ruskin is concerned with excluding from his definition any elements of sensuality and mysteriousness such as those that infiltrated Burke's definition. Thus he points out that "the beauty of the animal form is in direct proportion to the amount of moral or intellectual virtue expressed by it; and wherever beauty exists at all, there is some kind of virtue to which it is owing."[43] Ruskin's definition is in agreement with Burke's, for in both formulations gentleness and sweetness are characteristics of beauty; however, to Ruskin, these qualities are moral and divine, so that the female body cannot represent purity and virtue. Like Burke, he distrusts it and sees beauty only in the face; the beauty of the face reflects the virtues, while the body can display only corrupting influences. He disliked all representations of nude figures, especially that of the female, fearing that any portrayal could easily stray into that which is "luscious and foul."[44] Ruskin's attitude toward the domestication of women is apparent in *Sesame and Lilies*, which contemporary feminists have revealed as an argument for immuring women in the home. He believed that any vices would appear on the face; pride, sensuality, fear, and cruelty would "destroy the ideal character of the countenance and body," whereas "there is not any virtue the exercise of which, even momentarily, will not impress a new fairness upon the features."[45]

The Feminine Binary and the Discourse of Class

Ruskin also suggested that dark colors did not constitute beauty, thus upholding the connection of whiteness with purity and darkness with evil, a linkage that played an important role in the racial underwriting of Western colonialism. In *Modern Painters* he says that "the splendid colours of many birds are eminently painful from their violent separation, and inordinate variety, while the pure and colourless swan is, under certain circumstances, the most beautiful of all feathered creatures."[46]

Many nineteenth-century novels used the fair woman as the heroine and the dark one as the sensual or, in Victorian terms, fallen woman. White muslin, symbolizing virginity and innocence, was worn by many heroines, and the feminine virtues that were valued were quite Burkean because they included innocence, meekness, lack of opinions, general helplessness, and weakness. Thus in Charles Dickens's *David Copperfield*, Dora was a helpless toy, and in Thackeray's *Vanity Fair*, Amelia Sedley's charm was her submissiveness. Becky, though fascinating, was dark, of foreign ancestry, and lacking Amelia's submissiveness. Women such as Becky were seen as more alluring than the virtuous beauty, but less desirable for marriage and domesticity. In Wilkie Collins's *The Woman in White*, Marian is described as being dark and ugly, for she has "a swarthy complexion. . . . a large firm masculine mouth and jaw; prominent piercing resolute brown eyes; and thick, coal-black hair, growing unusually low on her forehead." The connection of darkness with exoticism arouses anxiety in the viewer, who sees her as "altogether wanting in the feminine attractions of gentleness and pliability, without which the beauty of the handsomest women alive is beauty incomplete."[47] Mrs. Gaskell's mill workers in *Mary Barton* are similarly dark and unbeautiful. Gaskell describes them in the following terms: "Their faces were not remarkable for beauty; indeed they were below the average, with one or two exceptions; they had dark hair, . . . dark eyes, but sallow complexions and irregular features."[48]

If only the domesticated and disciplined woman could be beautiful, then it was to be expected that working-class women lacked this beauty. Women who worked sixteen hours a day at sewing or in the factories for meager sums of money were neither submissive nor weak. Nor were many of them virtuous, for factories fostered an unbourgeois sexual freedom from an early age. Furthermore, the money to be gained from prostitution was competitive with that obtained from factory or home labor, and required far less effort. In fact, there were many reformers who reported on deplorable living and working conditions for the working-class woman, and who wanted factory reform not only because of inhuman working conditions but also because such conditions had disastrous effects on the morals of the women and on their domestic virtues.[49] Heidi Hartmann, arguing that patriarchy was an important element in capitalism, suggests that nineteenth-century culture saw that capitalism "threatened to bring all women and children into the labor force and hence to destroy the basis of the power of men over women (i.e., the control over their labor power in the family)."[50] Yet the patriarchal family relation was also beneficial to capitalist structures, since it ensured that women's labor was cheaper and they were more vulnerable to exploitation.

To judge women by their physical beauty was central to class formation, especially since working women, worn out by hard work, childbearing, and undernourishment, could not possess the kind of beauty that the more comfortable life of upper-class women allowed. Furthermore, it was not only physical appearance that mattered; if that were so, it could not be normative. But when virtue became a part of beauty, it meant that all women could hope to attain this beauty even if their physical appearance could not be called beautiful. Thus beauty as a normative concept seemed to transcend class even while it did not do so. In both physical appearance and morals, the chances of working women being beautiful were limited. If only the domesticated and disciplined women could be seen as beautiful, then it was to be expected that working-class women lacked this beauty.

Comparisons of factory workers with "savages" were also quite pervasive. It was believed that the heat of the factories had effects similar to the heat of the tropics, and both fostered promiscuity. Judith Walkowitz notes that the literature of urban exploration and tourism to the slums of London utilized the anthropological gaze to constitute the poor as "a race apart, outside the natural community."[51] Though modes of disciplining varied in England and in the colonies, since the British did not provide the working conditions, educational institutions, or welfare services in India that they did in England, the impetus of civilizing uncultured bodies was similar. Therefore the opposition of East and West London took on, as Walkowitz suggests, "imperial and racial dimensions" within which the two parts "imaginatively doubled for England and its empire."[52]

Efforts to civilize the working classes involved the movement to get working women into the home as servants for their husbands and in line with patriarchal culture, and teaching women the domestic virtues. This move to improve the conditions for the working classes included laws for shorter working hours for women, classes to teach them sewing and cooking and home skills, and the fostering of home conditions that would make them better mothers and wives.[53] The effort was in response to what was seen as the indifference of women toward their children, the lack of interest in the home, which tired

women treated merely as shelter, and the dangerous ways of financially independent women who had no reason to be subservient to
men. A consequence of such factory reforms was that married women
who had earlier been financially independent of their husbands thus
became their domestic servants, while men gained control over tech-
nology, production, and marketing.[54]

Charles Dickens was in the forefront of such reforms of working
women and prostitutes, for he found beauty in women who had
become virtuous after repentance and suffering. His interest in the
female criminal, whom he saw as the pathological opposite of healthful domesticity, contrasted for instance in Rose Maylie and Nancy of
Oliver Twist, led him to visit numerous prisons, mental asylums, and
other rehabilitational institutions on his travels in the United States. In
the Eastern Penitentiary in Pennsylvania, where all prisoners were
kept in solitary confinement, Dickens found that the prisoners were so
full of misery that it was painful to look at their faces. However, on
looking at three young women in adjoining cells, he found that "in the
silence and solitude of their lives they had grown to be quite beautiful."[55] Their suffering seems to have brought them to beauty. While
the male prisoners come to have "appalling countenances" because of
the misery of prison life, the women come to have beauty. Prison life,
said Dickens, "humanizes and refines" the faces of the women.[56]
Condemning the solitary confinement used in many prisons, Dickens
paradoxically endorses such a practice for women by suggesting that
it makes them virtuous and beautiful. Silence, loneliness, and confinement have rehabilitated and humanized these women. Thus for Dickens, if it is not healthful domesticity that beautifies women, if it is not
incarceration in the home, it is incarceration in the prison that does so.
Beauty thus becomes indicative of women's moral health; it symbol-
izes effective control over their moral and physical nature.

The Feminine Binary: Colonialist Discourse

Colonial reform movements in India, though careful to claim that
they were working with and within indigenous beliefs, used the discourse of English patriarchy and the popular Victorian belief that

women, like Indians, were children. While Indian women were seen as "half-devil, half-child," Englishwomen were "half-angel, half-child."[57] They were represented as passive and as victims—the ideal of nineteenth-century English culture. Kenneth Ballhatchet's work on the control of prostitution in India under the Raj reveals that the Contagious Diseases Act, which was used in England to exert state power and control over those women who lived outside the domestic sphere, was also used in India to control the Indian prostitutes who lived around army barracks.[58] Lata Mani's research on sati reforms in nineteenth-century India reveals that within colonial discourse, Indian women were denied subjectivity; they were seen as victims, even when they resisted sati. Denial of subjectivity to women was the practice of a colonial British culture that saw men as individual, autonomous subjects and that had divided women into the infantilized angel of the house and the victimized whore. Further, even though the British expressed horror at the practice of sati, they divided the practice into the good, legal sati, which involved the voluntary submission to death, and the bad sati, which involved coercion.[59] Mani reports that often the good sati was described in the British newspapers in a nonhorrified way, showing that for English culture, a voluntary sacrifice or submission of a woman was to be praised. The submissive, bourgeois Englishwoman was to be horrified at the practice of sati but also to admire such submission. Sati became a lesson in barbarism and in female obedience. Thus colonial reforms were attempts at extending patriarchal power to Englishwomen as well as to those colonized peoples whose practices seemed to escape it. Colonial reform movements placed Indian women under new forms of patriarchal oppression while purporting to free them from the power of Indian men.

The support in England for such reforms came from the representation in travel and colonialist literature of the "oriental woman" as the opposite of the bourgeois, domesticated Englishwoman. Although travelers often found picturesque scenes in the area termed "the East," they did not find beauty as easily. If they traveled in the biblical lands of Egypt or Palestine, they found beauty because of historical associations with Christianity. For instance, Thackeray found beautiful the landscape near Jerusalem, with "the land in graceful undulations, the towers and mosques rosy in the sunset, with no lack of verdure, especially of graceful palms."[60] Other landscapes were beautiful if they presented opportunity for economic profit.

Harriet Martineau, an ardent believer in free trade, saw fertility as beautiful on her travels. She admired the rich green fields of the Nile valley and the verdure of India. The connection between beauty and fertility was emphasized also in Cook's tourist handbook for 1897, which described the land on the banks of the Nile as "glowing with beauty and fertility" even though it was surrounded by "scorching deserts and barren mountains."[61]

By describing the rich and verdant scenery of India, and thereby showing its potential, Martineau suggests that the British must civilize this land and gain profit from it. The beauties of nature, that is, the land's potential for development, become justification for British colonial rule. In two books, *Suggestions towards the Future Government of India* (1858) and *British Rule in India* (1857), written after the Indian mutiny in 1857 and when the question of the future of India was raised in the English Parliament, Martineau combines aesthetics, politics, and economics to argue for the civilizing of India by proper colonial rule.

According to Martineau, the territory enclosed by rivers in India is "rich and populous" and the effect of the landscape is one of verdant growth, with huge trees, oleander blossoms, ripening apricots and pomegranates.[62] She points out that "nowhere is there a region more splendidly wealthy by nature"; its wealth is incalculable for "the most moderate estimate would look like statistics from the desk of Baron Munchausen."[63] While emphasizing India's vast resources, Martineau points out as well how much of all this is being wasted, a waste that can be reclaimed by British rule. For instance, she mentions that grain was being sowed "all mixed" and pulled up separately with "infinite waste of time and produce."[64] She points out, as well, that this wealth is in "that accessible state which our public works will soon realize." Thus she concludes: "If well governed, India must yield occupation and subsistence to hundreds of millions of human beings, at home and abroad."[65]

The necessity of holding India is obvious to her because of the wealth it will bring to England. Colonial rule will "call millions into

existence at home . . . , and to improve the lot in life of millions more."
Martineau says that "so clear is the prospect of a doubled, a 5-fold, a
10-fold, a 20-fold, income from India when colonization and commerce have had a free course," that it is "a political object . . . to
develop intelligence and industry of inhabitants, and [their] . . . peace-
ableness and loyalty."[66] If this is accomplished, the income to British
officers, both civil and military, and to their dependents will be, Martineau calculates, £10 million per annum. Though even with improvement, India "can never become . . . another England," yet there will
be "surely sufficient honor and profit for the proprietary country."[67]
In Martineau's writings on India, the aesthetic pleasure in the wealth
and fertility of its landscape comes from its economic potential.

Similarly, the beauty she finds in Egypt, as described in her travel
narrative *Eastern Life: Past and Present*, comes from its verdure and
its richness. She likes the present richness of Egypt and the religious
ideas of the past. She notes that there is no hunger or poverty in Egypt
and people appear "sleek, well-fed, and cheerful." She claims there is
more disease and poverty in England, for "I have seen more emaci-
ated, and stunted, and depressed men, women and children in a single
walk in England" than she saw in all her travels in Egypt.[68] Even her
companion, Mr. E., claims that "he had never seen so rich an expanse
of country" as was visible in the Nile region.[69] Her comparison of
England and Egypt suggests that one important justification for colonization was that it would improve the lot of the poor at home, both
by emigration as well as the increase in commerce and industry from
colonial markets abroad.[70]

The perception of beauty in the fertility of the landscape and its
potential for production suggests that for these travelers, lands were
appreciated for some of the same reasons that landscape was seen as
beautiful in England: its ability to fit into the patriarchal culture and
capitalist economy. To call a landscape beautiful was usually to suggest reasons for its domestication and colonization. Similar to the way
in which the English landscape was called beautiful if it showed green
fields and working peasants, this landscape was beautiful if it displayed the possibility for profit. Calling it beautiful also made it seem
less alien, for it signified the possession of familiar qualities such as
fertility and verdure. Along with familiarization, however, beauty

also suggested a controlled region, for no object could be beautiful that did not conform to the English ideals of usefulness and order or submission to such order.

What is noticeable in the passages from nineteenth-century travel narratives that include the description of foreign landscapes as beautiful is that the people of those lands are not seen as beautiful. A fertile land whose beauty is apparent and visible is different from the people, whose opacity is an obstacle to the construction of a harmonious society. Consequently, the landscape is separated out from the culture that it nourishes; land and people are divided in order to suggest the lack of fit between them. The inhabitants of these countries are implicitly alienated from the land in which they live; quite often landscape descriptions ignore any human figures, showing them as truly blank spaces that await the colonizer. Whereas Englishwomen reflect the beauty of the English landscape, Muslim, Arab, Indian, or African women do not reflect the beauty of the landscape in which they live. If they do mirror their environment, they portray the waste fertility of the jungles and forests; such women do not reflect the ordered productiveness of fields and woods, as does the virtuous Englishwoman.

Thus there is an important difference between perceptions of the beautiful in England and in the colonized and potentially colonizable countries: whereas land and people were seen as a unity in England, they were dissociated in alien lands. People were exotic, as were urban and hidden spaces such as bazaars and harems, for they were unknown and mysterious and sources of anxiety. The logic of transparency works here as well. Open fields and vistas that promised production and fertility and were open to view were beautiful, since they were seen to be needing the English to begin production.

It is not surprising, therefore, that there were far fewer representations in nineteenth-century travel narratives of "Eastern" women working on farms and fields than there were of Englishwomen, although such work was done by peasant women all over the world. Popular portrayals of Asian women showed them in harems and houses, in poses either erotic or idle; mostly upper-class women were described. Travel narratives also emphasized such roles, suggesting that these women, unlike the English, were wholly given over to erotic pleasures; the only work they were shown doing was ornamenting themselves. Thus the discrepancy between beautiful landscape and nonbeautiful and exotic women suggested that the people were not suited to the land; its value, as was often suggested by English travelers and those providing justification for imperialism, could only be brought out by the hardworking English. Here once again the idea of work and industry is valorized, as it has been done for the English working classes, but now in contrast to the industrious English, the idle East is shown, all the more to emphasize the value of work and to reveal it as an English characteristic. Furthermore, it was believed that since people in Asia were lazy and idle, it could not be left to them to get the maximum economic profit out of their lands; it was the industrious English who would be able to do so. For instance, the presence of the colonizer was justified by showing that Indian women textile workers, so important to British economic profit, were idle by nature.

Yet it must be kept in mind that despite the prevalent nineteenth-century discourse of work, the idealized, beautiful Englishwoman was one who was idle, who had servants for housework and did not work outside the home. Thus it was paradoxical to find fault with all "Eastern" women for the very quality that made Englishwomen beautiful: a life of leisure and submission to men. Yet the important difference presented to English readers was that the bourgeois Englishwoman's leisure was combined with a nonsexual morality of wifehood and motherhood, while "exotic" women were believed to be sensual with a sexuality that was seldom represented as being connected with motherhood. The discourse of race was thus refracted through that of labor. Whereas the married, middle-class Englishwoman was thought of as being uninterested in anything erotic, the woman of Asia was endowed with all the sensuality that the Victorian period repressed in its own culture but that it thought available in women of the lower classes and of "Southern lands."[71] Trollope's portrayal of the exotic Madame Neroni in *Barchester Towers* who, though English, is ruined by her stay in Spain, represents this view. She is sensual, barren, and, like an odalisque of orientalist paintings, spends her days reclining on a couch with a number of men around her.

Yet another reason why Asian women cannot be beautiful is that the English believed Asians lacked the proper idea of beauty. They believed such people lacked aesthetic perception. The universalizing of the Western, upper-class aesthetic had been visible in Burke; it does not disappear in the nineteenth century, for imperial power makes explicit what was only implied in Burke. For instance, Kipling's paternalistic attitudes toward the Indians, as well as his indictment of what Indians consider the norm of beauty, disqualifies them from participation in governing themselves. Kipling shows that the natives of the East cannot be judges of improvement or progress, since they lack the ability to make aesthetic distinctions. This inability is evident in the dirt in which the Indians live. Kipling describes the landscape of Calcutta, for instance, as that of filth, both moral and physical, which the "natives" cannot recognize is pathological; he suggests that it is only the English who can clean up this dirt. Though Kipling claims that he prefers the colors of the East, "the blistering blood-red under fierce sunlight that mellows and modifies all," to the "pale greens and sad reds" liked by the English, he implies that the love of passionate colors evident in the people of Asia is more the effect of nature than a consciously created aesthetic.[72]

The Indians, Kipling suggests, do not possess canons of taste. A prostitute who is beautiful by Indian standards is a "Fat Vice" to Kipling. The only woman that he finds beautiful is one that he says is "surprisingly different from all that experience taught of the beauty of the East." This beauty he describes as one that is not particularly admired by the Indians themselves, but is the beauty "that Byron sang of."[73] Kipling suggests that what seems aesthetically valuable to Indians is mere sensuality; such attitudes were common in English accounts of Indian art and functioned to contrast the divine and transcendent qualities of what was believed to be of highest aesthetic quality, such as classical Greek art, to Indian art. Many British novelists withdrew all sympathy for Indian art and culture because of what they saw as its licentiousness. One such writer, Flora Annie Steel, believed that the difference in the "sense of colour" between the Indians and the English was because of differences in sexual temperament attributable to racial characteristics; in one of her stories she states that "the difference between a brown and a white skin was the outward sign of the vast difference between sentiment and sheer passion."[74]

How this cultural superiority combines nationalism, imperialism, and racism by the end of the nineteenth century to create particular patriarchal discourses that discipline women in many locations is apparent in the writing of Rudyard Kipling. Home and harem, transparency and opacity, are all constructs visible in the way in which Kipling describes Indian women and Englishwomen, England and the United States, the land where Kipling spends some years of his life and where he feels he can find a transparent society.

For Kipling, the Indian prostitute cannot be called beautiful; in fact, he finds it difficult to see beauty in any prostitute. It is not surprising, therefore, that when he sees a Eurasian prostitute in Calcutta, he is appalled. He suggests that she has succumbed to the filth of the city itself, that she has "stooped to this common foulness in the face of the city," and that she has "offended against the white race."[75] Kipling wishes to believe that no white woman can be a prostitute, for it arouses the terrible specter of miscegenation as well as obscures the racial contrast between the virtuous Englishwoman and the virtueless Indian woman. An English prostitute he meets in Hong Kong is an even greater shock to him, for she has not even the partly Asian blood of the prostitute in Calcutta. The English prostitute in Hong Kong, who is also drunk when he meets her, leads him to comment that such a woman could cure all desire for sexual pleasure. He remarks, "if a man wishes to get out of pleasure with it [i.e., vice], let him go to Hong Kong." Conceding that "to one who has lived in India, [it is] something shocking to meet again Englishwomen in the same sisterhood," he comments that "if this be life, give me a little honest death."[76] Kipling wishes to establish that for an Englishwoman to fall to prostitution is so against the norm of her race that it is a fate worse than death. Such a belief was implicit in his warnings to Englishmen against miscegenation, for he cautioned each one to "keep to his own caste, race and breed."[77]

Kipling's aesthetic unites the representation of beauty with morality and with the law of race, though not of nationality that is open to transformation into race, as with Ruskin's "truths." Beauty, according to Kipling, is apparent only within his own race. In fact, he suggests that racial homogeneity is an element of beauty, and only within people of one's own race can that domestic beauty be found that makes a place or person into a haven. Rousseau's perfect republic is only possible with like-skinned people, not merely with like-minded ones. On his journey through the United States, narrated in *From Sea to Sea*, Kipling finds such a haven.[78] Since he believed the United

States was composed of immigrants from western Europe, he felt they belonged to the white race too. Thus he feels a sense of comfort and community in the little town of Musquash, near Chicago, even though he does find it tainted by "economic, business, mercenary America."[79] Kipling writes of Musquash:

Imagine a rolling wooded English landscape, under softest of blue skies. . . . The golden-rod blazed in the pastures . . . and the cows picked their way home through the twisted paths between the blackberry bushes. . . . All summer was in the orchards and the apples—such apples as we dream of when we eat the woolly imitations of Kashmir were ripe and toothsome. . . . Everybody in that restful place seemed to have as much as he wanted. Everybody knew everybody else intimately . . . here were Americans and no aliens—men ruling themselves, by themselves and for themselves and their wives and children—in peace, order and decency.[80]

For Kipling, this landscape, like that of England, is one of belonging and comfort. It has the familiar elements of a rural idyll: sunshine, cows, verdure, fertility. His description of the American / English countryside creates the picture of a rural idyll that is domestic, orderly, and peaceful, and this English America is seen as a perfect democracy. No class conflicts, such as those belonging to the reality of English life, or racial conflicts of Indian life, mar this landscape. Kipling's insistence on the sufficiency and homogeneity of this society evokes the dream of the perfect social contract in which citizens can assemble, regard themselves as a single body, and are sufficiently alike so that they are capable of exercising this single will for the common well-being.

Such a beautiful landscape could be found in America because of the racial homogeneity of a small town like Musquash; even though the racial homogeneity of England enabled such landscapes to be found in England as well, the conflicts of class and the politics of England were deeply disturbing to Kipling. He disliked socialist ideas, condemning them in a story called "My Son's Wife" as the "fevered breath" that needs to be brought back to health. His ideal, classless society was a bourgeois as well as patriarchal dream, where each class and gender had an assigned place.

Kipling's arrival at this English landscape came at the end of his journey through India, America, and South Africa. Though he had

called each of those places home during some part of his life, in the
end he went to England, where he remained until his death.[81]

The Feminine Binary:
The Discourse of Imperialism and Nationalism

At the same time as the "civilization" of working-class women was
under way in England, it was being carried out in the foreign lands
that were under British control. For just as the English working classes
were believed to be corrupt and degenerate, so were the inhabitants of
many of the lands of the so-called East. Like the English working
classes, they could not be beautiful because of their supposed lack of
moral virtues; they had to be colonized in order to be improved, and
this process involved the imposition of English patriarchal culture and
its capitalist economy. Yet the strategies used in the colonies were
quite different from those used in England, since racism provided the
rationale for changes in the colonial space.

Just as the movement toward domesticating working-class Englishwomen was an attempt at beautifying them into disciplined bodies
within a patriarchal culture, the move to "civilize" "Eastern" women
functioned to make them less opaque, to strip them of their veils, and
to remove them from harems where they lived lives hidden from the
European male. As Barbara Harlow suggests, "more than analogy
links the imperialist project of colonizing other lands and peoples with
the phantasm of appropriation of the veiled exotic female."[82] The
exotic, so European in its opacity, allure, and evil, was the aesthetic of
a civilizing endeavor that saw itself as the remover of darkness and
mystery.

If despotism embodies this opacity, then the harem, as a displacement of European monarchy, becomes a space that most clearly de-
picts this mode of control. Such a view is apparent in its earliest forms
in Montesquieu's *Persian Letters*.[83] There the harem is in disarray, with
fomenting rebellions, wives with no love for the husband / master,
intrigues, and crises. Such despotism in the domestic space embodies
the orientalist view of the harem. To this, in Montesquieu's inaugural
text of the European Enlightenment, is compared the dream of a
transparent society, one where self-government is done out of love.

Lisa Lowe has suggested that *Persian Letters* "allegorizes the problems and tensions of eighteenth-century France."[84] While it no doubt does so, the allegory is also directed at domestic despotism and the potential loss of masculine authority. The harem stands for the domestic space of home and nation, so that despotism is revealed as dangerous for order and peace. A transparent society of representative government and its counterpart in the home and marriages that are companionate serve as the solution to this despotism; here transparency implies an ability to govern through knowledge rather than through domination. In places that are seen as unknown and opaque, colonization becomes a way to render transparent that which is threatening. This principle of surveillance is what unites the disciplining of European middle-class women, the working classes in Europe, and the people who are colonized, though the technologies of power were different.

The veil and the harem were fascinating to European culture because they stood for the opacity that they believed marked what was radically different from Western culture. To remove these was to civilize the colonies, the first step toward creating a pacified, unthreatening, transparent populace, a need most obvious in the case of India from the middle of the nineteenth century, after the First Indian War of Independence in 1857. What was suggested in the travel narratives of writers such as Harriet Martineau and Rudyard Kipling was the oppression and incarceration of the "Eastern" women, an oppression that disguised the oppression of Englishwomen and gave English readers a false sense of their own unoppressed state. The harem was presented as a space of nonfreedom, evil, and idleness, where the greatest evil of all, sexual relations between women, occurred. To English patriarchal culture, this was, of course, the greatest evil, since a society of women was a threat that could only be expressed in terms of forbidden sexuality. For the harem was a place where women lived without men in a community of women, whereas the domestication of women within the nuclear family in the industrial states separated women and isolated them in their homes. As Leila Ahmed suggests, the harem need not be seen as a space of greater oppression; it could also be an area where "female relatives of a man . . . share much of their time and their living space, . . . which enables women to have frequent and easy access to other women in the community vertically, across class lines, as well as horizontally."[85] Despite Ahmed's view, it is difficult to adjudicate whether the separation of the sexes was more oppressive to women than their isolated incarceration within the nuclear family with its ideology of companionate marriage. Nevertheless, this female society was defined in English terms as a zone of evil, not to be replicated or condoned.

The seclusion of women in a separate space in the house was also given other terms in other places. Forms of veiling such as *ghunghat* or *purdah* signified this seclusion. In India it was the *zenana* or the *antahpur* that took on the symbolic differential function of the harem, even though the description of Hindu women in the nineteenth century in India was quite distinct from that of women in the Turkish or Egyptian harem. Despite their specificities, all these forms of seclusion of women from the public sphere or from male society were taken as a problem and as evil. While the harem women in orientalist texts were seen as promiscuous, duplicitous, and often as lesbians,[86] those in the Indian zenana were seen as passive and exploited as well as duplicitous. Englishwomen, lay and missionary, writing about India all referred to this space as dark, evil, dirty, confining, prisonlike, even though women's spaces did include the roof areas of houses and the inner courtyards.[87] The pleasures and joys of life in the antahpur are recorded in the writing of many Indian women, as are the restrictions. Mary Frances Billington writes in 1885, for instance, that the "bibighar or woman's home" was "architecturally and artistically its meanest part."[88] Malavika Karlekar points out that Indian reformers often blamed the behavior of women in the zenana as the reason for their oppression rather than the customs and conditions of patriarchal culture.[89] Consequently, for Indian reformers, the reform of the antahpur became essential.[90] This was done by the English and Indians through discourses of science in the name of improving practices of childbirth (the influence of the local midwife was seen as pernicious), of domestic hygiene (domestic science becomes a cornerstone of women's education by the end of the century), moralistic literature, and dress that in certain parts of India by incorporating some features of Western dress attempted to be respectable. The relative autonomy of the woman's world was threatened by such discourses, and the multiple discourses of colonial power infiltrated these domestic spaces. Even though it is important not to deny the oppressive nature of this world for many women, the representational practices of both the reformist and the colonialist were also objectifying and problematic. The English missionaries took on the task of fostering the ideology of Victorian domesticity in India, aiming to demonstrate to families that girls who had been to mission schools made superior wives and mothers.[91] Modernizing the domestic spaces was an important task.

The desire to remove the opacity of the women's space was also one to place "exotic" women under modes of patriarchal control that were quite different from indigenous patriarchal practices. Though Ester Boserup suggests that the usual result of colonization was the institutionalizing or increase of male power,[92] such claims suggest problematically that patriarchy was not a problem before colonialism, considering that anthropological inquiry is so mediated, and much remains to be done regarding the study of women's lives prior to, during, and after colonization. Yet what can be said is that colonialism certainly did not reform patriarchal power, despite the claims of English writing on colonialism. For economic reasons, and for ensuring the acceptance of the colonial regimes by the colonized male, patriarchy continued unabated, as feminists such as Pandita Ramabai (as I reveal in later chapters) would later argue, though it was transformed in many ways according to class lines and historical circumstances. According to Heidi Hartmann, because the colonial state is interested in the alienation of tribal lands and labor power, it "finds it convenient to use the traditional gender division of labor and resources in tribal society and places them in a hierarchical relationship, both internally and externally."[93] Yet the colonial state also created conditions for transformation of gender relations. For instance, in North India, the British government intervened in family and cultural practices to suggest that the seclusion of a woman was a problem only when they found out that agricultural productivity, and their revenue, was not as high as it could be with the contribution of women's labor.[94]

Many studies of contact and transformation of specific Indian patriarchal forms by colonial patriarchal ones are now being done, showing how, for instance, emerging nationalisms, in response to the need for removal of colonial power, created "traditions" that involved altered and new forms of control of women. Other studies record the impact of developmental and modernization policies on women's

lives. However, none of these studies suggest that colonial rule less-
ened or removed patriarchal oppression. Some of the changes under
colonial rule that continued the oppression of women include the
introduction of models of companionate marriage with its homo-
phobic heterosexual norms, as in English society, to the bourgeois
middle classes in India as an alternative to the Indian family structure's alternate heterosexuality. In matrilineal areas of South India,
female claims to maintenance under joint family ownership were
replaced by new revenue settlements and laws that gave male heads of
households sole property rights.[95]

The Feminine Binary: Indian Nationalism

The complex nexus of discursive practices that construct the home
and the harem as a binary includes the ways in which this binary is
taken up by Indians as well. The "woman question" was one that
vexed both Indian men and women as well as the British colonialists.
For the nationalists, the concern is the place of women within the
imagined nation-state, an imaginary that is visible as an upper-class
patriarchal discourse. The sexuality that is seen as the problematic
aspect of women's lives forms the opacity that is to be removed if the
transparent nation is to be gained and to become a reality. For instance, as Tapan Raychoudhuri shows, even as Bankimchandra Chat-
topadhyay, the foremost Bengali writer of the nineteenth century,
approves of Western notions of equality between men and women,[96]
he still sees sexual relations, even between husbands and wives, as a
threat.

Partha Chatterjee, in his essay, "The Nationalist Resolution of the
Women's Question," suggests that the material/spiritual division
was taken up by Indian nationalists as analogous to the division between the private and the public, the inner and the outer, the *ghar*
(home) and the *bahir* (outside).[97] Chatterjee argues that the problem
of women's role within nationalism was resolved by constructing the
space of home as the repository of nationalist culture and the embodiment of the spiritual element that characterized India, while the West
was supposed to be symbolic of what was material. If the home was
the space of women, then the protection of home, of the spirit, was a

central concern. Chatterjee's essay is limited in his regional emphasis on one class of male writers in Bengal who wish to deny, while using the Victorian binary of public and private spheres, that the home is infiltrated by colonial formations just as much as the market. Yet it is useful to suggest that such an alteration of British discourse was done by some Indian reformers in an attempt to erase women's sexuality, agency, and emerging modernity. Here the "home" and "harem" division is utilized in a different way: while Indian women embody the "home," Western women then become, in their mingling freely with men and women, symbols of the "material," of the "world" as opposed to the spirit; Englishwomen are believed to be sexually promiscuous, as were the women in the harem. Any Indian woman who read novels, used Western cosmetics and jewelry, did needlework, or rode in open carriages was believed to imitate Englishwomen and consequently was ridiculed; forms of sexuality among Indian women were ignored. Unfortunately, Chatterjee does not present the vociferous and highly charged contestations of such discourses by many Indian men and women nor the debates that fracture the binary. Chatterjee points out that it was believed that Western women were fond of useless luxury and did not care for their homes. This inversion of the English discourse of women, work, and beauty reveals not a colonial mimicry, but a reconstitution of colonial paradigms that created a nationalist culture that utilized women as grounds for a discourse rather than as subjects of it.[98]

Just as the discourse of the woman "caged" in the harem, in purdah, becomes the necessary Other for the construction of the Englishwoman presumably free and happy in the home, the discourse of the Englishwoman's association with men and women becomes, for Indian nationalism, a sign of depravity. The "purdah" construct of the English imperialists becomes the "home" of the Indian nationalists; Indian women's location in the women's part of the house becomes the symbol of what is sacred and private for Indian nationalist culture. The colonialist's use of Englishwomen as signs of the advanced state of their civilization is seen by Indian nationalists as the depraved state of Western culture. For all these discourses, women's changing role within nation and culture is the issue, one that is fraught with anxiety and fear. *Memsahib* comparisons abound in the literature written by Indian men; and it is by comparison with this *memsahib* that roles for

Indian women in the nationalist struggle can be contained and regulated. For instance, Kundamala Devi writes in 1870, "If you have acquired real knowledge, then give no place in your heart to Memsahib like behavior."[99] The memsahib as shameless, immodest, and sexually promiscuous was a powerful formation for disciplining women in India. Even an admirer, like Swami Vivekananda, of what was often seen as the more egalitarian nature of Western society could write the following of the women in London, rearticulating the fear of women's opacity as symbolized by face powder:

> Here come the hussies with parasols
> Their heads in pretty bonnets
> Tonnes of flour on each face
> Who knows from how many baskets.[100]

Yet despite this opposition to the memsahib, it is also clear that Victorian notions of respectability had a powerful impact as well. Emerging Indian patriarchal discourses could not place all women in the spiritual realm, for clearly there was also a need for a new model of secular femininity. The discourse of modernity required the construction of the middle-class woman, like the Victorian ideal, as docile, gentle, asexual, and nurturing.[101] Victorian values were absorbed but placed on Indian women while suggesting Englishwomen did not have to keep to these values. In both Victorian and Indian cultures, it is clear that transnational influences and knowledges are seen as threatening in terms of enabling forms of sexuality for women that are not sanctioned by the dominant patriarchal culture. Bankimchandra Chatterjee's writings reveal this concern with women's sexuality. In his novel, *Anandamath*, it is not the domestic space that is of concern but the sublimation of sexuality by both men and women.[102] While women have to contain their sexuality, men have to protect themselves from such a threat. Other writers and thinkers, such as Dayanand, were also concerned with women's sexuality and how it had to be managed. Susie Tharu suggests that Toru Dutt, the first Indian woman poet who wrote in English, turned her heroines into virtuous Victorians.[103] The lack of middle-class bourgeois "respectability" of women artistes, courtesans, poor women, and women from lower castes came to be seen as a threat by the middle of the nineteenth century such that forms of sexuality were disciplined in new ways. In

Bengal, for instance, with the creation of a powerful *bhadralok* (urban middle class) through colonial education, a concerted effort was made to suppress forms of popular culture, both religious and secular.[104]

Home and harem were useful spatial tropes by which female subjects were constructed in both England and India within a colonial context that linked patriarchal practices. Class and gender formation functioned to provide bodies for a disciplinary aesthetics that modified itself according to context. How Englishwomen negotiated with these practices forms the topic of the next chapter.

Chapter 2

Empire and the Movement
for Women's Suffrage
in Britain

~☙~

For feminist individualism in the age of imperialism, the stake was the making of human beings. That meant the constitution and interpellation of the subject not only as an individual but as individualist.[1]

As I have suggested, the Burke-Ruskin model of beauty, which emphasized purity and spirituality as prerequisites, operated somewhat differently in the colonial arena. Colonized women, and here my focus is on Indian women, were never seen as beautiful in the way Englishwomen were believed to be. Flora Annie Steel, the English woman writer of colonial India, like many other travelers of the time, portrayed the licentious women of the East in order to emphasize the nonsensuality of Englishwomen; the necessity for Englishwomen to be pure and moral was inscribed by the opposition between women of the East and the West. What was suggested, as well, was that sexuality for the sole purpose of production of children was the role of Englishwomen, in contrast to the nonproductive sexuality of the Eastern woman that was devoted to the pursuit of mere pleasure. Ruskin's law of nationality in the colonial context becomes more simply formed as a law that is plainly racist, for Kipling and Steel were writing at the height of England's imperial power. That imperialist attitudes were repressive for women in England is suggested by the fact that Steel disliked the rise of the women's emancipation movement in England during the nineteenth century, believing that such women only desired sexual liberation, while she believed that marriage was "a duty to the race" and was unrelated to sexuality, or "intense personal pleasure," as she called it and of which she disapproved.[2]

While Steel, Kipling, Ruskin, and Burke can be seen as writers invested in English patriarchy as a central element in the formation of Englishness, it is important to also look at the writings of those opposing or ambivalent to patriarchy. In this chapter, I examine texts from those who were seen as suffragists as well as those who were not suffragists but were involved with various women's reform movements in England. If, as I and many others have suggested, masculine ideology is central to imperial discourse, what then is the relation of those who oppose patriarchy to imperial structures, to colonization, and to English imperial nationalism?

The implication of feminism within imperialism and racism at the present time demands such questions. For it is only by looking at the discursive spaces that feminisms occupy, spaces that are imbricated within other discourses of state and nation, that we can see feminisms not as orthodoxies, but as ongoing practices of locational politics, as the work of Caren Kaplan reveals in regard to contemporary U.S. feminisms.[3] What Lata Mani calls their "multiple mediations" therefore need to be examined in order to formulate progressive politics.[4] It is clear that understanding of one's own oppression does not result in understanding of all oppressions; feminism, for instance, did not create an automatic antipathy toward imperialism in late nineteenth- and early twentieth-century England. To believe in the liberatory possibilities of a singular identity politics is to simplify enormously the connections between the state, different social divisions, emerging identities, and various subject positions occupied by women.

However, it would also be inaccurate to see the English suffragists' politics of imperialism as similar to that of upper-class and bourgeois Englishmen. While Victorian imperial culture inculcated a belief in English superiority because of race and civilization and created orientalist notions of other "inferior" cultures, bourgeois Englishwomen fighting for their rights used nationalist rhetoric for vastly different reasons than working-class Englishmen, for instance. Their utilization of the discourse of beauty, domesticity, and nation reveals a specific class and gender position.

Even for suffragists such as Josephine Butler, beauty was normative and the surface manifestation of inner qualities. Thus in arguing for the education of women and the amelioration of the conditions in which poor women lived, Butler praises women who are "happy, industrious workers" and possess "that kind of beauty of face and mind which an earnest life imparts and which is never seen in an idle or frivolous woman."[5] In opposition to popular notions of beauty, she argues: "Who has not felt that the attractiveness of our better-class women, who often lead the life of butterflies, is spoiled by the vanity and egotism which so easily take possession of minds devoid of great thoughts, and deprived of the invigorating influence of work." An important strand of the discourse of beauty is apparent here: the connection of beauty with transparency, which by valorizing the discourse of work for women, still connects beauty with virtue and utility.[6] Butler's views uphold the idea of beauty as normative and as an aesthetic that seems to break down class and race divisions even while it implicitly upholds them. Though Butler identifies virtues different from those of Burke or Ruskin, since she believed the best virtue was hard work rather than submission, she too sees the domestic virtues as the best virtues of a woman. For her, work was an important component of domestic life since the life of a working woman in a family was nothing but hard work.

What connects Butler with the other nineteenth-century writers was her concern for describing the domestic as the proper role for women, and the English nation as a domestic space. For Butler's introduction to collected essays by prominent suffragists and their supporters, *Woman's Work and Woman's Culture*, is a discourse on women as part of religion ("Christian women," "Christian community") and nation ("our fair England"). Also continuing that comparison of women and landscape, through which "improvement" becomes a metaphor for reform, she suggests that the present condition of women in England is like a "blight over so many estates in our fair England."[7] Arguing for teaching women different trades so that they can support themselves, she positions herself as one who knows the value of "home," saying "I believe that Home is the nursery of all virtue, the fountain-head of all true affection, and the main source of strength of our nation" and that she speaks from "the heart of my beloved home, with my children around me. . . ."[8] Attempting to change the notion of the "domestic" as involving work in conjunction with freedom from dependency on a man, she argues that the "highest beauty will be found to rest upon the greatest utility," using a Benthamite argument while making distinctions in class and race necessary to her discourse. Thus in her essay, while revealing that among tens of thousands of prostitutes, more than fifteen hundred were found, in an inquiry, to be under fifteen years of age, she says, "Think of this, you mothers who are living at ease, in your pleasant drawing rooms, with your tender darlings around you!"[9] Distinctions of class are also accompanied by comparisons with differences of race, where Englishwomen (masculinized) are different from (emasculated) "flaccid Brazilian creepers which cannot exist without support" and similar to slaves who freed themselves through searching in the Bible for arguments against slavery.[10] A discourse of religion and race is essential for constructing this nationalist female subject.

Butler's attitude toward empire is clear in her crusade against the Contagious Diseases Acts in India, which she took up after the successful abolition of these acts in England. Antoinette Burton, in her essay, "The White Woman's Burden," writes that even though Butler was concerned with the oppression and exploitation of her Indian "sisters," she saw the cause of Indian women as a means of ensuring "the well-being of their own England."[11] Burton argues that Butler termed Indians "fellow subjects," thus repeating gestures of imperial citizenship that denied power differences between Indians and English. Thus in suffrage literature, feminists claimed their rights to citizenship on the grounds of being part of the "political nation and empire."

Burton's argument about the participation of English middle-class feminists, which is central to notions of feminist subject formation in England, is important in examining the role of English women travelers to Asia and Africa and the connection between English feminism and imperialism. However, the relation between British middle-class women and Indian women within a nexus of colonial power relations is central not only to British feminist subject formation but also to the construction of all British female subjects. Thus it is not only feminists who refer to Indian women as "exploited" and "oppressed" but all middle-class British women who do so; British feminist discourse is thus on a continuum with other discourses within England, though the subjects' positions are different. Notions such as companionate marriage are formed in relation to oriental despotism and the harem, and this form of marriage suggests new ways for women to position themselves in English society within the domestic space. The construction of the harem as a space of female incarceration within "traditional" and "unprogressive" "Eastern" societies uses a contrast with the "freedom" of European women. New strategies of disciplining societies through knowledge and surveillance rather than through domination are evident in the binary of freedom and unfreedom that marks colonial discourses on women in India and that enables female subject formation in England.

Jane Eyre in the Colonies: "Helpmeet" and Comrade

Englishwomen who traveled to the colonies were perceived as intrepid pioneers whose accounts revealed the dangers and discomforts they had to undergo. Their efforts showed them to be able, like Englishmen, to withstand the rigors of life in the supposedly enervating and harmful climates of Asia and Africa. Participating in the project of colonization as travelers, missionaries, teachers, and ethnographers, these Englishwomen broke down the bourgeois ideals of the "angel in the house" and helped, implicitly and explicitly, in the cause of women's suffrage in Britain. Their narratives showed their attempts to be the equals of bourgeois and upper-class Englishmen and superior to many peoples of the world. By doing so, they also became part of the nationalist discourse of empire.

Charlotte Brontë's *Jane Eyre* reveals this perception of the pioneering Englishwoman and is a text that has caused much discussion in the area of feminism and imperialism in the context of English literary studies.[12] When Jane is asked to join in missionary work with St. John Rivers, she believes it to be a life of work and sacrifice. However, she feels she can perform this vocation only as a comrade of Rivers. Missionary work is, to her, an alternative to marriage and family life. Despite the fact that the colonies were seen as places where Englishwomen were to be protected from the rapacious and oversexed "natives," imperial needs came to require Englishwomen in order to keep the colonists from cohabiting with "native" women. Jane, acting within English imperial and racial beliefs but trying to break gender norms, is willing to go as the equal of Rivers. Instead, Rivers asks her to accompany him to India as a "helpmeet and fellow-labourer," defining this position as that of a wife whom he can "influence efficiently in life, and retain absolutely till death."[13] Rivers's needs are those of the colonial state. Realizing Rivers's will to dominate, his "hardness and despotism," which recalls the colonial trope of the oriental despot, she refuses to go as his wife. As his comrade, on the other hand, she feels she can endure the life of a missionary, "cross oceans with him . . . toil under Eastern suns, in Asian deserts," and even admire him as long as she can remain free and "still have my unblighted self to turn to."[14]

Her offer to be his equal, to be his comrade with "a fellow-soldier's frankness, fidelity, fraternity," as she describes it, is rejected when Rivers makes her wifely subservience essential to her becoming a missionary.[15] What is made evident in this episode is Jane's strength, which is opposed to Rivers's problematic desire for domination. His recourse to conventional sexual morality is contrasted with her independence and willingness to work in India with him. Male superiority is questioned in the context of missionary work, where it is implied that Englishwomen also possess the capability for such work. More importantly, the Englishwoman's position in the colonies is clearly delineated here. Deemed inferior by Englishmen who see women's subjugation and peripherality as an intrinsic part of the hierarchy of a masculine nation and empire, Englishwomen see the colonies as a space to prove their capabilities and their participation in the work of the nation for civilizing the "natives."

It is also important that Brontë's text then goes on to show that, refused her terms by Rivers, Jane becomes instead the wife and comrade of Rochester, who is weakened through his connection with the colonized woman, Bertha Mason. Jane can be comrade to Rochester when the increasing interest in women's concerns and capabilities combined with the Enlightenment ideology of equality turns marriage into companionate marriage.[16] Within such a conceptualization of marriage, Jane and Rochester provide a new bourgeois heterosexual couple, the emerging notion of the nuclear family of the nineteenth century. Furthermore, imperial masculinity, condemned in Rivers's case, is endorsed in Rochester's, when it is not autonomous but is needy. Jane becomes the comrade and wife of the Englishman harmed by a colonized, dark woman. Englishman and Englishwoman support each other to form a new version of the domestic unit in the domestic space. Whereas Rivers allows Jane the role of a missionary only when it is combined with that of a wife and mother, in England the strong

Englishwoman can be wife and mother and a comrade (though the last occurs only within the ideals of a heterosexual, companionate marriage) in order to nurture and care for a masculinity wounded by the colonial encounter. What is implied is that a strong nation is to be made up of Englishmen and Englishwomen who are comrades; Englishwomen are as central to the formation of empire as the men.

However, the role of "helpmeet," despite Jane's implicit superiority, remains a problematic issue, for she does not break out of the domestic space. Few women, even those more involved in struggles for Englishwomen's rights, were able to do so. Yet within the narrative of *Jane Eyre*, Jane's subject constitution becomes central, through opposition and comparison with Bertha and through the battle for her equality with Englishmen who wished to dominate her. Peripheralized herself by a patriarchal culture, Jane's peripheralizing of Bertha Mason enables her entry, however partial, into the colonizer's masculine world and her sharing of Rochester's imperial subjectivity.

The colonies become, therefore, doubly important in showing the capabilities of Englishwomen. As liminal spaces, they can be proving grounds for Englishwomen's attempts at equality with Englishmen, their superiority to colonized men, and their ability to be a part of the project of empire conceived of as a heterosexual and masculinist project. As dangerous spaces, they show the vulnerability of English masculinity and the attempts of Englishwomen to control and share this masculinity that is essential to the English family and nation. Many texts, such as those by Richard Francis Burton, which delineated a colonial space of homosexual masculinity, no doubt compounded this threat. The text thus questions the necessity for the colonial project to be a purely male one, while questioning the subjugation of Englishwomen. However, it does not question the imperial project itself, since it is this very project that enables the subject constitution of the bourgeois Englishwoman.

In her essay, "Three Women's Texts and a Critique of Imperialism," Gayatri Spivak suggests that *Jane Eyre* is concerned with the constitution of Jane's subjectivity as "female individualist" through the Othering of Bertha Mason by the operation of "imperialist axiomatics."[17] While, as Jenny Sharpe suggests, the Indian woman remains the shadowy double of Jane, Jane's superior position is not as evident as Spivak suggests.[18] Her subject constitution occurs through comparisons and opposition to the Englishmen in the text as well as through Bertha. It is only because she is deemed inferior by her countrymen, in both her gender and class position, that it becomes essential for Jane to establish herself as a subject. To do this, she claims her class and racial superiority in order to accede to the position of Rochester's comrade by the end of the novel. As comrade, Jane's position supposedly becomes different from St. John Rivers's version of a good missionary wife, the subservient "helpmeet." However, the "imperial axiomatics" that allow her to claim her subject position at the same time keep her within the domestic space. Her subject position remains problematic, even at the end of the novel.

The process by which Jane is created as the Other of Bertha in order to constitute herself is called "worlding" by Spivak. By this term she means the ignored and imperial use of colonized people for the formation of the Western subject.[19] This "worlding," as in *Jane Eyre*, was also an intrinsic part of the English movement for women's suffrage, which started around 1860, over a decade after the publication of *Jane Eyre*, in 1847, when women in England fought for their rights with frequent references to the subordination and incarceration of Asian women. At that time a supporter of women's rights such as John Boyd-Kinnear could ask in an essay published in 1869 on "The Social Position of Women" whether forbidding women from participating in issues outside the home was not equivalent to placing them in a harem: "Do we not in truth reduce them to the mere slaves of the harem? Do we not, like those who keep such slaves, deny in fact that they have any souls? What can they do with souls, if nature means them only to be toys of our idle hours, the adornment of our ease and wealth, to be worshipped as idols but never taken as helpmates, permitted at most to gaze from afar at the battles of life. . . ."[20]

By contrast with the inhabitants of the harem, Boyd-Kinnear suggests that Englishwomen are not "idols" or "toys" or objects for "adornment," but must be seen as "helpmates" who participate in every aspect of an integrated public and private life. His definition of the "helpmate" is very different from St. John Rivers's subservient "helpmeet," though both terms reveal that in no case were Englishwomen to lose their roles as nurturers or be the equals of men in the public realm. The woman in the harem is also present in this statement, for it was the "Eastern" woman who was believed to be the "toy" of the despotic husband; such women were thought to spend all their time in the harem adorning themselves, indulging in lesbian sexual practices that were deemed unspeakable by the English patriarchy. Englishwomen were to be different.

Nation and Empire: Suffragists, Pioneering Women, and New Perceptions of Women

The idea of the Englishwoman as one who had rights, powers, and capabilities that reached those of Englishmen emerged from contrasts with Asian women. It also emerged from the accounts of adventures of English women travelers, emigrants, and explorers whose adventures showed that they could be the equals of Englishmen. Travel that was secular, for reasons other than pilgrimage, was taken to imply a mobility that was synonymous with freedom and rights for women. Women in purdah, supposedly without this mobility, believed unable to move out from their homes, were considered without such rights or freedom. The contrast supported the belief that to be able to travel was to be free from gender constraints. As travelers, ethnologists, missionaries, and reformers, Englishwomen could show their equality with Englishmen by participating in the colonial project that was defined in purely heterosexual, masculinist terms as a "penetration" and "mastery" of "virgin" territory or of feminine and weak cultures. By such participation, they could uphold their supposed racial and national superiority over Eastern women that, many Englishwomen felt, justified their possession of equal rights with men. Women such as Hester Stanhope and Jane Digby, who traveled to the Middle East and lived among the Bedouins, became famous for their ability to do so; they proved that they could live the life of the "Other" as much as men such as Richard Francis Burton or Charles Doughty.[21] They proved too the power of an Englishness that could be supposedly inviolate while living and being in the "East," which was depicted as the antithesis of the "West,"[22] even while their narratives were gendered to show the extra effort required to do so and the difficulties faced by women attempting to live in these lands. Their Englishness, though seen as inferior to that of Englishmen, supposedly made them superior to any "native" man or woman. The popularity of travel narratives, and the fame of the women travelers, who petitioned to be members of the Royal Geographical and Anthropological Societies and thus opened more doors for women, contributed to perceptions of Englishwomen, their freedoms and their abilities, that supported the battle for women's suffrage in England.

Many Englishwomen in the nineteenth century, even those who were sympathetic to the issues of women's rights in England, saw Asian women with great contempt, thus reinforcing their own freedom and superiority. Women who stood for women's rights, the "new woman" at the turn of the century, and women travelers to Asia demonstrated what was seen as the Englishwoman's mobility—her adventurous, pioneering, mobile spirit. All these women saw the "oriental" woman as an example of submission that symbolized what they were fighting against and what they did not wish to be: the immobile women, in seclusion at home, without any rights that brought them to the public arena. The orientalist trope of the "veil" and the "harem" was thus essential to such a discourse. As a part of the "civilized" culture, which perceived itself as superior in being against despotism and promulgating representational government, Englishwomen were seen as free and therefore different from Asian women. The contrast between the English female traveler and "Eastern" inhabitant of the harem emphasized the mobile-immobile, free-unfree opposition that was part of the structure of colonial relations.

Though they were alive to the subordination of Asian and English women, those nineteenth-century Englishwomen who fought for their rights were not against the project of empire. For most of them, empire was a matter of pride as well as a policy that did not need contestation. It was important to see themselves as part of a "civilizing" nation, for that could imply a nation that would not subjugate or exploit its own people. Being part of the empire also gave them a sense of racial superiority that enabled them to feel their own worth and equality with men. Even Annie Besant, who fought for women's suffrage, was against direct British rule of India, and became an important figure in the Indian movement for independence, was well known as one of the most famous and remarkable women in the world. Her openness to Hindu culture and religion came more from a problematic universalism rather than from a reaction to British values. She fought for India's Home Rule and for its status as dominion or commonwealth but was not comfortable with a struggle for complete independence from Britain.[23] It is important to remember, however, that Annie Besant, as well as Margaret Cousins, the other British woman who was vital to the beginnings of Indian feminism, were both Irish so that they were more receptive to anti-English and anti-colonial movements.[24]

Most of the "pioneering" women (as the women travelers were often called) were supportive of the imperialist project; they called upon the same positive-negative dichotomy of masculine-feminine functions and abilities as did those who opposed granting English-women any voting rights or any measure of equality. As a consequence, they did not extend their protest to a critique of industrial economy or patriarchal systems, nor did many of them protest the interrelated notions of class and race hierarchies that supported the culture of colonialism in England. By retaining these hierarchies, and supporting the masculinist project of colonialism, the suffrage movement was able to evoke nationalist sentiment by making itself distinct from the colonized women even while indicating their exploitation and thus their similarity to them. Racial superiority and national pride, so integral in the habitus of empire, was often used as the basis for the demand for women's votes.

The nationalist discourse of the Englishwomen's suffrage movement is only recently being scrutinized by scholars. Yet when English-women's rights to vote and for equality are made through and against the discourse of the confinement of colonized women, and within the view of nation as empire, these national and racial components must be examined. For instance, at the fifth annual conference of the Women's Labor League in January 1910, a Mrs. Annot Robinson from central Manchester argued that the enfranchisement of women was "a burning question for the country, for the race, for women and children."[25] Even during the First World War, opposition to the women's vote came from those who argued that since women had not fought in the war or defended the empire, they should not have the vote.[26] Furthermore, an imperial, masculinist nationalism would also have functioned to repress alternate forms of sexuality within England, participating in the increased surveillance of gendering sexual practices.

In many ways it was remarkable that many advocates of women's suffrage were pro-empire, for their opponents included die-hard colonialists. Yet empire figured in the debates for women's rights, for it was a symbol of masculinity, while giving the vote to women was believed to result in the emasculation of England. Thus it is not surprising that many prominent men who were pro-empire were anti-suffragists. A list of antisuffragists published in 1910 and 1911 by the *Anti-Suffrage Review* lists Kipling, Cromer, Curzon, and Joseph Chamberlain, all men who had much to do with England's imperialist policies.[27] For these men, the empire was a symbol of masculinity and Englishwomen were the keepers of morals and the angels of the house; colonial matters, involving miscegenation and the darker mysteries of exotic life, were not to touch these women, as Kipling's fiction reveals. Furthermore, women were considered unqualified to make decisions in the masculine enterprise of empire. For instance, a member of Parliament, Mr. J. A. Grant, said in the House of Commons in 1913: "In controlling a vast Empire like our own, an Empire built by the mental and physical capacity of men, and maintained, as it always must be maintained, by the physical and mental capacity of masterly natures—I ask; 'is there a place for women?' "[28]

Such ideas had earlier gained prominence in the writings of Mrs. Eliza Linton, who wrote misogynistic and anti–women's suffrage tracts in the 1870s and 1880s, calling the suffragists "wild women" and "shrieking sisters." In 1889, she argued that women's suffrage would blur sex differences and create a nation of emasculated men and mannish women. Virile England would become "a feminine nation pure and simple."[29] Being both an antisuffragist and an imperialist, she supported "the manly doctrine of readiness for war . . . and the steady expansion of the Empire."[30] As her biographer records, she saw foreign policy in terms of (hetero)sexual stereotypes, arguing also that home rule was not for the "feminine" Irish, who should stay under the "manly" control of England.

Since the suffragists were equally pro-empire and had similar orientalist views, Linton was answered by Millicent Fawcett in terms that did not radically change the argument.[31] Fawcett pointed out that though Turkey was a country that oppressed its women terribly, it was also the most effeminate, again showing a feminine nation to be a problem. She dismissed the idea of any sympathy between women since the feminine men of Turkey were shown to be exploiting the women of Turkey. Thus feminine characteristics were indicated as being responsible for oppressing women, even while colonial discourse claimed that masculine penetration was a civilizing venture for the amelioration of the "natives." Though refuting the argument that enfranchisement of women was emasculating to the nation, Fawcett yet believed that Turkey was a feminine nation, showing that she too saw the colonized and Eastern counties as effeminate, and also upholding the claim that the project of colonization was a virile one. Thus both pro- and antisuffragists saw the colonized nations as feminine, leaving unchallenged the notion of empire-building as a masculine endeavor or as a problematic project. Fawcett's argument, in which Turkey became a "feminine" nation, indicates the ways in which race distinctions undermined the status of women even while it appealed to nationalist rhetoric in order to show the worth of Englishwomen. What Fawcett implies is that Englishwomen are masculine on the basis of race, while the Turkish men are feminine; it is unclear what gender Turkish women are. In such a comparison, however, the denial of Englishwomen's votes and rights threatened the status of England as a "civilized" nation by showing racial unity being broken by the gender division. However, such a threat was always contained by the appeal to national and racial superiority that makes England a "masculine" nation of hard workers who can obtain empires. This masculine status is, by the logic of such suffragists, not threatened if Englishwomen are given the vote.

Thus neither side broke out of orientalist perceptions of the "East" that were based on notions of race and gender. In fact, for the suffragists, the purdah system of Asia and the Middle East was the example that most eloquently argued for women's rights, while antisuffragists like Mrs. Linton claimed that do-gooders in the colonies who condemned the purdah system did not understand that women in purdah were happy to be protected. Both sides saw imperialism as an admirable venture: for Mrs. Linton it protected "native" women; for Fawcett, it worked to reform their lives. As recent historiography has shown, colonial reform movements simply changed the nature of Indian women's subordination; they did not achieve much in giving them self-determination or rights.[32]

Even John Stuart Mill, whose inclusion of women's suffrage in his platform in 1865 inaugurated a concerted and systematic battle for women's suffrage in England, was a supporter of colonization. This support of colonization was clearly stated in his *Principles of Political Economy*: "There needs to be no hesitation in affirming that Colonization, in the present state of the world, is the best affair of business, in which the capital of an old and wealthy country can be engaged."[33] Colonization became also a solution to the continued exploitation of Englishwomen in the sewing trade, in governessing, domestic service, and the factories, as well as the problem of numbers of poor women in workhouses and in the streets. The Malthusian perception of the sheer numbers of women who were poor and exploited led to a belief in the need to relieve the crowding of the English cities by emigration. More space, available in the colonies, would ease the burden on England and give employment to those left behind. The solution to the exploitation of women was to be an expansion of the nation and its markets.

In light of such domestic problems, most suffragists favored the idea of empire, since many of them saw it as an opportunity for bettering the lot of poor and unemployed women. Isa Craig, who in 1858 joined the famous Langham Place Group led by Barbara Bodichon, presented a paper on "Emigration as a Preventive Agency" at the National Association for the Promotion of Social Science, which was later reprinted in *The English Woman's Journal* in 1859.[34] In this she argues that crime is a result of unemployment and the colonies are the perfect place to provide this employment. Another member of the Langham Place Group, Maria Susan Rye, in 1861 organized the Female Middle Class Emigration Society to supervise the welfare at sea and in the colonies of women emigrants. In an essay entitled "On Assisted Emigration," published in *The English Woman's Journal* in 1860, she remarks that greater enthusiasm about emigration needs to be generated. She writes that it is a mystery to her that "any nation possessing such magnificent colonies as ours should hold such varied views and display such apathy on the subject of emigration as is shown in England."[35] Since many women were exploited in the colonies in Australia, Canada, and New Zealand, or lived there under tremendous hardships,[36] it is not surprising that the poor and working classes were hesitant to leave for unknown dangers. Yet Rye saw emigration as the way to alleviate the overpopulation in England that crowded cities like London, while "the colonies, quite as much our own though they are thousands of miles away, remain year after year uninhabited wastes without man or beast."[37] Rye's words reveal the nationalist pride of ownership in the colonies that the suffragists had. Moreover, the inhabitants of these lands were either invisible or non-human; to Rye, as to most of the English, these lands were empty and available for colonization.

Even those women who did not think emigration was the solution for the "superfluous women" were not opposed to colonization.[38] Jessie Boucherett, opposed to the emigration of women, thought that it would be extremely advantageous if more men were made to emigrate, for then employment opportunities would increase for the women remaining in England. Furthermore, she believed that the pioneering work of colonization was better done by men, for "in uncivilized regions there is a vast amount of rough hard work to be done that can only be done by men, and is better done by men unencumbered by wives."[39] For Boucherett, therefore, the setting up of colonies was a masculine task and an important part of the role of a "civilized" nation such as England; she writes that "a vast army of pioneers are employed all along the borders of civilization."[40]

The division of the world into "civilized" and "uncivilized" regions, in which the latter have to be settled and "tamed" by Englishmen, was part of the habitus of the suffragists. In such a discourse, national pride was dominant, even when English patriarchal attitudes toward Englishwomen and the plight of tens of thousands of women in England were being deplored. With such views on emigration and empire, the fight for women's suffrage became a struggle for the improvement of the nation. Boucherett therefore says, "What a strange spectacle does the great English empire present to the world! Savages doing Englishmen's work abroad; men doing women's work at home; and women starving, begging, and sinning, because they can get no honest employment."[41] What is called upon is the image of England as a powerful nation and as an empire that needs to be set in order. In such an empire, the sexes in England must each have an assigned place in order to prevent any poverty.

In this formulation, furthermore, the English empire consisted of savages, Englishmen, and Englishwomen. Women of the colonies have no place in this view of the empire, for the gender of the "savages" is of no concern; "native" women are invisible but at the same time symbolize the "savage" customs that mark by contrast the racial superiority of English culture that should and could allow equality to its own women but paradoxically does not. Thus Boucherett claims that if Chinese men were less lazy they would emigrate and not have to drown their superfluous female infants. She suggests that Englishmen, being hardworking and solicitous of their women, must emigrate in larger numbers and improve working conditions for Englishwomen. The imperial discourse of British "industry" versus "Eastern indolence" is here utilized by the suffragists to suggest the need for Englishmen to emigrate. Female infanticide in China becomes a "savage" custom that is contrasted to the "civilized" practice of emigration and colonization.

Though emigration occurred in large numbers to the supposedly "empty" lands such as Canada and Australia, many more women went to colonies such as India after 1860, when the question of Englishwomen's suffrage was becoming important. Their presence did not affect English notions of racial and cultural superiority. Instead, their presence in larger numbers created an even greater division between the Indians and the English, for most Englishwomen lived in English communities along race and class lines without associating with the "natives."[42] Protection of English womanhood endorsed many forms of racial discrimination; their presence in the colonies was, as Ann Stoler points out, "intended precisely to enforce the separation between Asians and whites."[43] Though themselves subject to many restrictions, Englishwomen nevertheless participated in the colonial habitus of racial and class divisions. Any solidarity with Indian women was forestalled by racial divisions as well as the imperialist discourse of competition for Englishmen as the objects of desire for both Indian and English women. Such a discourse is visible in the many fictional narratives depicting the Englishman rescuing the "native" woman. Moreover, the separation of the English residential areas from the "native" bazaars did not allow for the mingling of the colonizing and colonized women. The creation of new towns, some in the hills away from what was perceived as the crowded and unhealthy plains, enabled the English to live separated from the Indians. Many hill stations were inhabited mostly by Englishwomen through the summer months, while the Englishmen carried out their colonial duties, enduring the heat and the proximity of Indians.[44] Though, as Helen Callaway argues in her study of Englishwomen in Nigeria, the

Englishwomen were not responsible for race and class hierarchies in the colonies, their presence resulted in a "new structural alignment of the society brought about by official decisions not of their making."[45] Control over Englishwomen in the colonies was essential to the maintaining of European group integrity.

As Callaway's book reveals, Englishwomen in Nigeria participated in the colonizer's discourse of empire as a "civilizing" process in the twentieth century, even though many of them had personal and close relationships with Nigerians. Most of them believed that their presence was beneficial and crucial to Nigerians. Callaway writes, "Few Nigerians today would fail to appreciate the value of such medical work, though they might criticize it on grounds of 'too little and too late.'"[46] Though beneficial, such work was also crucial to the formation of the imperial subjectivity of the Englishwomen and to new perceptions of their abilities. As Callaway suggests, "This was a time when European women came into their own, as single women and wives, in both professional and voluntary work."[47]

John Boyd-Kinnear in 1869 had envisioned women who did not only "gaze from afar at the battles of life."[48] The women who went to the colonies participated in the project of empire, a project that was integral to the formation of English culture and nationalism. The Englishwomen who came to the colonies for philanthropic reasons did not see "native" women as their equals. Charlotte Brontë's Bertha Mason as an insane and pathetic "Other" to Jane Eyre is indicative of such attitudes. These Englishwomen, appalled at what they perceived as the terrible conditions of colonized women, took on projects to help them, often with the conviction that, first, these women were unable to help themselves, and second, that they were helping to civilize these countries. Women such as Rose Greenfield helped open one of the first women's medical schools in India, though it had not been long since Englishwomen themselves had gained access to medical education in England.

Though we read that these women were appalled at the condition of women in India, it is ironic that they should have thought so, for conditions for women in England, especially those of the working class, were quite oppressive too. Such attitudes toward "native" women worked, in some instances, to disguise and, in other instances, to bring to prominence problems in women's condition in England, while promoting the discourse of colonialism as a civilizing venture. Philanthropists as well as missionaries, who came from the English middle and upper classes like the colonists, supported the notion of England as a civilized and civilizing country. Nor did they see colonialism as anything but a glorious enterprise. The goal of the Order of the Daughters of the Empire, which collected funds for female education and medical help in India, was to foster loyalty to the crown. All these women working for the improvement of the "native" woman believed that colonial rule was essential for any improvements in education and medicine, as did those working for women's rights in England.

Suffrage, Socialists, and the Pankhursts

The question of empire, therefore, worked in several ways within the suffragist movement. There was little consciousness of any solidarity on the part of Englishwomen with the oppressed in the colonies. Yet there were class comparisons made between the English poor and the slaves (in the Abolition debates) and with the uncivilized "natives," most often when it became necessary to reveal the plight of the English poor. The participation of the labor groups in the suffrage movement, where universal suffrage was a goal, no doubt was responsible for the focus on the English poor. Yet by the end of the nineteenth century, some suffragists were breaking off alliances with the working class and the concerns for the poor that had formed many of the women's unions. This break came to a head when the suffragettes, the women involved in the suffrage movement, in the Women's Social and Political Union cut off ties with the Independent Labour Party, though there remained other working-class women's groups (Women's Labor League, Women's Trade Union League) that were committed to suffrage. This formation of one important and prominent section of the suffrage movement as a middle-class women's movement without alliances with other movements is visible in the political efforts of the most famous suffragettes, the Pankhursts.

Emmeline Pankhurst and her daughters, Christabel and Sylvia, were at the forefront of the movement for women's rights in the early twentieth century. Though they presented a united front in many of their struggles, there was a wide division between them. Emmeline and Christabel dissociated themselves from the Independent Labour Party and from working-class concerns, a change that was quite radical since Emmeline and Richard Pankhurst had been active in the Party. Christabel believed that women's concerns did not get priority in such an alliance, and she felt that membership in their organization, the Women's Social and Political Union, would increase if ties with labor were broken. In fact, when this was finally done by 1906, women of the middle and upper classes joined the group and many wealthy supporters donated money, which they would not do to a labor-affiliated organization.[49] Christabel's single-minded approach was to work for the vote for women; she believed social reform would have to wait.[50]

On the other hand, Sylvia remained devoted to socialist ideals, believing that the Labour Party, with all its shortcomings, was the only party that would support women's suffrage. She detested what she saw as her sister's "incipient Toryism."[51] During the First World War, when the suffragettes halted their campaign, Christabel made speeches about the "German peril" while Sylvia believed that women, especially the suffragettes, should be antiwar. Thus she spoke at and organized anticonscription rallies.[52] In 1918, when a bill was passed to give the vote to all men over twenty-one and to women over thirty who were university graduates, local government electors, and the wives of graduates and electors, Sylvia was one of the few suffragettes who protested such discrimination.[53]

While Christabel became both pro-empire and anti-Bolshevik, Sylvia was the opposite. She became a communist and later on, with the Italian aggression in Ethiopia, a strong antifascist. She remained antifascist and supported Haile Selassie in his years of exile and his return to power. She ran a newspaper in London that was devoted to the Ethiopian struggle, and later on published books on Ethiopia, criticizing British policy in Africa. Yet Sylvia Pankhurst's enthusiasm was often misplaced, for she went from being a communist to a monarchist who supported Selassie even when he was most autocratic.[54] Pankhurst's support for Ethiopia can be seen as a wild enthusiasm that blinded her to what was actually going on; she had great faith in the emperor even when he was back in power and it was clear he was not helping to improve the lot of poor Ethiopians. Despite her feminist credentials, she was blind to the everyday lives and needs of Ethiopians, and especially the women. Yet she did involve herself in the antifascist struggle, in anti-Stalinism, in fighting apartheid in South Africa and British imperialism in India. Christabel, on the other hand, became a Second Adventist, lecturing in the United States and Canada about the Second Coming and arguing that it was not women but the Second Coming that would save the world.[55]

When one reads Sylvia's writing about England's colonies, her anti-imperialism is clear. She is, in fact, one of the few English feminists who wished to build alliances, with the Independent Labour Party and socialists in England during the suffrage movement and with the people of the colonies whose exploitation under imperialism she attempted to understand. She used colonial discourses to argue against imperialism, much as Indian nationalists were doing at the time. In a book entitled *India and the Earthly Paradise* (1926), she described the various ways in which imperialism had made Indians poorer and disrupted their land tenure systems in the name of private property and for the advantage of the English merchants and corporations and the Indian princes.[56] Like Max Muller, she sees India as having degenerated from a golden Aryan age, but she also suggests that the English were responsible for the present state of India. She sees a connection between modes of knowledge that are Eurocentric and the problems of colonial rule. Perceptively, she argues that British reliance on written laws of Manu, rather than on unwritten customary law, a reliance that was "a natural outcome of their training," had led to their upholding of what she calls "the reactionary Brahmanic code of Manu." She argues that "the control of a people by a superposed alien power must always be prejudicial to progress" (90–91).

Her Marxist concerns emerge in this book on India. It is, she says, the "great capitalist corporations" in England that are the moving force in the English government's policies in India, and the interest of "the toiling masses" are opposed to those of the corporations and of the ruling princes whom the British support (534). The missionary project in India is doomed, according to Pankhurst, because the "European missionaries, and above all the British, have treated the Indians as a lower race" (3). Thus their teaching of brotherhood does not work. Under British imperialism, India was, she says, "torn, burdened and plundered by gradually extending wars of conquest, was drained by taxation, was prevented from taking any steps to conserve her industries, which were harassed and even forcibly suppressed by the alien conquerors, anxious to make her a dumping ground for their own goods" (286). She quotes a member of the Bengal Civil Service who states, "The British government has been one of the most extortionate and oppressive that ever existed in India" (273).

Though her concern is more with the exploitation of millions than with the conditions of women, she does not neglect them. However, she can only represent Indian women within the tropes of colonial discourse, thereby recuperating the difference in power that she attempts to undermine. She covers the colonial and reformist concerns with women's condition in India; she talks of sati, child marriage, widow remarriage, and so on. Companionate marriage with free choice of partners is the ideal she presents as an alternative to the Indian system. This leads her quite often to idealize the Western woman's life and abilities in comparison to that of Indian women, leading to the characteristic amnesia about women's conditions in Britain. Describing problems in child marriage customs, she claims, "No decent West European mother of sane mind permits her daughters to be thus victimized." Yet later on she is more self-conscious, for she mentions British satisfaction with their own ways of living: "The more homogeneous people of Britain, where the capitalist system and a strong centralized government have long obtained, are but too easily taught to believe that theirs is the only form of virtuous marriage, the only true religion, the only right and proper organization of society" (173).

Like more recent feminists, she focuses on those ways of living she sees as alternatives to the patriarchy of England. These are the matrilineal systems prevalent in some parts of India. She argues that the British system of property ownership by males only disrupted such systems to the detriment of the women; she suggests that in communities like the Nayars, "where women occupy the superior position under native law, British law givers frequently defy native law, and relegate the women to the inferior position" (290). British rule, being patriarchal, is shown to be against any move to emancipate Indian women, for, Pankhurst states, "British courts have usually accentuated what was harshest towards women in Indian law and practice, and in case of doubt have generally discriminated against them"

(210). She reveals that patriarchy, being an important part of the economic and social structure of Britain, has been imposed in various ways in India, so that the condition of women has not improved under British rule. Thus she claims that "The British-made law for India was . . . approximated to the law of modern England, which permits a man to bequeath or give his property as he pleases, leaving his wife and children penniless" (104). It is important to note here that her concerns for women in England and in India enable her to understand colonialism as a means by which English patriarchy was being extended to India, so that she identifies the connections created by colonialism. While other feminists compared patriarchies, Pankhurst saw how English patriarchy could adversely impact the lives of Indian women.

Sylvia Pankhurst's concerns reveal a trajectory that connects the struggle for women's rights and freedom with other struggles for freedom. It suggests that some feminists in England could construct a historiography that connected "East" and "West" by showing connections between patriarchal power in England and colonial practices. It suggests that not all Englishwomen were in favor of imperialism and empire, that their opposition to patriarchy and government in England led them to be radicals who fought against all kinds of oppression. They recognized that patriarchal power was oppressive and exploitative not only in England but in the colonies, and that opposition to one meant opposition to the other. Despite such a radical understanding, Pankhurst too could not see Indian women in terms outside the discursive practices of colonial discourses.

Yet she remained a radical, in opposition to the militant suffragists who turned the movement into a middle- and upper-class issue. Most of them did not even argue for equality with men on every level, for the home and domestic life were still considered sacred. Concern for women in the colonies remained more a matter of private charity than a matter of policy. Few Englishwomen were interested in learning about the lives of women in the colonies, for they were content with the popular orientalist notions of purdah and seclusion that travelers and orientalists had emphasized. Few women, travelers or feminists (including even Sylvia Pankhurst), mention meeting women from these countries. If they do, they present them as "natives," never by name nor as personalities who differ from each other. Empire remained a place to send indigent women and a dumping ground for what had no place in England, and the Orient became a symbol of female seclusion and oppression that Englishwomen were believed unable to live under and that suggested the need for their emancipation.

Gender, Travel, and Feminism

Underlying the demands for Englishwomen's suffrage and equality were new perceptions of women's capabilities. English women travelers participated in such perceptions even if they were against women's suffrage. An example was Flora Shaw, who was a pioneer in women's accomplishments. In 1888 she traveled to Egypt as the accredited correspondent of the *Pall Mall Gazette* and the *Manchester Guardian*. She was the first woman to give a talk at the Royal Colonial Institute in 1894.[57] A fervent supporter of empire and of Cecil Rhodes, she later became colonial editor of the *Times*. There she reported on political events as well as on topics such as life in a harem. Despite being an example of a pioneering woman, Shaw was antisuffrage and pro-empire. She later married Sir Frederick Lugard, who became governor-general in Nigeria, and gave lectures and wrote articles on Nigeria.[58] Thus women who were against women's suffrage also promoted the cause of women's suffrage by contributing to new ideas of women's abilities. Such ideas were intrinsic to the formation of English female subjectivity in which empire was an important element.

For the many women travelers who went to Asia and Africa to escape circumscribed lives in England, these lands became places that, on the one hand, proved women to be equals of men including taking on the role of the colonizing male. Travel became synonymous with political freedom because its Romantic discourse enabled them to label their escape from some domestic gender constraints "freedom," though this freedom was only that of becoming a version of the imperial Englishman. As Dea Birkett points out in her book, *Spinsters Abroad*, women such as Marianne North, Mary Kingsley, Isabella Bird, and Gertrude Bell traveled within a colonial habitus of racial superiority, a superiority that opened many doors for them in the era of English imperialism. Thus even if they disliked the life of the colonial settlements, where they did not fit the role of the women who needed to be protected, they nevertheless used their belief in racial superiority to travel. Escaping their gender roles, they took on their racial ones. As Birkett states, "Raised in a Britain of confidence and Empire, expansion and conquest, they shared common perceptions of a foreign and, as yet, untouchable world."[59] Thus the colonial realm and imperial habitus underwrote their travels as well as their perceptions of the people they met on their travels. At the same time, their achievements contributed to a belief in the capabilities of English-women. Their travels made them anthropologists and botanists and allowed them to participate in the scientific discourses that could show them to be the equals of Englishmen.

Though Birkett is clear about the imperialist beliefs of these women, she yet makes claims about their being quite different from the men and ignores the imperial and Romantic structures that defined travel. She claims they traveled without the definite goals that many male explorers had. Further, she suggests they learned to brave dangers, to value being alone rather than feel lonely, and to have control over their lives. All this was empowering for the women who learned through their travels how strong they could be in enduring and living through many adventures. Yet for the Englishmen too, the braving of the dangers of travel became an imperial strength that justified imperialism. In fact, the escape from England, the alienation felt at home, the freedom gained from travels, and the value of solitude were intrinsic to the male Romantic traveler from Byron to Burton.[60] For instance, Alexander Kinglake writes in his very popular travel narrative *Eothen*, "I can hardly tell why it should be, but there is a longing for the East, very commonly felt by proud people when goaded by sorrow."[61] The difference for these women was that they were alienated at home because of their gender; however, this alienation did not necessarily make them either anti-imperialist or empathetic toward women, either Asian or English. In fact, Gertrude Bell, the famous traveler who lived many years among the Bedouins, blamed the Englishwomen in the colonial settlements in Egypt for creating an exclusive society and taking no interest in Arab life. She claimed that such attitudes had brought about the downfall of the British government in India.[62] Bell saw herself as different and superior to the Englishwomen who had accompanied the colonists.

Even Mary Kingsley, who was remarkable in her examination of the hypocrisy of the project of "civilizing" the natives of Africa, believed that imperial rule could be beneficial. She proposed that good science and ethnology would lead to better rule and the good trade that could benefit both English and Africans.[63] Though opposed to many forms of English superiority in which Africans were seen as childlike or savages, she became herself an example of the mobility and ability of Englishwomen to be travelers and ethnologists; she showed that women could even advise the English government in the masculine project of colonization.

Despite this belief in a good imperialism, Kingsley was anomalous in her respect for the many different peoples she encountered on her travels. For the most part, English women travelers were not exempt from the imperial habitus. Belief in their racial superiority led to a belief in the inferiority of their colonial subjects. Taking on the male role, they felt much superior to the Asian and African women. This was evident in their comments on the women in harems. They had access to places that Englishmen did not have, a fact that contributed to the complicated nature of Englishwomen's participation in the discourse of empire. Yet in describing the harem, which they could enter because they were of the same sex as the inhabitants, they used many of the stereotypes of the male empire builders. At the same time, they tried to demystify this symbol of "Eastern" and female "mystery," which impacted adversely on their own lives as women. What Malek Alloula in *The Colonial Harem* describes as the object of the imperial, male gaze was somewhat different for the imperial European woman in its elimination of the erotic and the mysterious and the emphasis on the prosaic and unadmirable nature of the women behind purdah and their lives.[64]

In fact, it is in these descriptions that the problematic of gender and race in the discourse of empire becomes visible. While showing women in the harems to be victims of oppression by "native" men and thus that gender divided the colonized peoples, they suggested the "native" women were lazy, like their male and racial counterparts, and thus inferior. However, this became a characteristic of the "feminine" nations, as Millicent Fawcett had called them, that was to show the superiority of the English but problematize notions of women's abilities. In effect, the harem became a racial sign for "Eastern" culture that erased the gender similarity that enabled Englishwomen to enter. That both "native" men and women were feminine was emphasized by the fact that in purdah, women lived in the company of other women, making the harem a sign of a "feminine" society. Flora Shaw, in her dispatches to England, described the women living in harems in the following manner: "plain women, dressed in vulgar adaptations of European clothes, sat about listlessly hour after hour, with neither work nor entertainment to enliven the long days."[65] Edith Durham claimed that the conversation of the women in the harems, who were kept, she says, "mainly for breeding purposes," were "much like what that of a cow might be, could it talk."[66] Harriet Martineau described women in Egyptian harems as "wholly and hopelessly baulked." As Dierdre David suggests, Martineau saw them as "grotesque in their unnatural isolation and enforced companionship of each other." Describing what she sees as their indolence and their "ample flesh," she thinks of them as "baulking human progress."[67] Such descriptions are markedly different from those of male travelers, for whom entering the harem became a symbol of imperial powers of penetration.

While for the European male, the harem symbolized mystery and allure as well as female subservience and unfreedom, for the Englishwomen the harem became an example of the consequence of the denial of freedom to women as well as the problem of the inferior races. Birkett shows that women travelers often compared Asian and African women's lives to theirs and thought that they were free in comparison, even though they were traveling to escape their own circumscribed lives. Martineau's description of the harem women as "baulked" emphasizes this freedom.

For the suffragists, however, the stereotype of women's seclusion in the Middle East and Asia suggested the need for women to be employed, vote for their rights, and participate in public, and not merely domestic, matters. The evils of purdah, the harem, and sati, so obsessively described by English travelers and so much a part of orientalist knowledge, were seen as an example of not giving women the vote and as the result of a despotism that denied freedom to women.[68] Barbara Bodichon in one of her lectures even called the men of England "Hindoos" for oppressing Englishwomen. All Asian women were believed to live in seclusion; rich and poor, working class and aristocracy, all were thought to have the same life. Bodichon also suggested that Asian women liked their seclusion, and that the habits of submission made them servile, as it did the "vast population of Asia," who did not desire or value "political liberty"; for instance, she refers to the lives of Algerian women as an "idle, slovenly existence" that European women were ameliorating in a female civilizing endeavor. She suggested that some Englishwomen who were anti-suffragist were in a servile state comparable to that of all Asians.[69] Servility and laziness were synonymous, as were mobility and freedom.

Harriet Martineau and Empire

The complex relationship between issues of gender, imperialism, and race is apparent in the work and life of Harriet Martineau. An ardent believer in empire and free trade, and in maximizing British profit through empire, Martineau was also a supporter of the women's suffrage movement. She campaigned against the Contagious Diseases Act, supported the Women's Suffrage Society, encouraged efforts to obtain qualification for female doctors, and was a supporter for better female education and employment. She also traveled widely, being interested in foreign affairs and political economy. In two books, *Suggestions Towards the Future Government of India* (1858) and *British Rule in India* (1857), Martineau combined aesthetics, politics, and economics to argue for the civilizing of India by proper colonial rule.[70]

Martineau was unconcerned with the exploitative effects of colonial rule in India, seeing it only as a civilizing and improving project. Invested in showing that productivity would increase only by colonization, Martineau saw Indians as ignorant of economical and industrious methods. She paid no attention to women working on farms and fields, although such work was done by peasant women all over the world. Few travelers mentioned such women. Honoria Lawrence (1808–1854) was one of them, though even she does so quite cursorily, more interested in recording her own experiences rather than in describing the people of India.[71] When she does turn to Indian women, she represents them in ways that had become increasingly popular: showing them in harems and houses, in poses either erotic or idle. It was mostly upper-class women who were described, for few of the lower classes or village women lived in the kind of seclusion and idleness that became a symbol of oriental women.

More typically, Martineau ignores the female population of the lands she travels to. More interested in ancient monuments and history, she does not have much interest in Egypt's modern inhabitants. When she does mention native women, it is almost always in denigration. She is appalled by what she sees as their lack of morals, their idleness, and their unhealthy, confined lives. She describes a meeting with some "Jewesses," mentioning their lavish and expensive dress and ornaments. Their painting of the eyes she finds "somewhat deforming" and their painting of the eyebrows even more offensive, stating that "nothing can be more disagreeably absurd than to see this artificial thoughtful frown on the excessively silly and inane face of an Eastern woman."[72] Since paint is associated with desire to hide the inner faults that appear on the face, as with the English prostitutes, she cannot appreciate such ornamentation. She finds their habits even worse, for she states contemptuously that "their health is bad, of course, as they have no exercise but shuffling over their marble pavements in splendid style."[73]

The confined Egyptian woman is contrasted with the freedom of the Englishwoman, especially of the writer who is free to travel to these lands. Such orientalist representations of Egyptian women make the Englishwomen feel free and disguise their own subservience in their patriarchal culture. This misrecognition was, of course, central to imperial culture in England in which the superiority and freedom of European forms of civilization was the rationale for empire and for an English nationalism for which empire was a cornerstone.

Chapter 3

The Guidebook and
the Museum

⁂

*We then have a contested cultural territory where the people must be thought
in a double-time; the people are the historical "objects" of a nationalist peda-
gogy, giving the discourse an authority that is based on the pregiven or constituted historical origin or event; the people are also the "subjects" of a process
of signification that must erase any prior or originary presence of the nation-
people to demonstrate the prodigious living principle of the people as that
continual process by which the national life is redeemed and signified as a repeating and reproductive process.*[1]

The dream of the transparent society at "home" was integral to the
construction of an English identity and of English nationalism in
the age of empire. If the Englishwoman's identity was constructed
through nationalist and imperial discourses, then nationalism is the
imaginary not only of the dominant groups within a society, but also
of the participation of nondominant groups for the formation of their
own subjectivities. This participation constructs these imaginaries
through various and competing agendas and agents. As I have argued
in earlier chapters, so it was with Englishwomen, mainly bourgeois
women, who participated in the discourses of imperialism in order to
insert themselves into a Selfhood that gave them the rights denied by a
patriarchal culture.

Thus national identity, as English identity, was utilized and recast
by women such as Harriet Martineau who saw clearly that English
laws were unjust to them. Writing travel narratives, as did so many
women who went to foreign lands, women such as Martineau constructed not only a female Self but an *English* female Self, one that
shared in the discourses of Euroimperial travel, but in a specific gen-

dered and classed way. Since the aesthetics and geography that travelers and tourists followed was itself imperial and English, these narratives were ideologically mediated. Aesthetic perception had not been separately constituted from ideological constraints; class conflicts and emerging conditions within England, as well as politicized understandings of new lands, had been integral to scientific observations as well as to cultural productions.[2] These contexts influenced the modes, rules, and institutions of travel that would be a crucial aspect of Victorian and imperial culture. The emergence of travel guidebooks reveals this political aesthetic, indicating the domestication of foreign lands and the centrality of the culture of travel within national and imperial ideology. The aesthetic of the picturesque, which interpellated subjects through imperial and class divisions via binaries such as subject and object, seer and seen, was crucial for the culture of travel, to English culture as well as to the emergence of the consumer by the end of the nineteenth century. This aesthetic, as one that enabled travel and observation in the eighteenth and nineteenth centuries, created differences on the basis of "taste" that were implicated within other distinctions by race, gender, class, and nation.[3]

Many scholars have written about imperialism as a concern of the upper classes and as an issue that was outside the experiences of working-class men and women. Yet many others have shown how imperialism was the locus of new forms of nationalism and patriotism that were manifest in all classes of English culture from the second half of the nineteenth century. John Mackenzie, for instance, in *Propaganda and Empire* and *Imperialism and Popular Culture*, systematically reveals the pervasiveness of representations of empire and colonies as part of English upper-class and working-class cultures. He argues that a "generalized imperial vision" was part of popular culture among all classes so that it is difficult to presume a working-class culture that is unconnected to an imperialism shared with other classes.[4] In doing so, Mackenzie presumes that classes are formations that are predetermined, instead of seeing these as dynamic and historically changing. Yet knowledges and socioeconomic conditions that were linked to imperialism were integral to the formation of classes; internalization of these conditions further consolidated certain social divisions and recast others.

Thus working-class English women and men were interpellated as classed, gendered, and sexualized subjects also through discourses of empire within a domestic culture of travel. The ways in which they saw themselves as imperialists were no doubt different from the mercantile class or the aristocracy. However, the many forms of popular culture, the kinds of education that were given by the state and by the church, and, as I argue in this chapter, by travel guides, by museums and their guidebooks, turned all the English into classes through differential relations to various notions of "culture." What is evident is that shifting and emerging class interests, such as distinctions between tourists and travelers, the emergence of the Cook's tours, the working-class "improvement" societies, and "rational recreation," brought certain sections of the working class into a culture shared with other classes, one that contained common notions of England and its relation to other parts of the world. To be English was to incorporate in some form the class- and gender-specific subject position of what Mary Pratt calls a "Euroimperial traveler." The consciousness of a heterogeneous racial and national subjectivity that saw itself as English interpellated tourists and travelers, albeit diversely, and all those at "home" who consumed the books and objects of travel.

The trajectory of imperial interests suggests how such imperial subjects came into being. By the middle of the nineteenth century, as British colonial interests took stronger hold, knowledge of colonized and colonizable cultures was believed necessary in order to govern correctly.[5] More of the British public absorbed such knowledge in various ways through travel books, exhibitions, newspaper accounts of politics and imperial ventures, children's books, didactic and "improvement" literature; the list of ways in which the empire became a part of the British imaginary was endless.

It is in aesthetic and cultural productions, as Pierre Bourdieu suggests, that class divisions are reinforced precisely because they are concealed. As Bourdieu puts it, "art and cultural productions are predisposed, consciously and deliberately or not, to fulfill a social function of legitimating social difference."[6] Rather than legitimating preexisting social differences, they also generated divisions and consolidated others for various purposes. Moreover, the methods by which class divisions were formulated and disguised in order to create nationalist culture helped to create the nineteenth-century "Englishman" and "Englishwoman" to whom imperialism became acceptable, if not natural. Yet class division was not the only space within which the colonizing dispositions of the English were created, for the domestication of women, the regulation of sexuality, the division between private and public, between the home and the marketplace were also part of the habitus in which the individual subject was formed and which replicated the divisions of race and gender which were the nexus of colonial power relations.[7]

Within the discursive formations that comprised Victorian culture, the colonies were "civilized" by a venture that resulted in their commodification, while the British public was educated through a knowledge that involved their own commodification while it suggested their ability to reify the non-Western "Other." In his analysis of the Exhibition of 1851, Thomas Richards suggests that displays of imperial power were a precondition of consumerism, for they "proved once and for all that the best way to sell things to the English was to sell them the culture and ideology of England, its plans for commercial dominance, its dreams of Empire, its social standards, and its codes of conduct."[8] Within the context of an imperial nationalism, the consuming subject could come into being.

As Timothy Mitchell argues, the image of the Orient was constructed through the related ways of representing the world that appeared in museums, exhibitions, schooling, tourism, stores, fashions, and the commodification of everyday life: "Everything seemed to be set up before one as though it were a model or picture or something. Everything was arranged before an observing subject into a system of signification, declaring itself to be a mere object, a mere 'signifier' of something further."[9] Spectator and consumer were related figures, yet class, gender, and sexuality functioned to create various recastings and refigurations into discrete but related imperial subjects. What Mitchell calls the "exhibitory order" had emerged from Romantic relations to the world, such that empire became a means to acquire goods whose specularity was central to both the British Museum as well as to the formation of the department store.

Matthew Arnold, writing in 1867, believed that the upper classes could uplift the lower by teaching them culture and inculcating in them aristocratic qualities.[10] In *Culture and Anarchy*, Arnold implied that "civilizing" the lower classes involved emphasizing their differ-ence from the upper, as well as from those seen as "Barbarians" and the "Philistines."[11] In claiming that his idea of "culture" com-prised that of the whole nation, Arnold reinscribed its class origins. Furthermore, Arnold believed the middle and lower classes of En-gland needed insertion into a culture in order to be part of a nation. Without this, they would be dangerous. For Arnold, culture was "the most resolute enemy of anarchy, because of the great hopes and designs for the state which culture teaches us to nourish."[12] Culture will develop, according to Arnold, the national spirit that will pacify the masses and make England "a great nation."[13] He believed that education would, above all, teach the culture of nationalism, which, as aesthetic education, implied the perfection of both individual and state.

Arnold's beliefs reflect the ideological underpinnings of the public museum in the nineteenth century: the rise of nationalism disguised differences of gender and class and promoted the hegemony of the aristocratic, patriarchal "culture" disseminated through the museum, a hegemony that helped formulate and reproduce class and gender differences. Though Arnold had suggested that the availability of culture signified the democratization of England, what it effectively concealed was the social reality that a large number of working-class men and women had no part in such a culture. The possession of cultural capital in the hands of the dominant classes was presented as a disinterested and gratuitous sharing of national wealth. This mis-recognition of class and gender divisions was necessary for the opera-tion of the sphere of symbolic and cultural goods.

In his landmark work, *Imagined Communities*, Benedict Ander-son includes a section on museums, showing how the "museumizing imagination" enables the iconography of the nation to be infinitely reproducible and thus concretized in innumerable settings.[14] What he does not ask is how various groups that supposedly comprise the nation read or interpret this iconography, nor how different readings construct the national imaginary. An important question becomes how various readings of the iconography of the nation interpellate social divisions such as class and gender. Furthermore, the "mu-seumizing imagination" does not only represent itself, it represents many others. How it represents others is an important part of nationalism, as are the ways in which diverse readerships are created around this iconography.

In examining the representation of objects from different countries in Victorian museums, I will focus on guidebooks to the British Museum not only to answer how objects are read and interpreted but also how subject positions are formulated through an aesthetic education. I will explore both the commonalities and the divergent locations from which the spectacle of the museum is read.

Guidebooks and Englishness

As an embodiment of aesthetic classifications, the British Museum exhibited and represented the world through certain objects to which some general guidebooks directed the public. A very selective, dichotomized taxonomy was thereby created, which presented not only a history of the whole world but also that of England, for it inculcated the opposition of Self and Other, subject and object. Such an opposition was crucial also to a national pride in English ability to gather knowledge and display the world in glass cases. While the function of the museum was to assist in the education of the public, the aesthetic judgments passed on domestic and foreign artifacts in the museum's guidebooks and catalogues reveal that it disseminated a schematic aesthetic that inculcated class, gender, and racial difference.

For museum-goers, guidebooks worked to sublimate the alienating practices of the museum, an institution formed by collections given by the aristocratic patrons and named after them, such as the Hamilton, Elgin, and Towneley collections. They contributed to the consolidations of a larger section of the middle classes and to the reduction of working-class radicalism that occurred by mid- and late nineteenth century. They mediated between those with "taste" and the "vulgar," a mediation central to both class and gender formation, and therefore reveal the role of aesthetics in the social conflicts of nineteenth-century England.

For the casual visitor, the museum did not aim at inculcating specific knowledge; it aimed at inculcating general ideas, creating general sensations—all within a short time period. It propagated a generalized idea of the new and unknown world and, for easy and quick consumption of British Self and foreign Other, it provided easy stereotypes and homogenized ideas; it suggested, above all, the availability of the treasures displayed within it. Within the British Museum, the public was "civilized" by means of an aesthetic education that involved showing the non-Western world as uncivilized. Thus, while the East was "civilized" by a colonial venture that resulted in its commodification, the British public was disciplined through a knowledge that involved the reification and domestication of the non-Western "Other"; such a process involved also the misrecognition of such a binary within England itself. Everything in the museum, as well as in stores and exhibitions, created a distance between viewer as spectator / subject and display as object.[15]

Such a culture at "home" in England was a change from as well as a continuation of certain Romantic attitudes and linked to Romantic aesthetics that marked a specific form of modernity. By the end of the nineteenth century, campaigns for sexual purity and a greater surveillance of sexual practices had occurred along with greater demarcation of home / domestic space from public arenas that were integral to gendering practices.[16] While the Romantic travelers such as Lord Byron had, by their very popular portraits in "native" costume, displayed their merging with a different culture as an English ability, for English women travelers this sublime experience was believed to be rather dangerous.[17] There were some women, such as Jane Digby and Isabelle Eberhardt, who became notorious for "going native," but for the most part, the many Englishwomen who went to Asia and Africa kept their clothes on. The reasons for this were linked both to nationalism and gender; for "going native" meant not only having sex with "native" men (same-sex relations were tacitly believed only for traveling English men rather than for women, even though such acknowledgments were contained within upper and working classes, rather than in the bourgeoisie), but also that such relations could be a threat to national identity. Since a racialized nationalism relied upon women and their bodies to symbolize both "home" and "harem," the symbolic markers for both these signs needed to be kept separate.[18]

In the early part of the century, the ability to conceal Englishness became itself an English masculine quality. This ability was exaggerated in explorers and settlers rather than in the tourists, and it revealed the anxiety to remain uncontaminated, especially sexually, by a different culture.[19] The authority of these Romantic travel narratives came from the narrator / perceiver's ability to experience being both Self and Other and thus to describe the Other with a more authentic knowledge.[20] Romanticism, in its emphasis on the representation of the language of "real" life and "real" passions of other people, sought what was authentic because of a felt alienation from it. The travel narratives' claim of authenticity, which was validated through the travelers' living the "real" life of alien peoples, was, consequently, Romantic. To be able to pass as a "native" became the sign of successful merging with the foreign culture. Such merging authorized the travelers' representation of native life and culture. It is not surprising, therefore, that the fame of many travelers was a result of successful journeys disguised in "native" clothes.[21] Travelers like Burton, Doughty, and Lane became famous because they went in disguise to places that were forbidden to Christians or Europeans. Burton wrote of his exploits in harems, of the lure of the Arabian Nights, and of his ability to penetrate into an unknown Eastern life. He traveled in disguise in the countries of Arabia and India while gathering anthropological and political information. In an account of his career, we are told that he returned from his journeys "with a rich budget of news and information, which proved not a little useful to the local government . . . he arrived at secrets which were quite out of reach of his brother officers and surveyors."[22] Yet a polymorphous sexuality came to be considered a threat with the emergence of the homosexual as a marked category; for instance, Burton was thrown out of government service because he was believed to have had homosexual relations with "native" men and boys. Also his notion of the "Sotadic zone," that sexualized geography of the Middle East where homosexuality flourished, was not well received, for his writings were heavily censored by his wife and by others. Suspicion against him arose because of his intimate knowledge of the boy-brothels of Karachi; he had been sent by Charles Napier to investigate them because Napier believed that his troops were being corrupted by them, but then was thought to have become much too knowledgeable and therefore untrustworthy.[23]

While Romantic travel, as practiced by upper-class Englishmen in the Victorian era, merged the search for authenticity with that for political information in the interest of imperialism, tourism, seen as the ability and power of a great many men and women to move around various countries in groups, was no less a display of English power. Tourist guidebooks by the middle of the nineteenth century made available a new kind of middle-class English identity, including information on clothes as a visible index of that identity. While such information was necessary for tourism to be coded as pleasure / comfort in contrast to exploration or adventure, it reveals also the impetus within Euroimperial travelers of both sexes to have and present particular forms of control over every situation they encountered along the way. Within touristic modes of travel they did so through representing themselves as spectators / consumers / imperial subjects by visual identification through clothes, mode of travel, and places to visit or stay. Ali Behdad, in his book *Belated Travelers*, recognizes this mode of travel as desire for and commodification of the Orient as disappearing exotic.[24]

For Englishwomen in particular, the display of national and racial identity as superiority was believed to be critical and was marked on bodies and behaviors in specific ways. In her two-volume travel account, *Eastern Life: Present and Past*, Harriet Martineau reveals the significance of clothes while traveling, stating that no Englishwoman should alter her dress during her travels, for the change might imply her rejection of English ways. Martineau states that the Englishwoman could not look like an Eastern woman. Eastern costume will "obtain for her no respect, but only make her appear ashamed of her own origin and ways. It is better to appear as she is, at any cost, than to attempt any degree of imposture."[25] In an appendix to her book, she advised women travelers to dress in gloves, brown holland dresses, straw hats, thick-soled boots and shoes—just as many items as would be worn in England. The only Egyptian adaptation was the tarboosh instead of a cap indoors or in the tent; the intent to hide the hair remained. She advised travelers to eat and drink "as nearly as possible, as one does in England." She did, however, recommend the use of tobacco in the water-pipe for "refreshment and health" in order to offset the fatigues of travel. The necessity to look in command in foreign countries was important to Martineau, suggesting that for English travelers, national identity was as important, during this time when increasing numbers of English men and women were traveling, as the need to investigate and explore foreign lands.

Martineau indicates the anxiety about loss of English identity aroused by travel to foreign lands. Clothing that was uncompromisingly English was one way to prevent any ambiguity regarding the reasons for travel, for then travel could not be interpreted as alienation from or rejection of England. Wearing "native" clothes, Martineau suggests, could be construed as a rejection of Englishness. While the European male explorer could wear "native" disguise to indicate his chameleon power to be both English and pass for a "native," the tourists traveling in groups presented themselves as English men and women who could travel and were thus distinctive from the inhabitants who, supposedly, lived and died where they were born. Most tourist guidebooks to Africa and India suggested, as did Martineau, that women travelers keep to English dress. Murray's 1858 guidebook to Egypt, one of the most popular series of guidebooks, stated that it was unnecessary to wear "Oriental dress," and that "a person wearing it, who is ignorant of the language, becomes ridiculous."[26] This guidebook suggests that change in dress was suitable only for those, men presumably, who intended to pursue a greater interest in Egypt than that of the ordinary tourist. It is clear that control over Englishwomen's sexuality, through the tourist's visual identification, was crucial for consolidation of imperial power in the second half of the nineteenth century, even though Englishmen's sexuality was also being policed in newer ways by the end of the nineteenth century with events such as the trial of Oscar Wilde.

The suggestion of some laxity in regard to Englishmen disappears toward the end of the century, by which time greater numbers of the English bourgeoisie were traveling to the East. The 1897 Cook's guidebook firmly laid down the rules for traveling dress: "For gentlemen, light tweed suits, and a flannel suit, with a suit of darker material for wearing on particular occasions. . . . Ladies are recommended to take a good woolen costume, not heavy; one or two of light texture; and a serviceable dark silk."[27] Cook's guidebook illustrated that there was no room for a choice in dress, for it contained no proviso as had the earlier guidebook. Murray's 1904 *Imperial Guide to India* suggested that if touring the plains of India in winter, "the traveler should wear much the same clothing as in a mild spring in England."[28]

This tourist is, however, not an unambiguous figure, for it is seen as part of mass culture and ridiculed by those who aspire to be "travelers"; the traveler is the lonely, alienated, upper-class, "cultured,"

Romantic individual. The distinction made between tourist and traveler within European modernism, as exemplified by Paul Fussell writing about the period between the Wars, for instance, plays on the differences between traveler / explorer and tourist as examples of high culture and mass culture respectively.[29] The disparagement of the tourist comes also from a supposed lack of individuality that is seen to be part of the "freedom" of mobility of the traveler, as opposed to the tourist slavishly following the guidebook and therefore unable to connect with the authentic or the "real" "native" culture. Class formations were the result of such distinctions, dependent on an erasure of the similarities between the tourist and the traveler.

There was much that linked these two figures. If tourists followed the guidebook, travelers followed other culturally specific rules of observation that laid down what could be a picturesque view or a sight worth seeing. Such views and observations were no less cultural metonyms and no more "authentic" than were the tourist's "sights."[30] Clearly, all these encounters were mediated by economic, political, and historical specificities that varied by gender and class. Whereas some guidebooks were designated for the "masses," others were meant for elites. Travel narratives, which covered the same ground and very similar views, also were guidebooks, for they too suggested where travelers could go and what sights they could see. The formulaic quality of many travel narratives published in nineteenth-century England suggests how much travelers followed each other.[31] Sets of instructions, such as Martineau's appendix, that reveal the continuity between the "traveler" and the "tourist" became separated into the guidebook. For the most part, the guidebook was seen as different from other forms of European travel writing. Yet the guidebook reveals that just as the tourist's "sights" are signs of having "been there" in a complex signification of class, gender, nationalism, and imperialism as it constitutes leisure within industrial capitalism, the European traveler's "observations" are markers of an upper-class or mercantile imperial mobility.

While there is a continuity between traveler and tourist, what the guidebook constructed, in its clear delineation of where to go, what to wear, and what to see, was a traveling subject as consumer and the sights as commodities.[32] Almost every person venturing out of England by the end of the century, in groups or by themselves, bought a guidebook, either one of the Cook's series or the Murray's or the Baedeker's. These guidebooks suggested what to wear, what to eat, how to travel, what to see. They contained brief histories, geographies, and ethnographies that governed what the tourists were to observe and to believe about the countries in which they traveled. Such guidebooks, along with the numerous travel narratives, created the image of the English tourist, who became at once the butt of jokes in *Punch*, but also an image in or against which all English tourists saw themselves. In addition, they created a consensus about what was observed by the tourists.

Consequently, part of the costume of the traveling Englishman included the guidebook, by which the English tourist could easily be distinguished anywhere in the world traversing the tourist geography prescribed in it. Murray's, Cook's, and Baedeker's guidebooks were to be found on these travelers; a writer on Swiss travel remarks, "'Murray's Handbook' soon attained great popularity among the ever-increasing throng of English visitors to Switzerland, and an Englishman came to be recognized as much by the possession of the 'red book' as by his inability, half contempt, half shyness, to speak the language of the country."[33] The inability to speak any foreign tongue, the inhibition against knowing any foreign language imperfectly, and the anxiety about not being able to pass for a "native" were as much a part of English identity as the separation maintained by clothes and guidebook. Consequently, the new subjects created by the guidebooks were both connected to and different from those created in and by the travelogues. Ali Behdad makes this point in examining the political and generic differences between the guide and the travelogue.[34] Yet what is also crucial is the relation between aesthetics, politics, and commodification within the context of nationalism and empire, and the emergence of gendered and classed subjects in this nexus.

The Genealogy of the Guidebook: The Picturesque and Politics

The guidebook of the nineteenth century shows clearly the tension between the display of national identity and the desire for the Other as it becomes coded in the primitive, in nature, in the exotic.[35] Whereas the English Romantic poets such as Byron and Shelley reveal this tension in their poetry, their nationalism is differently articulated through alienation from the social norms and values of upper-class English culture struggling against class conflict and the rise of working-class unrest in the nineteenth century.[36] Social unrest and the onset of industrialization as well as forms of urbanization are also connected to the emergence of the guidebooks, for these form the context of the aesthetic of the picturesque, an aesthetic that fueled new forms of travel and new appreciations of scenes that were hitherto ignored.[37] The genealogy of the guidebook can be traced from the aesthetic of the picturesque as it was formulated toward the end of the eighteenth century and the early decades of the nineteenth, an aesthetic whose central concern is framing and controlling alterity and heterogeneity. The mostly male aestheticians of the picturesque, who were concerned with the English landscape, such as Humphrey Repton, Richard Payne Knight, Uvedale Price, or William Gilpin, argued over its symbolical relation to England and its future; for Uvedale Price, for instance, earlier landscape gardening was too despotic, and its removal, like the removal of despotism in France, could lead to revolution.[38] Thus Price suggests that variety is to be encouraged in order to combat despotism; the picturesque embodies this variety as a society contains distinctions in class.[39] Such distinctions were to be encouraged and were part of society as it contained both "civilized" and "wild" elements.[40]

With the rise of tourism in the nineteenth century, the appreciation of the picturesque spread to a larger portion of society than the aristocratic men of taste who hitherto had been interested in aesthetic effects and sensations. Yet this taste did not permeate all classes. As John Barrell points out, English writers in the eighteenth century established a difference between the upper class, which could participate in the political and aesthetic discourse of civic humanism, and the working class, which was believed unable to understand it; what was suggested was the division "between liberal citizens and unenfranchised mechanics, both in the republic of the fine arts, and in the republic of taste."[41] The upper class came to include the bourgeoisie in the eighteenth century, for values, concerns of commerce, and the middle class were, by the middle and late eighteenth century, included in the discourse of civic humanism.[42]

Since the picturesque was not thought to be intuitively apparent to the viewer as was the beautiful, it required an education in taste. Even in the eighteenth century, it was an aesthetic that had to be taught and required knowledge, reflection, and fancy. This beauty of picturesque scenes could be felt, according to Gilpin, by "a very small number out of the great mass of mankind."[43] Uvedale Price suggested that a "picturesque eye" saw many interesting objects, whereas a "common eye" saw nothing but "ruts and rubbish."[44]

Travel guidebooks were the successors to those publications that described picturesque views in the eighteenth century, such as those written by William Gilpin, *Observations Relative to Picturesque Beauty*, and *Three Essays: On Picturesque Beauty, On Picturesque Travel; and on Sketching Landscape*, and those published toward the end of the eighteenth century and during the early nineteenth century that described Romantic landscapes and views. The most famous of the Romantic works was William Wordsworth's guide to the Lake District, which went through multiple editions. All of these books were meant to accompany the traveler who was normatively male, for they described the best routes to take, points of interest to note, or the exact position in which the traveler should stand in order to observe the best view. Wordsworth's book, *A Guide Through the District of the Lakes*, contained a section with the heading "Directions to the Tourist," and his preface suggested that the guide was intended to direct the visitor's attention "to distinctions in things which, without such previous aid, a length of time could enable him to discover."[44] This expert who "saves time" appears in all later guidebooks, maximizing learning in the minimum time, suggesting a change in the audience for these guidebooks from the gentleman scholar to the person who learns in moments set apart from the time devoted to his or her job or profession. Wordsworth's guide is also meant for the Romantic evocation of recollection for the person who has already been to the area, since it is intended to give the visitor's memories "a more orderly arrangement than his own opportunities of observing may have permitted him to make."[46] In this Romantic use the guide becomes a souvenir—a reminder and an ordering of memories of travel.

Wordsworth's *Guide* was one of the most popular guidebooks in the nineteenth century, when more and more Londoners went to the Lake District. The *Guide* was, according to Wordsworth, meant for people of taste "when travel is of the mind as well as of the body."[47]

The success of Wordsworth as poet and as publicist for the Lake District led to an increase in visitors, and the *Guide*, published in 1810, was reprinted in 1821; his publisher later included it with other guidebooks dating from 1842. While it contains detailed descriptions of scenes that can only be called picturesque since these are compositions and views that are suggested by Wordsworth to be fit subjects for paintings, it also includes suggested walks, views to be caught, and an itinerary "for the use of Tourists" that mentions distances and inns.

Despite the importance of the *Guide* in popularizing the area, Wordsworth was aware that the Lake District was changing with this influx of visitors.[48] In his book on the popularization of the Lake District, John Murdoch mentions that with the publication of William Gilpin's *Observations*, the Lake District became a place "crawling with upper class tourists all busy mounting elevated Stations, and chattering loosely about the prospect."[49] Toward the end of the eighteenth century, Murdoch reports, the wealthy had summer villas in the area, and by mid-nineteenth century, the Lake District was easily reached from London and Manchester.[50]

Such a loss of the "authentic" with the coming of the traveler, tourist, or ethnographer has been coded within European modernity as the progress toward "civilization" and as the loss of the "real" or the "primitive."[51] It is clear that even while Wordsworth sees the newer arrivals as less cultured, he sees them as part of a society that has to be educated, even though it is middle- and upper-class "gentry" who are moving in. It is for the service of this gentry that he writes the guidebook, since he wishes to improve their tastes and feelings so that they may enjoy the Lake District in the correct Romantic way. Thus he says:

It is then much to be wished that a better taste should prevail among these new proprietors; and, as they cannot be expected to leave things to themselves, that skill and knowledge should prevent unnecessary deviations from that path of simplicity and beauty along which, without design and unconsciously, their humble predecessors have moved. In this wish the author will be joined by persons of pure taste throughout the whole island, who, by their visits . . . testify that they deem the district a sort of national property, in which every man has a right and interest who has an eye to perceive and a heart to enjoy. (127)

Since the picturesque objects, as the rural poor were designated in this iconography, could not be self-conscious viewing subjects, Wordsworth's guidebook is intended, he says, for "minds of persons of taste and feelings for landscape." Not surprisingly, he opposed the influx of less wealthy tourists who would come by rail. He opposed the building of a railway into the Lake District and, in a letter to the *Morning Post*, protested against the development by saying that it would lead to an influx of railway visitors, who, unlike the "tourist" who had "taste," would "trivialize" the area by virtue of their lack of education or "appreciation" for the landscape. Wordsworth welcomes the tourist with taste but not the mass tourists who come by rail, showing how class divisions were being constructed through education in taste within the culture of travel.[52]

Wordsworth's guide was no doubt the basis for later works, such as the Reverend T. D. Fosbroke's *The Tourist's Grammar, or Rules Relating to the Scenery and Antiquities Incident to Travelers* published in 1826,[53] and for the travel guides that all Victorian travelers carried on their journeys. Fosbroke, who had earlier written such books as *The History of Gloustershire* and *The Wye Tour*, intended his work as a tourbook to be carried on one's travels. In his preface, Fosbroke states that he wishes to disseminate Gilpin's and his own ideas "of the Picturesque, and the Antiquities incident to Travelers; the result of which will, it is hoped, enable the Tourist to have a higher enjoyment of his excursive pleasures. . . ."[54] For the "excursive pleasure" of those who needed a concise, easily read guidebook and did not have an extensive education in aesthetics, Fosbroke simplified an aesthetic into a "grammar." The dissemination of the picturesque into all sections of the bourgeoisie continued in the nineteenth century.

Every book on travel included the description of scenes that had caught the eye of travelers taught to observe effects of nature and of the atmosphere. Sometimes these scenes were called beautiful, though this was not the Burkean beauty belonging to a domestic or divine world and comprising purity and virtue. This was picturesque beauty. It implied a scene that had novelty or variety and gave pleasure because it was a "composition" or a composed view. It included ruins and nature, always positioning the human against nature. It was a view encountered while traveling or moving through regions at home and abroad. One had to travel to encounter a picturesque view; the discovery of novelty and variety required travel. For instance, Bernard Cohn points out that for most of the first half of the nineteenth century, English travelers in India saw it mostly from boats, thereby emphasizing the separation of seer and seen[55] and, I might add, contrasting their mobility with the supposed immobility of the Indians.

The picturesque, furthermore, signified the hegemony of the "cultured" classes through the creation and utilization of aesthetic rules. The poor became aesthetic objects to be looked at and judged by their suitability as objects in a view; they could not be subjects since they were believed not to have the necessary education in taste to view the picturesque. Rural poor as well as urban poor came to be considered objects of spectatorship, since travel as mode of observation was undertaken in both city and country. For instance, George Sims in 1883 introduced his exposé of London slums, *How the Poor Live*, as a "book of travel," revealing the division between urban subject and object within class distinctions in England.[56] By eliminating the socioeconomic reality of their lives, the picturesque made the working class subject to the anesthetizing gaze of the bourgeoisie,[57] although the urban landscape of the industrial city, because of its believed alienation and inauthenticity, could not become picturesque. Sims, in his "travels" in the East End of London, found it hard to inject the picturesque into his revelations.[58] This picturesque gaze represented the working class and the poor within rural idylls, showing that their poverty was unrelated to the rule of the upper class and was merely caused by nature, or was a result of fate; it was in these contexts that the aesthetic of the beautiful was to merge with that of the picturesque to suggest a picturesque beauty.[59]

Yet Burkean notions of beauty and this nineteenth-century picturesque was split not only by class but by racial distinctions since what was not in England could never attain the transcendence of beauty. Even so, by representing the power of the upper class, picturesque landscapes and views transformed the poor as well as the non-Western "natives" encountered on foreign travels into elements in a landscape, within similar discursive practices that compared English factory workers to savages. As such, class difference and the poor's inability to travel became a source of pleasure.

While greater numbers of the middle class were learning the appreciation of the picturesque, the ability to undertake tours in search of it was beyond their capacity. As Thomas Wright, who called himself a "Journeyman Engineer," wrote in 1867: "What in fashionable society would be considered a holiday, the general body of the great unwashed, as at present constituted, cannot have. In the first place, the unwashed ones have not, as a rule, the means for a few weeks' residence at a fashionable watering-place, or a trip to some gay or picturesque part of the Continent; and even if they had the means and had learned the manner of 'doing the Rhine for five pounds,' they could not avail themselves of holidays of that kind."[60] Wright places picturesque observation as an activity of those with leisure and money, whereas the holiday activities of the working class are local picnics, seaside excursions, fairs, sports, and drinking. Wright points out as well that it is "vulgar or ridiculous" for a working-class woman to exclaim, for instance at the sight of the sea, "Is it not picturesque . . . ," whereas to call it "beautiful" would be in keeping with her position. What Wright reveals is that while it was necessary for working-class women to be acquainted with the disciplinary norm of beauty as a moral imperative, the picturesque, with its ambiguous aesthetic that endowed value on what was novel and different, was the domain of the upper classes.

Englishness and Murray's Guides

The demand for all guides and their place in Victorian culture may be seen through the history of John Murray's travel guidebooks. These began publication in 1836 and became the most famous English guidebooks in the nineteenth century. Murray was Byron's first publisher and Byron's poems and exotic tales were themselves travel accounts, including illustrations by Byron's traveling companion, John Hobhouse. Clearly, Byron's works had given an immense impetus to foreign travel.[61] Murray's biographer suggests the beginnings of the famous Murray's travel guides lie in Hobhouse's letter to Murray, in which he complained in 1817 that most books of European travel were inadequate, and that "if anyone writes a book of travels without telling the truth about the masters and the subjects in this most unfortunate country [i.e., Italy], he deserves more than damnation and a dull sale."[62] Hobhouse suggests that the emerging English traveler is one who may not only enjoy travel accounts in the armchair, but who also wishes to know what to expect on his journey. This traveler ventures into unknown territory not as an explorer, but as one who journeys in order to authenticate foreign territory as a known, social space. This space would have its living and moving arrangements all mapped out within the guidebooks in a familiar taxonomy that replicated the domestic, English space; even the mysterious would become familiar, when placed within a known aesthetic geography. The exotic would be domesticated, suggesting the ways in which English culture in this period would be receptive to creating colonies, to making other familiar spaces far from their own homes.

What is suggested through the guidebook is the increasing power of a class and gender able to appropriate and define a national "culture" in the Arnoldian sense. In a study of the English eighteenth century, Jon Klancher in *The Making of English Reading Audiences* refers to the role of newspapers and journals creating a "reciprocity of reader and writer" where "the audience exchanges places with the performers," providing "an alternative society of the text" where social differences were effaced. Klancher sees Arnold's notion of a unified culture as a way to rise above social conflicts and to bring together new audiences that arose in the nineteenth century.[63] Similarly, the guidebooks, in creating new forms of defining an English culture, also attempted to create a homogeneous "society of the text" in which the experience of a fairly wealthy Tory like Murray was replicated by middle-class readers, both men and women, within a noncoeval time and space. The guidebook suggests there is no disparity between the author and the public, and therefore posits a homogeneous society.

Such a strategy is also visible in Murray's account of the writing of his first travel guide, for Murray suggested that he had written about places that might most appeal to his readers. We are told that he had to "consult the wants and convenience of travelers in the order and arrangement of my facts," indicating the presence of the imaginary readers / travelers that he constructs, but who are somewhat less scholarly or "cultured" than he.[64] Here the guidebook is presented as a deliberate attempt at a transparent language, for Murray says that because of his desire not to bewilder the reader by "describing all that *might* be seen," he uses "the most condensed and simplest style in description of spatial objects." What Murray suggests is the fear of any referential proliferation that might occur in the reader / traveler who is faced with an alien landscape; the freedom to explore all possible readings might not only "bewilder" but might also be dangerous in a political period of radical upheaval and given the Tory fear of an increasingly literate mass audience. Heteroglossia, in Mikhail Bakhtin's terms, constructs class and nation but is feared and denied by the guidebook, which insists that it does not exist, that only one common language exists.[65] Thus the "simplest" style is used, making the claim of transparency, both as unmediated and as creating a unified society, and thus enabling the misrecognition of the process of selection and elimination that was involved. Whereas scholars such as Ali Behdad see the travel guide as a heterogeneous text that "frames its information through the dispersion of a plurality of voices and the exposure of their discontinuities," it is clear that the consumer of such heterogeneity sees them in the context of an imperial teleology that constructs subjectivities within a national imaginary.[66]

Even though Murray's audience is less traveled than he, he sees the user to be within his own class and circle. He claims that he tested his book by giving it to friends on their travels. The writer's reading is shown to be the only possible one, for it is tested by other readers. Murray says: "I proceeded to test them [his routes] by lending them to friends about to travel, in order that they might be verified or criticized on the spot. I did not begin to publish until after several successive journeys and temporary residences in Continental cities. . . ."[67] Here Murray claims that his reading is not that of an individual but of a community: his friends all traverse the same routes, presumably testing out hotels, the courtesy of landlords, the best routes to take. Furthermore, Murray suggests that the writing of the guidebook is a scientific process; repeated experiments, in the best scientific method, produce the same result, such that the guidebook aims to present travel and its interpretation of other cultures as fact.

To participate in this "culture" of travel was thus to belong to a class that shared its aesthetic, though differently, with the collector, the traveler, the scholar, and the tourist. Of course this new subject, which possessed a new kind of cultural capital, was a masculine one; yet women utilized guidebooks just as much as the men, even though special instructions were often given to women.

Guidebooks to the British Museum (1800–1826):
Neoclassicism and the Collector

Guidebooks to libraries and museums had been published before 1836, when the first Murray's guide appeared. The methods of museum guidebooks were the same as those of the travel guides, for all these works posited a homogeneous discursive community where the reader/user was treated as the perfect reader, receptive to the assumed transparency of a text that proposed to lay out an objective geography. To follow these guides was to be in the footsteps of the writer in an actual physical space, without straying into dangerous and undomesticated territory. The intention of museum guidebooks was the interpretation and description of the museum collection, in other words, the control of referentiality. Such a control was necessary since, in the collection, the object's removal from its use value, as Susan Stewart has suggested, enabled referentiality to become multivocal.[68]

One method by which the museum was interpreted to the public was through guidebooks. These catered to the casual visitor and pointed out the highlights of the museum, leaving the specialized scholar to pour over the more detailed catalogues. A number of these general guidebooks were printed, some by the New Library of Useful Knowledge, one of the many societies for disseminating knowledge to the middle as well as working classes. For instance, there was *A Guide to the Beauties of the British Museum* (1826, 1838) and *The British Museum in Four Sections or How to View the Whole at Once* (1852). Many more of these guides were printed and some went through multiple editions.

In 1808 the first *Synopsis* of the contents of the British Museum was published by order of the trustees. This was also the year in which the practice of issuing admission tickets was abolished, for admission had earlier been through application in writing that had to be approved by the museum officials. The officials were recognizing that they must cater to all classes of people. Compiled by the museum staff, the *Synopsis* was the first official publication of the museum meant for the general public and could be bought for a few shillings. Other museum publications at this time were the detailed catalogues that were records and descriptions of the collections and which were often given away to trustees. These were expensive and not meant as guides for the casual visitor to the museum. The *Synopsis* was one of the very few publications of the museum that gave general descriptions, for it was not until the end of the century that the museum would publish a number of descriptive guides meant for the visiting public for most of its separate collections.

Yet it was clear that the *Synopsis* was not sufficient to fill the demand for guidebooks to the museum, for a number of publishers in London undertook to print books that would be of help to the public in seeing the museum. One guidebook, published in 1826 by the firm of Thomas and George Underwood, was entitled *A Guide to the Beauties of the British Museum Being a Critical and Descriptive Account of the Principal Works of Art Contained in the Galleries of the Above National Collection.*[69] Though the author's name is not proffered, his credentials are: he is the author of *Beauties of the Dulwich Gallery* and *Beauties of the Fitzwilliam Gallery at Cambridge.* The price of the book was two shillings, and it therefore would not have been read by the working class. As Richard Altick points out, working-class readers, who often worked sixteen hours a day for two shillings or less, were only willing to spend a few pence at most for reading material; this guidebook would have been bought by a member of the middle class, or perhaps the lower spectrum of it, such as the prosperous artisan or clerk, those termed by Altick the "modestly circumstanced booklover."[70] This reader of modest income who constituted a huge market by the middle of the nineteenth century certainly did not include most of the industrial workers who lived in constant fear of starvation.

Catering to a wider public, the 1826 *Guide to the Beauties of the Museum* valorizes the discourse of labor which was so essential to Victorian bourgeois, industrial culture. The labor of collecting and describing was described as enabling the guidebook; this labor was also defining the emerging class of professional scholars, constituting new knowledges and new forms of masculinity, that became a part of imperial power. Ed Cohen has pointed out that whereas the 1841 census listed only the ancient professions such as law, medicine, and the church, the 1861 census included schoolmasters, professors, civil engineers, actors, authors, journalists, and musicians.[71] The 1881 census added even more professions to the list.

This new professionalizing, however, retained for its own authority the upper-class aesthetic and economic values. The writer of the Underwoods' guide replicates the endeavors of the travelers and collectors who obtained the artifacts in the first place, since he claims he has searched assiduously in the museum for the beauties that he now brings to the reader's notice. The writer will, we are told, "convey some of the impressions which he himself received, during a search, diligent at least, and often repeated, without which search the beauties here pointed out may have remained undiscovered" (1826, preface). This labor of exploration within the museum mimics but also compensates for the labor of the collector (since women had few rights of ownership of property, this collector was also a masculine subject), whose work in creating the collection includes the obliteration of the use value of the objects and the substitution of aesthetic value, that value which Stewart defines as "the value of manipulation and positioning." The guidebook thus disguises the fact that the collection comes into being by the abstraction of labor within the cycle of exchange;[72] it substitutes instead a masculine aesthetic labor that masks the alienation of labor within the process of production of commodities.

In addition, the writer of the Underwoods' guide claims his search for the beauties in the museum was "often repeated," and thus invokes the process of verification that seems to give his text scientific objectivity (1826, preface). This claim also suggests the assumed transparency of the text which underlay so much aesthetic discourse, since the writer claims, as had Murray in his travel guides, that he has often repeated his search in the museum only to reach the same results and the same interpretation. Such assumptions of transparency aimed at creating a more widespread aesthetic community by repressing interpretation. Guidebooks were not meant to be interpreted; the logic of their functioning was the suggestion of value-neutral description.[73]

The control of referentiality suggested by the guidebook and the creation of the male writer / collector / scholar as the origin of meaning in the new context of the museum are apparent when the writer of the 1826 museum guide states that he will enable his audience of both men and women to read the artifacts of the museum in the way that he himself has read them: "the writer of this guide would attempt to convey some of those impressions which he has himself received" (1826, preface). By pointing out "what the writer conceives to be the most striking and important objects," the guidebook attempted to control and direct responses to the artifacts in the museum, as well as to create a new context for the objects removed from their origins. The guidebook's intention was the control and standardization of the museum's ability to generate meaning, and consequently, of the museum-going public as well.

Like the traveler with the guidebook in a foreign country, this normative museum-goer comprised a new kind of visitor, one for whom there was limited time for education and enjoyment. This new visitor absorbed alien histories and cultures within the historical context of his own history, whose referent was, as Susan Stewart puts it, the interiority of his own self.[74] Thus the 1826 museum guidebook claimed that with its help even a one-day visit to the museum taught something. The guide is aimed, we are told, at those visitors who might leave "without gaining any permanent or distinct impression of what has been presented to them." It directs itself at "that numerous class of persons who have no time to seek out for themselves the peculiar beauties of this extensive collection" (1826, preface).

Furthermore, the primacy of the Self was suggested by the aesthetic that was disseminated by the guidebooks. Greek art, for instance, was interpreted as validating and inscribing English values. The neoclassicism of the first half of the nineteenth century was visible in the valorization of Greek art and its participation in creating an ideal "English" subject, unquestioningly masculine but one who was receptive to a "moral" art and who immediately recognized the "purity" of classical forms. Classicism was believed to be the apotheosis of all art forms, one that was seen as part of the European heritage. It stood as proof of the superiority of the West over the barbaric East; as such it presented one more reason for the civilization of the East through European colonization.[75]

Objects were therefore described and interpreted in ways that taught aesthetic appreciation to a public that had no aesthetic education, while paradoxically suggesting such a transcendent aesthetic did not need to be taught. The audience was instructed on how to "read" and interpret these objects, thereby forming their "taste" for them, by means of guidebooks that had already laid down their aesthetic judgments and therefore eliminated the necessity to interpret; the internalization of a naturalized aesthetic validated the guidebook.

Aesthetic education was also internalized in the form of moral lessons when, for instance, it was suggested that Greek art bespoke a rational control of sexual desire for both men and women, though differently. Erotic or sensual interpretations were suggested and negated; what was stressed was the "purity" and the transcendent value of classical art. A binary aesthetic, positive purity versus negative sensuality, was offered. As was common with Victorian definitions of beauty, even the objects that, we are told, could be "sensual" created the "intellectual" effect. A statue of a drunken fawn, mentioned in the 1826 guidebook, even though "redolent of wine and woods," was believed to have "an ideal grossness and sensuality belonging to it, unmixed with anything that could be called low or vulgar" (1826, 17). The division between purity and sensuality conformed to the gendered binary of virgin-whore, while the museum-goer occupied the position of a masculine, normative spectator / consumer of such aesthetic objects.

The 1826 guide directed its readers and viewers to notice this cerebral quality of Greek sculpture:

there is nothing more worthy of admiration, in the works of the Greek sculptors, than the exquisite purity and chasteness of their female forms. . . . The Greeks were in fact a people so wholly intellectual, that their idea of voluptuousness itself was an imagination rather than a sentiment. Perhaps not a single female statue . . . can be called voluptuous, in our sense of the term. The naked female statues of the Greeks, with all their resplendent beauty, do not appear to the mere bodily passions with half the mischievous eloquence that any given "Portrait of a Lady" does, on the chaste walls of a Royal Academy. . . . (1826, 13)

This conversion of what could be "sensuous" and "voluptuous" into the "intellectual" taught the museum-going, normatively gendered male, that having good taste and culture meant seeing Greek sculpture with nothing but the predefined aesthetic of beauty, whose divinity excluded the erotic. "Mischevious eloquence" and "bodily passions" were given prominence as well, but shown to be impure and problematic. The racial purity ascribed to Greek objects demarcated them from any nonwhite influences in constructing these as the heritage of the English. Here the Romantic tendency to convert material objects into metaphors of the Self extended into the Victorian practice of converting materiality, as the erotic element of the female body, into a representation of female purity that was aestheticized and consecrated. The white marble of the statues was utilized in a particular conversion, suggesting a racialized conjunction of purity and whiteness. The transformation did double duty in attempting to elevate both the disciplined, "pure" female body and the sculpture of Greece within a discourse of race and whiteness. The fact that these statues had been painted in their original state was ignored; the weathered historicity of the paintless, broken statues was emphasized instead.[76] Many Greek statues of naked figures were viewed through the same aesthetic transformation right through the nineteenth century.[77] Thus, aesthetic forms believed to be of the highest quality, such as statues from the Parthenon, were thought to exercise an effect of disciplinary purification; their aesthetic education was also a moral education and enabled the functioning of a patriarchal configuration that both suggested and repressed female sexuality. Classicism thus participated in the nineteenth-century ideology of the gendered opposition of Englishwomen, racialized as white and belonging to a "West" that unified England and Greece, as whores and angels of the house.

Such a gendering was integral to the discursive practice of "orientalism," that formation which underlay colonial ventures and by which, as Edward Said contends, the "West" represented the "East" to itself.[78] Such orientalism was created not only by representations of the East by itself, but by contrasting representations of East and West that replicated the aesthetic opposition of purity and eroticism. In the British Museum, Greek art functioned as a signifier of the former, while Egyptian art became that of the latter; thus contrasting values were given to them. Because it was believed to signify transcendent values, Greek art was thought to represent an "intrinsic" aesthetic contained in the objects themselves and thus immediately apparent, even to an uneducated viewer. Its excellence was believed, according to the 1826 guide, to lie in its "intrinsic merit," which "speak[s] for itself" (38). Egyptian art, on the other hand, was suggested as being *given* value by the collector, a value emerging only because it was displayed.

Believed to have display value and to lack intrinsic, transcendent value, Egyptian sculptures, it was suggested, did not have any elevating moral effect. They functioned, instead, as signifiers of materiality. Egyptian statues were described as repositories of erotic, sexual, and animalistic qualities—qualities that were shown to be the opposite of the sexual normativity of Greek statuary. Figures of Egyptian sculpture were thought, according to the guidebook, to represent "a phantasm and a dream" and not a reality, and were similar to those "which haunt us in that nervous affection called the nightmare" (1826, 30). Limited to the realm of nightmares, they became part of the unclaimed, "unspeakable" domain of aberrant sexuality. Their lack of what was "human" prevented them from being ennobling or educational. According to the 1826 guidebook, "We do not feel the least degree of human sympathy with the face [of an Egyptian statue], because there is nothing individualized about it"; instead of uplifting the viewer toward what is sublime, such art supposedly "exercises an almost painful and oppressive effect on the imagination" (33).

Egyptian characteristics, which were thought to embody a barbaric, nightmarish sexuality, became alien quantities belonging to the "East" and thus were separated from those of the "West" with its Greek "heritage." Not surprisingly, the 1826 guidebook suggested that England could itself be ancient Greece reborn. A statue of Acteon was described as having been executed "with great spirit and truth" (17). An ideal of human nature that was once "real" was conjured up as a contrast to life in the industrial age. As a result, an ideal classical form became conflated with and indistinguishable from what nineteenth-century England could and should be: classical art, supposedly the highest achievement of art, became a representation of England. The virtues represented by classical sculpture were believed replicated in the people of England; the likenesses of the statues were the men and women of England. While Egyptian sculpture was believed to have nothing that could be called "natural," statues of Jupiter and Apollo were, says the guidebook, "actual likenesses of men and women that most of us have seen in the course of our own lives" (1826, 13). Consequently, England was thought to embody this ideal and contain these "divine" forms; "classical" England was further differentiated from the "barbaric East." As Martin Bernal has suggested, the creation of a Greek "heritage" that was purely Caucasian and unmixed with Egyptian or Semitic influences had begun by the end of the seventeenth century and culminated in the nineteenth with a racist imperialist agenda.[79]

Such a rebirth was part of the neoclassicism of the early nineteenth century. It soon was incorporated into the very body of the British Museum. The architecture of the museum, which was rebuilt by 1852, was in the classical style, according to a plan created in 1823 by the Tory architect, Sir Robert Smirke.[80]

Working-Class Education
and Upper-Class Hegemony (1832–1850)

Yet even during the height of nineteenth-century neoclassicism, the education of the working class was of great concern. The fear of the mob, aroused by the French Revolution, was augmented by events such as the Peterloo massacre. The education provided by the museum was believed to be part of the process of "civilizing" the mob, though there were many in English society who opposed the policy of civilizing through education. However, despite Tory fear that the literate and educated masses might, armed with the weapon of knowledge, rebel against their betters, education was increasingly seen as an agent of pacification. Middle-class groups such as the Society for the Diffusion of Useful Knowledge, which published some museum guidebooks, believed that knowledge would provide "the means of content to those who, for the most part, must necessarily remain in that station which requires great self-denial and great endurance."[81]

Peter Bailey has argued that popular culture was increasingly subject to various forms of control from many directions, but that this control was by no means uncontested, nor were the emerging forms of working-class leisure conforming to bourgeois ideals.[82] Yet the attempts at pacification, evident in the British Museum and its guidebooks, represented the increasing hegemony of an upper-class definition of a "national culture." The attempts at pacification led to a consolidation of a "cultured" class with the negotiated participation of a section of the working class bent on improving itself. No doubt other sections of the working class opposed this notion of a national "culture"; yet their participation in empire has been addressed by scholars such as Penny Summerfield, who has examined the jingoism and imperialist discourses of music-hall entertainment toward the end of the century. J. A. Mangan argues that imperialism was a bridge between the classes; he shows that, for instance, both the state school system and the public school system disseminated a crudely militarist imperialism.[83] Yet imperialism was interpreted, disseminated, and negotiated through specific class interests even while the ideology of the superiority of English race and nation was ubiquitous and diffused.

For instance, the state-sponsored education, in which Arnoldian ideas were incorporated, would have had a widespread impact even though it was not without its opposition from some working-class radicals. It was not surprising, in light of exacerbated class tensions and the aims of groups such as the Society for the Diffusion of Useful Knowledge, that working-class radicals were suspicious of the educational policies of the government and these groups. Thomas Hodgskin wrote, in *Mechanics Magazine* in 1823, that "men had better be without education, than be educated by their rulers; for their education is but the mere breaking in of the steer to the yoke." He argued that the government merely wished "to control the thoughts and fashion, even the minds of its subjects," in order to continue that "most pernicious practice . . . of allowing one or a few men to direct the actions and control the conduct of millions."[84] Thus the concept of "radical education" came into being, by which radicalism developed its own agenda of "really useful education," one that separated itself from education provided by the state and focused instead on political knowledge, socialist principles, and labor economics.[85]

Hodgskin, along with the editor of *Mechanics Magazine*, J. C. Robertson, founded the London Mechanics Institution in 1823.[86] "Rational recreation" was considered essential, and many workingmen's improvement societies were set up in the 1820s and 1830s, with libraries and lectures as the means for learning.[87] Not all workingmen remained part of such institutes, for many of them were alienated by the absence of democratic management and the emerging rigid censorship of discussion and reading.

Working-class distrust of the education offered by the societies extended to a distrust of other institutions as well. Thus Richard Cobbett, member of Parliament for Oldham, argued in 1833 that money requested from Parliament for the runnning of the British

Museum, especially the one thousand pounds set aside for cases of dead insects, could better be spent on starving weavers.[88] The other Cobbett, William, was equally against public money being given to the museum. That same year he spoke in the House of Commons questioning which class of people the museum served: "Why should tradesmen and farmers be called upon to pay for the support of a place which was intended only for the amusement of the curious and the rich, and not for the benefit or for the instruction of the poor."[89]

Though many radical sections of the working class distrusted institutions such as the museum, there were those who were interested in what it offered and a very large number who came to museums and fairs by the end of the century. The secretary of the London Working Men's Association presented a petition for the Sunday opening of museums, arguing, as had the middle-class societies, that "the best remedy for drunkenness is to divert and inform the mind."[90] These reasons for museum-going were different from those of the bourgeoisie or the scholar or the aristocracy. There were accounts of working-class visitors to the museum, even though many of these accounts deplored the presence of such visitors. The British Museum guidebooks reveal that what the radicals had feared in state education was indeed correct: the aesthetic education provided inscribed class difference and presented the power and superiority of the aristocracy that could collect artifacts through various means from all parts of the world.

Admission to the museum had become far easier than it had been in the eighteenth century, when it could only be obtained by tickets applied for in advance with references.[91] By the year 1810, when the second edition of the *Synopsis* for the public was published, admission had become open to all persons on Monday, Wednesday, and Friday. In 1835, when the House of Commons ordered a committee of inquiry into the museum, the principal librarian was still resistant to the committee's recommendations to open the museum for public holidays and more days during the week. The librarian, Sir Henry Ellis, opposed having more public days, for he believed that the museum should also cater to the men of rank and to scholars, and he felt they should not mingle with the working class. He was against the opening of the museum on Easter, for then "the most mischievous portion of the population" could enter.[92] He did not believe that the collections would educate the public. As a Tory, his concern was the upper classes. He claimed: "people of a higher grade would hardly wish to come to the Museum at the same time with sailors from the dockyards and girls whom they might bring with them. I do not think that such people would gain any improvement from the sight of our collections."[93] His successor, Josiah Forshall, who was Ellis's assistant at the time of the inquiry, was also resistant to policies that would make the museum more accessible to the general public. When asked if the public in a free country was not the encourager of literature and science, Forshall replied, "Certainly, including in the word public those very persons of rank and wealth to whom I allude."[94]

Though for Forshall and Ellis, the "public" that mattered comprised the men of rank and wealth who they believed were most fit to visit the museum, the committee (and presumably the House of Commons, which had created the committee) had another definition for the word. Their interest was the poor, for they asked Forshall whether he believed that the function of the museum was to improve the "vulgar class," as he had termed it, that class devoid of taste. Thus, while museum officials and its trustees believed their public to be the men of "rank and wealth," the committee presumed it to be the "vulgar class." Consequently, at the same time that the House of Commons was interested in bringing the working class into a museum that was being supported, in large part, by parliamentary grants, the officials of the museum were interested in making it a more exclusive institution.

Such a contradiction was apparent in the guidebooks written by museum officials, which, while claiming their audience was the section of society that needed to be educated, as did the Society for the Dissemination of Useful Knowledge, created a culture in which the aristocracy became increasingly idealized. Thus, even though the increase of power of the middle class in Victorian England cannot be denied, the aristocracy still was powerful in the values of collecting and capitalism that it represented. "Men of rank and wealth," as Forshall called them, were enshrined as preservers of culture and as persons who placed national interest and national education before their personal needs. When museum officials who were opposed to the democratization of the museum wrote guidebooks that were meant for the lower classes, they represented the generosity of the upper classes who were willing to disseminate culture. The hegemony of the aristocracy was apparent within the discourse of education and during a period of changing class distinctions.

When the Society for the Dissemination of Useful Knowledge wished to publish guides to the museum as part of its Library of Entertaining Knowledge, it asked Henry Ellis to write the guide to the Elgin marbles, a guide that sold ten thousand copies. This was the same Ellis who had, in his evidence before the 1835 House of Commons Committee on the British Museum, shown his disdain for working-class visitors to the museum. The Society's guides, therefore, were no different from those published by the museum, to which Ellis also contributed. What these guides created was an aesthetic as national discourse that was produced by the scholars and the museum officials who saw themselves as guardians of culture and art, but which was consumed by the middle class and its less affluent sections as well as the better-off working class. Though this reading public suggested the growing fluidity of class lines in the first half of the nineteenth century, the population excluded from this consolidation of a growing "cultured" class that looked toward the aristocracy for knowledge on taste were the very poor. These were the consumers of the radical press and of the "penny dreadfuls," and they did not spend their money on "rational recreation" or improving knowledge.[95]

By 1845, though the Society for the Dissemination of Useful Knowledge had lost the audience to which it had originally directed its efforts, it had not failed in its purpose of education, for it had participated in the growing separation of the better-off sections of the working class from their poorer compatriots and united them with a middle class that was rapidly growing and anxious to improve itself, educationally and financially. It was to this increasingly powerful middle-class public that the Society directed its New Library of Entertaining Knowledge, a series of books on topics such as the *Backwoods of Canada*, *The Chinese*, *Biographies of Eminent Men*, *Criminal Trials*, *Pursuit of Knowledge Under Difficulties*, *Habits of Birds*, *Hindoos: Including a General Description of India*, Edward Lane's *Manners and Customs of the Modern Egyptians*, and the guidebooks on the British Museum collections.

The titles, their topics, and the treatment accorded these topics suggest ways in which knowledge of the British Museum and its collections was taught within the context of an orientalist knowledge of Egypt, as Edward Said reveals in *Orientalism* through his reading of *Manners and Morals of the Modern Egyptians*. The library presented a similar orientalist knowledge about India and China, an upper-class version of the penny dreadfuls, as in *Criminal Trials*, and the discourse of self-improvement, as in *Pursuit of Knowledge Under Difficulties*, in which the readers were given examples of historical personages who triumphed over poverty and adversity. What therefore was valorized was success, eminence, and those who had succeeded, along with information on science, highly orientalist descriptions of "exotic" cultures such as Egypt, India, and China, and books devoted to the improvement of taste, such as the guidebooks to the British Museum. Financial and scientific advancement reinscribed the language of educational progress, of geographic advancement, and, in the museum guides, of the improvement of arts from the early Greeks and the Egyptians to the peak of excellence in the sculpture of the Parthenon and the Elgin collection. Such narratives were combined with the presentation of the upper classes as the preservers of excellence: those who enabled such narratives to occur.

The guide to Egyptian antiquities in the British Museum, written by a G. Long and published in 1832, presented the world as a storehouse which supplied an "inexhaustible" number of collectible objects and which could provide many more such treasures for those capable of obtaining them.[96] Even though the titles of the collections in the British Museum proclaimed that only the very rich could do so, the guidebook suggested the possibility of collecting and of erasing the distinction between the collector and the viewer. While the British Museum was believed to contain the whole world, it also came to embody the power of Britain as a nation able to bring about this containment with the help of its wealthy collectors. Such a belief, accompanied in the 1832 guidebook by information about Egypt that showed its difference from the West, descriptions that were similar to those described in the 1826 museum guidebook published by Underwoods, helped lay the foundations of public support for later colonial ventures. Any examination of the histories of the collections reveals the interconnected politics of their acquisition, classification, and display.[97]

In this culture, men of taste, that is, the collectors, along with the scholars and explorers they helped to fund, formed the aristocracy, more acceptable because it did not seem to be founded on rigid class lines and because it seemed not a class aristocracy but a national one, with patrons collecting not to improve their own collections but that of the nation.[98] The power of this new aristocracy is visible in the museum guides of the Society for the Dissemination of Useful Knowledge. Sir Henry Ellis's two books on the Elgin marbles (1846) and the Towneley marbles (1848) suggested a veneration of the aristocracy that had brought these collections to England.[99] For Ellis, the museum could educate only because of the power and generosity of the wealthy. Thus these guidebooks claimed that the education of the public, and the idea of a "national" art and a "national" repository, could occur only because of the aristocracy. The elimination of class distinction through education, the emergence of nationalism, and the spreading of a classical education which hitherto had only been possible for the aristocracy were believed to have occurred with the help of the museum's collections. Class distinction became, paradoxically, by mid-nineteenth century, the method for the removal of class differences. Ellis's guides, therefore, made apparent the contradiction at the heart of the museum collection: the recuperation of class distinctions in the very process of removing them.

Both these books begin with their first chapters devoted to accounts of Lord Elgin and Charles Towneley bringing their collections to England. In the *Elgin and Phigaleian Marbles*, Ellis discusses the controversy surrounding the obtaining of the marbles, suggesting that Elgin did so out of concern that England had no classical models that could teach its artists and students, and that he had obtained the sculptures legally. He points out that Elgin had obtained the marbles also out of his concern for the sculptures themselves, since he had heard of the "almost daily injury which the originals were suffering from the violent hands of the Turks" (1846, 3). Ellis claims that since the Turks had no consideration for Greek statues, were "even in the habit of shooting at them," Elgin, as a lover of art, had no recourse but to save them (1846, 4). Thus while representing the Turks as barbaric people without any knowledge of aesthetic value or taste, Ellis exonerates Elgin from blame for taking the statues from Greece and describes him as the savior of art, one who ventures strategems and money in order to save the marbles for the education of the English.

Ellis ends the chapter by saying that Elgin's perseverance and taste have helped establish England's reputation as a repository of art: "The possession of this collection has established a national school of sculpture in our country, founded on the noblest models which human art has ever produced" (1846, 10). The aristocratic collector of the seventeenth and eighteenth centuries is here recast as a nationalist, one who collects not for his own power but for England and for the disinterested improvement of art and taste in its population. National pride becomes pride in the power of the aristocracy and results in the valorization of class difference.

Ellis's guidebook on the Towneley collection is also a testimony to the cultural power as aesthetic taste of the aristocracy which can, in England, reproduce the classical world even when faced with increasing industrialization and the growing strength of the middle classes. It opens with an account of the lineage of Charles Towneley. When he brought his collection to England, Towneley established, according to Ellis, a house for his collections in which the furnishings and decorations suggested that "the interior of a Roman villa might be suspected in our own metropolis" (1848, 6). The recreation of a Roman interior in England seemed valuable to Ellis because it became a setting that combined wealth and scholarship, taste and rank.

The Towneley guide is written by a staunch Tory seeing in 1848 that the museum was becoming more and more open to every kind of person, poor or rich, so that it seemed even more important to reclaim the world of art and culture as an aristocratic realm. At a time when bourgeois values were gaining dominance, aristocratic values became idealized.[100] In its valorization of classicism as the most essential part of an aesthetic education, the guidebook is therefore addressed to teachers of the classics and to those who wish to read and understand the classics. From the classical world they are to learn "how infinite in variety are simplicity and truth" and to "pay a tribute of thanks to the nobleman [Elgin] to whose exertions the nation is indebted for it [the collection]" (1846, 215).

The education disseminated by the guidebooks thus emphasized the importance of the wealthy collector and was reiterated by the museum's displays. Such an emphasis was evident by the titles given to exhibits: the Towneley marbles, the Elgin marbles, the Payne-Knight collection, the Christy collection, the Sloane collection. Each object in the museum came to be a mark of those who funded the travelers and collected the objects. As J. Mordaunt Crook reports in his book on the British Museum, "the age of the great private patron overlapped with the age of municipal enterprise," for the private patron was still a crucial factor in the development of the museum.[101]

The committee of 1835, concerned with issues of public education and access, had been aware of the problematic importance of the aristocratic collector, for they asked Ellis why portraits of the trustees and of benefactors were hung in the gallery of minerals in the museum. In 1850, at the hearings of another parliamentary commission on the British Museum, the keeper of the Department of Antiquities, Sir Charles Fellowes, commented that the Elgin collection would perhaps be better called the Athenian collection, and that collections would be better named chronologically or geographically than by the name of their collectors. Fellowes's suggestion shows that even though there were other ways of naming the collection, the museum continued to give prominence to its collectors, reminding visitors of the distance between the visitor and the collector.

Imperialism and Consumerism:
Class and Gender Distinctions within a National Culture

"Do you mean to say, that the behavior of the public, generally, is such as it ought to be in viewing the Museum?"

"Yes, the ignorant are brought into awe by what they see about them, and the better informed know, of course, how to conduct themselves. We have common policemen, soldiers, sailors, artillerymen, livery servants, and, of course, occasionally mechanics, but their good conduct I am very much pleased to see, and I think that the exhibition at the Museum will have a vast influence on the national character of Englishmen in general." (evidence of Mr. Samouelle, assistant in the Department of Natural History)[102]

In willing his collection to the British government, Sir Hans Sloane had desired that it be accessible to the public. When George II refused to buy the collection, Sloane's trustees petitioned the House of Commons, and by means of a state lottery and an Act of Parliament, the

British Museum was created. Since it was a collection set up by Parliament, it belonged to the nation and to the public. Consequently, its audience, educational function, and accessibility became sources of contention and anxiety. In the nineteenth century, committees set up by the House of Commons, such as the one that interrogated Mr. Samouelle, investigated whether the museum was endeavoring to educate all classes and how it was going about this task.

While there is no clear evidence of how many working-class men and women went to the museum, it is well known that they flocked in large numbers to collections such as the Exhibitions. Like the British Museum, these fairs exhibited objects and goods from many countries. The Great Exhibition, that collection of the spoils of empire displayed in the Crystal Palace, was a monument of consumption. It was a museum and a market, which signaled the era of the spectacle and from which advertisers and retailers learned that, as Thomas Richards puts it, "the best way to sell people commodities was to sell them the ideology of England."[103]

Excursion clubs were set up in 1841 so that the less affluent could save up to take package tours to these fairs, testifying to their popularity.[104] These clubs were originally a reform measure for the cause of Temperance, since it was hoped that wages would be spent on edifying travel rather than on alcohol. James Cook, a Temperance worker, took 165,000 people to the Great Exhibition in 1851 and set in motion mass tourism.[105] The number of visitors to the British Museum increased rapidly in 1851, the year of the Great Exhibition, when almost two million people visited it, more than the entire residential population of central London.[106] By visiting museums and fairs, a larger portion of the population was able to see objects and collections from remote parts of the world. These exhibitions were to have a great impact on Victorian life and culture, impacting the "home" as domestic space to replicate the power of empire. In such a space, Victorian interior design emerged, which in its crowded style simulated the juxtapositions of imperial objects in museums and exhibitions. Even in working-class homes, Jubilee souvenirs had a place.

The Museums Act of 1845 and the Public Libraries Act of 1850 enabled local authorities to build libraries and museums out of the public rates. Whereas in 1800 there had been fewer than a dozen museums, by 1850 there were nearly 60 and by 1887 there were at least

240.[107] The British Museum had grown immensely as well. A number of famous collections, from the royalty and the aristocracy as well as other collectors, had expanded such that in 1823, Montagu House, the first building to house the original collections, had to be rebuilt. The new building was completed in 1847. The number of departments steadily increased with the increase in collections. After 1838, when Anthony Pannizi became chief librarian, the book collection, because of stricter enforcement of the copyright laws, increased at the rate of thirty thousand volumes a year. A new reading room had to be added in 1857; the White Wing opened in 1882. Between 1880 and 1883 the natural history collections were removed to South Kensington.

Advances in public participation in libraries, fairs, and museums and the ascendancy of the department store occurred within the context of the decline of working-class radicalism after 1850, as well as the emergence of new forms of gendered consumption. Nationalism, as the misrecognition of class difference, contributed to this decline. Richard Johnson has suggested that after 1850 the alternative system of working-class "really useful education" supported by radicals such as Cobbett and by the Owenites and the Chartists was replaced by working-class demands for education provided by the state. Such demands came from popular liberal politicians and, much later, from the Labour Party. As Johnson puts it, while radicals, Chartists, and Owenites had all opposed state education except as the work of a transformed state, later socialists actually fueled the growth of state schooling by their own agitations.[108] Whereas the *Black Dwarf* had opposed the setting up of national libraries on the ground that learning should support itself, and other radicals had opposed state education on the Godwinian grounds of opposition to authoritative education, the acceptance and even the demand for state education signaled that the incorporation and the pacification of the working class had begun. After 1851, all classes were visiting the British Museum, though the numbers did not reach the peak of almost two million a year that occurred during the Great Exhibition.

It has been suggested that one reason for the rise in visitors was that the Great Exhibition contained displays of manufactured goods that were relevant to the social life of factory workers.[109] Yet this view does not explain why the British Museum became more popular when its exhibits did not change in any significant way. While other museums such as the South Kensington Museum (created by the planner of the Great Exhibition, Henry Cole) exhibited the products of industry and science, the British Museum did not change its displays to include popular objects. Though the increase of interest in museums in general created by Cole's exhibits may have brought in more people to the museum, other factors that contributed to the popularity of all museums may also have helped. The increase in earning power of all classes, in leisure time, and in literacy must be cited, as well as the greater acceptance of state interventions and institutions.

An important factor may be the continuity between the museum and the department store, as new forms of classed and gendered consumption came into existence based on a shared ideological aesthetic. Commodity culture was coming into existence through the transformation of high style.[110] The Victoria Jubilee ushered in a gendered commodification, where Victoria became at once the prototype of the female consumer, asserting the hegemony of the upper classes while creating a shared consumer culture, much as the museum had done. Regardless of the class she represented, she contributed to gendering the consuming subject.[111] What Thomas Richards calls a "jingo kitsch," the objects manufactured in commemoration of the Jubilee, connected home and harem, nation and empire, by moving objects of empire into the home.[112] Judith Walkowitz has suggested that the new public space for women, a "heterosocial space" that emerged during this time, included the music hall as well as the theater, department store, museum, library, and public transport.[113] The specularity of these spaces no doubt brought about a sense of an urban, mass, commodified culture as a characteristic of the imperial metropolis, within which classed, gendered subjects could exist as consumers.

To claim the necessity and the success of the museum and library laws, the Select Committee on Public Libraries was told in 1849 that the character of the workingman had improved in recent years both "in a moral and literacy point of view." By 1852, it was believed that the British Museum had become successful in educating the public. The preface to an 1852 guidebook to the museum, published by the New Library of Useful Knowledge, another series of books aimed at educating the middle and lower classes, begins with an enthusiastic counting of the steady increase in the number of visitors to the museum, a counting that reinscribed the participation of the working class in the dominant culture.[114] It is "wonderful" that 53,912 people came to the museum in one week; what is even more a matter of wonder and jubilation is their "perfect propriety and decorum," which is "highly creditable to their good taste and feeling" (1852, 13). It was felt that the "mob" had been disciplined by seeing and acquiring knowledge and information. To indicate the success of the museum the guidebook of 1852 continues: "formerly the English populace was a mere mob—a mischievous assemblage, incapable of appreciating the beautiful or the good, or of behaving with common decency in public places; and upon this plea they were virtually excluded from inspecting not only the mansions of the nobility . . . but our noblest national treasure" (13).[115] While suggesting that it was merely a lack of proper behavior that prevented the "mob" from participation in the glories of the nation, the writer states also that increased participation can come about now that the lower classes have shown civilized behavior in the Crystal Palace during the Great Exhibition of 1851. The "mob" has also behaved with propriety in viewing the "houses of the aristocracy, several of which have been liberally thrown open to their admission" (1852, preface).

It comes as no surprise, therefore, that the guidebook of 1852 concludes happily: "Verily this is an age of progress, and the conviction of this truth . . . that the sympathies of the rich and the poor are identical. . . . That we are all of one common nature, let us still further show [by acting on] the maxim of universal love" (13). Thus the union of rich and poor is believed to have taken place only through the much greater wealth, learning, and condescension of the wealthy.

The guidebook suggests, further, that with its help, the objects in the museum are now accessible to all visitors, much as the Exhibitions, missing price tags, suggested. The guidebook proposes to give visitors "a general idea of the nature and amount of the treasures that lie within their reach" (1852, 5). It points to a world of objects "within the reach" of the visitor, proposing the possibility of ownership even when the separation of viewer from artifacts kept in glass cases, of visitor from the collectors whose names were enshrined in the museum displays, negated such a possibility. Viewing was only "at a glance," but the objects were not "within reach," that is, they could not be owned except through a national collective ownership. The promise of democratic ownership connected the museum with the exhibition and the department store.[116] The museum displayed realms of knowledge that had earlier been hidden from the general public and provided the proximity of valuable objects that without any possibility of possession aroused the pride of national ownership.

The advances made by women included their presence not only in the streets and stores but also in the previously male sanctum of the British Museum Reading Room, which became a trysting place for heterodox men and women; letters complaining of such an intrusion appeared in the *Pall Mall Gazette*.[117]

The viewing public, both male and female, felt pride in the collections, without realizing that they were looking upon products that exemplified their own alienation, for the products included in the collection would be property created by the division of the worker from the product of his labor (1852, 16). Yet selling the idea of a lack of alienation would be central to an imperial, nationalist, consumer culture. The guidebook of 1852, by pointing out the harmony and unity in the nation, collapsed the difference between capital and labor. It thus seemed to reunite the workers with the product of their labor. Yet the reconciliation was proposed through the promise of ownership, which, though national, suggested that all people could own property, a relation very different from the reconciliation of labor value with use value wished for by early-nineteenth-century radicals. This new form of ownership promised, to all visitors to the museum and to the greatly increasing audience which included the working class, the breakdown of class divisions through the creation of a new homogeneous class of the consumer. Thus one important factor within English nationalism was the emergence of the consumer.

The consumer was a product of the collection because, as Susan Stewart argues, the consuming self constituted not by the production but the consumption of goods is the result of alienation. This alienation emerges from the abstraction of labor from the process of production of the collection.[118] The separation of labor from product, and of object from production, resulted in the creation of a self that could only overcome alienation by consumption. Gender difference could, for example, be sublimated by shopping, which emerged as a female activity in the 1870s.[119] The existence of the public collection, in which objects seemed to be produced magically, signified the subjects who were not the producers but the "inheritors" of value. And because the labor of the consumer was the labor of "magic" and not of production, the collection came to signal the economy of consumption. Such a relation is suggested in the 1852 guidebook, signaling the decline of working-class agitation and the rise of state education, as well as the increased commodification of social relations which signals the emergence of the consumer. While guidebooks before 1850 carefully included narratives of the labor of collecting and writing to mediate the radical disjunction of the object from its origin and production, even though what was produced was not use value but display value, the guidebook of 1852 contains no such narrative.

What it provides instead is a narrative of magic and transformation, that is, the consumer's labor. There are no accounts of the acquisition of objects, as in Ellis's books. What is mentioned is that when objects arrived at the museum—and we are not told how they arrived there, since the writer merely quotes from the most current edition of the *Synopsis*—the museum had to be made bigger. If a narrative is given, and this occurs in the description of the Lycian Room, it is one of accident and chance, and not of labor or hard work. Sir Charles Fellowes, we are told, made the "discovery" as a "result of mere accident," for while traveling in Asia Minor he "happened to alight upon the ruins of an ancient city." Being "struck with the beauty of the sculptured remains" he made drawings of these and took them back to England. There it became "immediately apparent" that these were the ruins of the ancient capital of Lycia (1852, 27). In contrast to earlier narratives of learning and acquisition, all of Fellowes's responses are unpremeditated, easy, not sought or worked for. The Lycian collection thus becomes a narrative of chance, of a magical transformation of ruins stumbled onto by chance into beautiful remains that have value.

The narrative of transformation becomes also the narrative of the process by which the museum educates. The education does not occur by the conscious mental labor of the viewer but by the effect of the proximity of objects. By the visit to the museum, says this guidebook, "the mind of the visitor will become gradually the recipient of an invaluable variety of information and knowledge, and will find itself qualified, in a superior degree, for historical, artistic and antiquarian pursuits, should inclination and circumstance prove favorable" (1852,

5). The public would be "civilized" by viewing the objects in the museum, objects that suggested their own commodification.

While working-class agitation decreased by the end of the century, the movement for women's rights and equality became increasingly vociferous. Working-class women had always been seen as threatening to upper-class male conceptions of the domestic space. For instance, the strike of fifteen hundred female card-setters in West Riding, taken as an indication of female independence, was seen to be "more menacing to established institutions than the education of the lower orders."[120] Yet suffrage movements became predominantly middle class, even though gendered, classed forms of resistance in terms of agitations by laboring women continued.

Whereas I have suggested in an earlier chapter that empire, nation, and race provide the site of enunciation for feminist subjects, consumer culture, also producing imperial subjects, presented another public space for middle-class women, along with philanthropy that was aimed at reducing the alienation of the poor.[121] The gendered consumer, predominantly the middle- and upper-class woman, was the target for goods displayed in the exhibitions and stores. Department stores provided a series of services and comforts for women that would recreate a homelike atmosphere,[122] domesticating the public space of the market. Liberty's Eastern Bazaar was the first to market the romance of the East to Londoners, a romance that in earlier decades had been sold by returning memsahibs in the form of shawls and jewelry to middle-class women.[123] Philanthropy, aimed at the poor in England and unfortunate "sisters" in the colonies, was seen by middle-class women to be a recreational activity equivalent to shopping.[124]

As socialist women's groups and women's labor groups continued to struggle against capitalism and consumerism, it cannot be said that there was no working-class agitation in the latter half of the nineteenth century, for there were champions such as Morris and Ruskin of working-class causes. Morris was against what he called "keeping art vigorously alive by the action, however energetic, of a few groups of specially gifted men and their small circle of admirers amidst a general public incapable of understanding and enjoying their work."[125] He was also aware of the danger of the working class's striving for this elitism; in an 1885 essay called "Useful Work Versus Useless Toil," he warns against what he sees around him: an economic system in which the working class did not strive for socialism but for participation in capitalism. Thus he remarks, "Civilization has bred desires which she forbids us to satisfy, and so is not merely a niggard but a torturer too."[126] Morris was opposed to the inclusion of art and its knowledge as one of the goods of a consumer civilization.

Yet Morris did suggest, perhaps as a way to turn the alienation implicit in the museum and the elitism implicit in classical art into an oppositional tool, that workers should visit museums in order to learn of the time when art and work were one and gave pleasure. He believed that great works of art, such as Greek sculpture from the Parthenon, could teach the working class to know of that great time and be discontented with the present. For Morris, therefore, the museum could inculcate revolutionary awareness. Yet even when Morris recommended that workers visit museums in order to learn of art that combined work and pleasure, he acknowledged the problems of the museum, that is, it decontextualized art and presented it as alienated from labor by displacing it from where it was produced and placing it in an artificial medium. He says, therefore, "nor can I deny there is something melancholy about a museum, such a tale of violence, destruction, and carelessness, as its treasured scraps tell us."[127] Morris was aware that the museum's "scraps" hid a history of violence, even though he wished to utilize it for giving the working class a revolutionary education. Yet Morris did not connect the violence of the museum with the violence of imperialism.

Such a contradiction indicates that working-class movements in the second half of the nineteenth century were less powerful than those of the early nineteenth century since they were more intertwined with the power structures of the dominant classes. Women's movements also continued to struggle with large fractures within them; the conflicts of the Pankhurst sisters, with Christabel as apologist of empire and Sylvia in a missionary-benevolent opposition to it, symbolize some of the struggles going on at the time. Yet, despite such struggles, the education of the working class by means of institutions such as the British Museum and the department stores continued and furthered the rise of imperialism, another function of nationalism. The British subject alienated and made into a consumer by her or his own commodification saw other races and other peoples also as commodities. The British Museum had shown the world to be a store-house of goods, and imperialism and the acquisition of artifacts for the museum became synonymous processes. When guidebooks from the end of the century mention how objects are acquired through military conquest, they elide the labor and cost of acquisition by suggesting its ease. The preface of the 1899 museum catalogue describing antiquities from Benin contains a narrative of their acquisition in which the reader/viewer is told that the objects have been obtained "by a recent successful expedition sent to Benin to punish the natives of that city for a treacherous massacre of a peaceful English mission."[128] The destruction of Benin City is shown to be a punishment to its natives that "made accessible to students of ethnography the interesting works of native art which form the subject of the following pages."[129] The ease of this acquisition, the erasure of labor, is suggested when the cost of the acquisition, in human lives, time, and money, is not mentioned. An 1890 guidebook to the museum, after a preface that lists its collections, adds that the main part of the Egyptian collection was laid "by the acquisition in 1802 of the antiquities which passed into the possession of the British army on the capitulation of Alexandria in the previous year."[130] In these catalogues of the late nineteenth century, the military might of a colonial power is given credit for enabling the collection and preservation of objects. Since display value in the collection comes from the transformation of goods into artifacts and art, military conquest becomes a source of aesthetic value, one that is easily converted into economic value.

The British Museum was an imperial project also because it embodied a love of order, what Walter Pater described as the "element of classicism." The world was reassembled in the museum as an ordered construct. The love of variety, that function of the power of capital through the acquisition of goods, was the aesthetic of the imperialist collector; it enabled the collecting of objects that could be put in order within a familiar taxonomy. Bachelard, in *The Poetics of Space*, mentions that Robinson Crusoe reconstructs a world from objects that he transforms magically. The British Museum did the same. It collected objects that were believed to have obtained value only by being placed in the museum collections. Taken out of circulation in their original economic and cultural spheres where they had use value, they were placed in another economy in a different form. However, what was suggested was that they had been transformed into use when they were made objects of knowledge; without this new use value they were merely the dirt that awaits transformation into gold.[131] Thus the British Museum constructed a world that showed what was unknown and alien as being constructible. The "East" and the "Other," made into interchangeable entities, were spatially and temporally frozen into artifacts within the museum.[132]

The British Museum also provided a discourse of communication with the rest of the world. Like Jules Verne's traveler in *Around the World in 80 Days*, whose house was filled with speaking tubes and clocks, communication as well as movement in time and space was proclaimed proven by the collection of objects in the museum. The unmoving, frozen spoils of travel showed the mobility of the English collectors. The visitor, armed with the guidebook, who perambulated through the museum past the atemporalized, stilled artifacts, imaginatively traversed the geography of Euroimperial travel. A visit to the museum was like a guided journey to foreign lands.[133] Here lay the ivories from many "dark" places; the spoils of travel, like the novel and the travelogue, narrativized the "Other." The "rescue" of personal fragments, which for Walter Benjamin gave the private collection its ability to provide rebirth and renewal, was, on a public and national level, an imperial ordering.[134]

PART II

Euroimperial Travel and Indian Women

Chapter 4

The Culture of Travel and

the Gendering of Colonial Modernity

in Nineteenth-Century India

The idea of the copy that we have been discussing counterposes national and foreign, original and imitative. These are unreal oppositions which do not allow us to see the share of the foreign in the nationally specific, of the imitative in the original and of the original in the imitative. . . . This schema is also unreal, and it obscures the organized cumulative nature of the process, the potent strength even of bad tradition and the power relations, both national and international, that are in play.[1]

In two of his essays, Sudipta Kaviraj has attempted to define the "we" that became articulated in nineteenth-century Indian writers, a "we" that has often been described as nationalist.[2] His framework is rather narrow—he examines only Bankimchandra Chattopadhya in depth so that he refers only to a single though complex notion of identity in middle-class colonial Bengal, and he does not see gender as one aspect of the political construct he examines. But Kaviraj's work makes some crucial points. First of all he distinguishes a nationalist consciousness from an anticolonial consciousness, which he argues is not nationalist in that the nation-state is not imagined yet as a possibility. Then he argues that notions of community much before they become nationalist have to be looked at carefully to see how they are created. Thus he sees two kinds of communities, "fuzzy" and "enumerated."[3] Earlier communities are fuzzy in two ways: first, because "they have fuzzy boundaries, because some of the most significant collective identities are not territorially based," and second, "because those communities, unlike modern ones, are not enumerated," with the consequence that a notion of a collective will that could be mobilized is not present. Such a notion of community is antecedent to nationalism but is not nationalist by itself. Thus he argues, "their sense of community being multiple and layered, no single community could make demands of preemptive belonging as comprehensive as that made by the modern nation state" (66). Nationalism comes into existence when the fuzzy community becomes enumerated.

The notion of enumeration poses its own ideologies, which Kaviraj does not go into and which must also be examined to understand specificities of communityness of a particular nationalist form. Nevertheless, the idea of a fuzzy community is helpful to the purpose of understanding prenationalist or extranationalist forms of identity in India, especially gendered ones. Even the anticolonial consciousness that Kaviraj reveals in the writings of Bankim does not account for the complex sense of a Self in Toru Dutt or even in Behramji Malabari, both of whom do not oppose British rule as clearly as does Bankim. Yet both construct forms of identity that reveal emerging understandings of what it means to be "native." Being native, having a native place, being "home," mapping one's land—all of these can be seen as attempts to articulate a sense of Self and community that are not as dominant as those articulated by Indian nationalism's canonical male texts. The term *fuzzy* is appropriate here, in that these notions of "we," so clearly visible in articulations of home, of what is not-home, of binaries such as urban / rural and India / England, of public and private spheres, are not synchronous. Within these conflicting, "fuzzy," and emergent notions of the national Self or Selves, modernity is an important issue.

The relation between modernity, reformist movements (especially on the "woman question"), and nationalism in India has engendered much interest, as is clear in the work of such scholars as Uma Chakravarty, Susie Tharu, KumKum Sangari, Partha Chatterjee, Sumit Sarkar, and Sudipta Kaviraj, among others.[4] The general view is that modernity was seen as a condition for nationalism, even though scholars disagree on the forms and the content of the modernity as well as its intersection with localized and indigenous practices. Sudipta Kaviraj, for instance, points out that "it was clear by the early twentieth century that Indian nationalism was marked by a deep attraction for modernity, it saw independence as a condition for achieving modernity."[5]

The South Asian historical view that colonialism and modernity were in collusion is foundational in my analysis of colonial traveling subjects since discourses of travel created new forms of historical self-consciousness that were modern. This modernity came from the imposition of European modernity which was in a hegemonic relation to it; as Tani Barlow suggests when speaking of East Asia, "Asian modernities perform their own recodings of the discourses of modernity within a hegemonic, capitalist world. Modernities in East Asia were undertaken in multiple, overlapping colonial dominations and participated in the shaping of global forces under numerous local exigencies it behooves us to understand."[6] The framework of colonial modernity, utilized by much recent historiography on South Asia, requires that we look carefully at the subjects created out of this modernity (as were the traveling subjects who are the topic of this chapter) and the discourses and contexts that created them. In this chapter, I look at gendered constructions of the "we" that colonial modernity gave rise to. I examine various appropriations of the European culture of travel as it was negotiated by Indian men and women under colonial rule. I argue that this form of travel, as it is reconstructed in terms of other traditions of travel and socioeconomic contexts, enables a mode of conceptualizing a Self that utilizes European Romanticism in conjunction with local cultural practices whose outcomes are quite different. The question then is how these new notions of the Self are created and what they consist of.

I argue that in order to understand this question, we need to understand above all that colonial modernity is a gendered issue, that is, the Selves that are created are gendered selves. The collection of essays *Recasting Women* has inaugurated such a project and scholars such as Dipesh Chakrabarty have added to it by discussing reconstitutions of domestic space under conditions of colonial modernity.[7] An attention to notions of travel that become altered in many ways during the nineteenth century in India can reveal how this colonial modernity created these gendered selves through the comparative framework of East and West and its homologies such as unfreedom and freedom that European modes of travel encouraged. Since forms of European travel above all created the demarcations between "home" and "abroad" through comparative perspectives dependent on the binary of Self and Other, the utilization of this binary by Indians was central to creating new forms of the Self.

The comparative framework, especially, enables the conceptualization of what is "home" and what is not. Women such as Toru Dutt (1856–1877) conceive of home as a problematic space that is both an embodied space of unfreedom and a spatial and temporal articulation of a Self. For Behramji Malabari (1853–1912), reformer and columnist, "home" is to be mapped in concentric circles of belonging, where the core is the place where one is born, spreading out to a regional and national identity. For Malabari too, the comparison between India and England enabled by European travel, of India with England, is central to the construction of an Indian Self.

"Home" and its distinction from abroad / market or from "harem" was a concept-metaphor that was fundamental to the comparative framework of colonial modernity. The formation of colonial subjects and the effects of English education resulted in the internalization of modes of travel and the formation of traveling subjects that are modern. Yet colonialism constructs something else: a colonial modernity that is seen as inexorable but foreign, as a hegemonic formation that is accepted in its epistemological framework that defines the relation between colonizer and colonized as a binary opposition, even while colonial domination is refused at many levels.

In the European culture of travel, mobility not only came to signify an unequal relation between the tourist / traveler and the "native," but also a notion of freedom. This freedom was directly related to notions of England as a "civilized" country in which parliamentary rule signified representational politics and the voice of the citizens. Paradoxically, even Englishwomen who were not able to vote participated in the discourse of "freedom," thus implicitly validating the discourse. Although believed to be ever present for the English, this "freedom" was especially dominant within the discourse of travel, for it was there that it was manifested and constructed within the discourse of English imperial nationalism through the contrast of the English as "free" with "Eastern" people as "unfree." Rule of the people in England was contrasted with the "despotic" and "monarchical" rule within non-European countries. Utilizing the prerevolutionary ancien régime in France as a universal model for all despotisms, parliamentary democracy in Europe was contrasted with despotism of non-European rulers of all kinds. The darkness and opacity of this despotism was seen as the past of Europe, and English travelers and colonizers believed in the superiority of their form of government as one that benefited all people rather than just a few. As Lisa Lowe points out, for the writers of the Enlightenment such as Montesquieu, despotism was "the Other of the French political system, figured in the Orient of Persia" in works such as *Persian Letters*.[8]

By the end of the eighteenth century in Europe, a new notion of "freedom" was constituted as mobility also through Romantic constructs (spurred in England by fervor for the French Revolution), which required a merging with nature and which enabled the enjoyment of land and new places in new ways. Freedom, within the European Enlightenment, was seen as a natural right, one that in Romantic philosophy was essential for the unalienated Self. With the rise of Romanticism, Europeans had new reasons to venture into areas that no one hitherto had desired to visit. Romanticism, combined with the scientific imperative, enabled exploration and mapping in the search for the noble savage, for the "Other" required by the Romantic Self to be complete.[9] This was a search for the past, for what was authentic in contrast to the alienation of the industrial age, and led to a new perception of nature within the discourse of the needs of the all-important Self.[10]

In this chapter, I turn to those who utilized these discourses of travel for different ends. These were travelers from India, men and women. As the colonized, they incorporated Western structures of travel but could not and did not deploy them in similar ways. For the most part, many of these travelers worked within agendas through which they tried to establish their new relations to colonial contexts, to English education, and to conceptualizing themselves in new ways.

Even though, for many Indian women and men, travel became a method through which education and certain forms of agency could be acquired, it was complicated both by imperial notions of travel within which Indians were seen as being liberated by European modernity constructed through notions of education and progress, and by the Indian travelers' desire to take advantage of these discourses but for various ends that reconstituted and sometimes, though not always, subverted European cultural superiority. Furthermore, travel was not always seen in terms of European Romanticism by those who were not educated in British literature or through English education, since for those outside European notions of travel, mobility and movement did not carry the same meanings. Nor did the concern for imitation or comparison become as much of a concern as it did for the upper classes or for such groups as the Bengali Bhadralok.[11]

Just as Englishwomen utilized the discourse of colonialism and nationalism in order to construct themselves as subjects, Indian women of the upper classes, who were of the higher castes as well, utilized European Romanticism. Toru Dutt, whom I will be speaking of at length in this chapter, absorbed and deployed English Romantic notions of Selfhood, of the land, and of the discourse of freedom as mobility in order to be able to construct her own sense of Self. Since she was educated in English literature, was reading the literature of empire, and came into frequent contact with English in India and England, she felt the need to construct such an agency. In examining the ways in which Toru Dutt participated in the European culture of travel, we can see not only the kinds of epistemic violence, as Spivak calls it, that is demanded by this insertion, but also the results of this violence in the reconstruction of new gender, caste, and class categories out of preexisting gender, caste, class, and familial ones.[12] That is, a Bengali woman such as Toru, having had an English education, utilized the culture of travel to see herself as a subject and as modern, and in doing so enabled the reconstruction of cultural formations relating to gender; traveling to England, remaining unmarried, and learning English were all practices that were new to women of her class and caste. As has been suggested by many scholars, this modernity, which recast various social divisions, became central in anticolonial and nationalist responses.[13]

This alteration in the discourse of travel occurred because English Romantic notions of travel were reconstituted within the context of very different cultural assumptions and formations of travel that were part of Indian cultures, as well as within the context of the new relations between the state and its people through colonial interventions in the economic and social realms. The demands of colonial power structures altered many of these assumptions while also challenging, in some instances, the discourse of freedom as mobility. Among the upper classes, travel had a different valence in regard to freedom, but the hegemony of Western travel was apparent among Indian elites in that both freedom and education through travel, which had antecedents in the Grand Tour as well as in the discourses of anthropology and exploration, became tropes for many English-educated Indians as well as for the English.

Restrictions for Caste Hindus on Crossing the Black Water

If European notions of travel were intrinsically linked to modernity, colonial modernity, as the way in which modernity was imposed in colonial contexts and utilized by colonized peoples, was apparent in the new ways in which people from India traveled. These changes ranged from the new forms of employment available to middle-class men, new locations for legal and registration work related to land—both of which changed people's relations to their villages and cities—to the emerging ways of living for women accompanying the men to places of employment in the colonial bureaucracy or even staying home by themselves. There were new ways of traveling enabled by the railways and roads being constructed by the colonial regime and by the different conceptualization of the West, of England, of Europe, and of America that colonialism brought to the people of India.

For those Indians who were Hindus, travel overseas violated religious and caste laws. It was seen as a religious violation even when eating beef, which was also proscribed, was not. Yet these views began to change by the last decade of the nineteenth century. In his *History of Hindu Civilization during British Rule*, Pramatha Nath Bose writes that "the present practice is to excommunicate those who go for purposes of education or travel to Europe or America."[14] While suggesting that this proscription may have been due to the belief that forbidden food or food not prepared under correct caste conditions would be consumed during such travel, Bose considers the travel proscriptions to be a contradiction because dietary restrictions do not, in and of themselves, cause excommunication. A proposition to remove this sea voyage restriction upon condition of keeping caste rules was rejected in the Sixth National Conference. However, in 1894 a resolution passed at a provincial conference in Bengal enabled sea voyage. In part the resolution said: "in the opinion of this Conference, the time has come when, having regard to the important political, educational and industrial issues which are involved, practical steps should be taken to give effect to the sea-voyage movement among Hindus, by organizing at an early date a trip across the seas to be undertaken by Hindus, due regard being had to Hindu customs and usages."[15]

Since access to higher education, the British civil service, and professions could not be obtained under colonial rule without trips to England, it is understandable that such a resolution was passed. It is also understandable that there were such restrictions for upper-caste Hindus against sea voyages, for until mid-century, only the poor, lower castes, and of course, non-Hindus went on overseas voyages to Europe as servants and sailors.[16]

While Muslims did not have such proscriptions, their notions of travel to foreign lands were structured within religious notions of the hajj, that is, as pilgrimage, a form of travel widely shared among people of all religions in India. Moreover, for traders from India, movements from the subcontinent to Africa and other parts of Asia had been going on for centuries. Trade routes between India and what is now the Middle East had a long history, for instance, that had reached its height in the Mughal period. Muslim and Jewish traders had had cordial relations with Indian merchants and a thriving trade that was interrupted and overtaken by Europeans. Within this trade, Indian merchants and slaves would also have moved across the oceans and land masses of West Asia.[17] The travels of Ibn Battuta and Al-beruni, for instance, record these trading caravans' movements and a very different notion of travel of Muslims in India that focuses on religious differences rather than racial or cultural ones understood within a hierarchy.[18] Yet, under colonialism even longstanding trading practices and movements related to commerce were altered, leading to new identities and relations between communities and trading partners. Traders of all religions within India had to respond to changed relations between politics, commerce, and agriculture during the nineteenth century.[19]

Even though these changed trading forms are not my focus, the changed nature of employment under colonialism had a more direct impact on forms of travel for middle- and upper-class men and women. These new forms of employment and education also signified class mobility in that they implied entry into the English educated classes. Moving to Calcutta from the villages for education or employment for many Bengali males marked such mobility.[20] For upper-class and caste Hindus, going to England for higher studies was a means for getting jobs or advancement in the colonial bureaucracy and signaled prosperity and high status. It also meant that they had to perform atonement on their return. Furthermore, restrictions for Hindus against sea voyage may have had much to do with concerns with Westernization and the desire on the part of many sections of the populace to maintain gender and caste structures in the face of European colonization. These caste restrictions did not weaken until the end of the nineteenth century, when more Indians began to travel overseas. Whereas earlier, those who violated such caste rules were put out of caste, this practice, as suggested by the 1894 resolution, weakened by the end of the century when, for instance, Hindu society in Bengal could not expel all those who had traveled abroad.[21] Furthermore, sea voyage also began to be seen as an issue of modernization that was integral to progress. Thus in the debates on the sea voyage issue, one tract argued that "as society advances gradually in religion and morals, the objections against sea-voyages will disappear . . . so long as the full measure of advance is not attained, so long it will be impossible to make sea-voyages acceptable to society."[22]

Furthermore, for many poor men and women, such restrictions may not have been relevant to the economic forces governing their decisions. Since the eighteenth century, as Rosina Vizram has revealed, the English had taken Indians to England as servants and sailors. Women went as nursery attendants and maids, and many of them were abandoned and ill-treated and left to find their own way home. Men and boys went as sailors, servants, and exotic pages. Many were virtual slaves, for they were not paid and could not leave their service. None of these early visitors to England went for the education that motivated middle-class and upper-class Indian travelers at the end of the nineteenth century. Furthermore, caste restrictions were, in many instances, not the decisive factor in their lives because they were either not Hindus, were not caste Hindus, or were too poor, lacking many choices under British rule.[23] Another category of persons for whom travel did not imply upper-class understandings of education was the indentured labor from India who were taken to various British colonies after the abolition of slavery.

Indian Travelers:
English Education and Indian Masculinity

Yet where European travel made its impact on the colonized in India was by altering modes of observation and creating new relations of Self to history among those classes and castes directly influenced by English education.[24] The new perceptions constructed colonized subjects with altered relations to their own land. These perceptions were also essential in creating new forms of knowledge for the colonized. In *Masks of Conquest,* Gauri Viswanathan argues that English education created a historical consciousness that "was intended to bring the Indian in touch with himself, recovering his true essence and identity from the degradation to which it had become subject through native despotism." Such an education presented itself as "restoring Indian youth to an essential self and, in turn, reinserting him into the course of Western civilization."[25] Further, it inculcated a historical consciousness that was part of the Enlightenment, even while it purportedly left "native" cultural practices untouched. In addition, the consistent, pervasive, and ongoing construction of knowledge as an understanding of the division between "native" and "English" or "European" was one that informed all discourses in the colonial context and was part of the comparative method essential to colonial discourses. Viswanathan's use of the male pronoun in the quote above indicates that this subject of history was also masculine. For such a subject, the new concepts of Self and community came out of the movement from the multiple fuzzy Self, as Kaviraj calls it, to a more mapped (rather than enumerated) and clear idea of community. The relation of the English-educated male elite with the English rulers comprised not only a utilization and adaptation of a hegemonic English culture and values that constructed modern masculine subjectivity, but also one that argued for equality from / with the British. Thus the terms of colonial modernity, termed "tragic" by some scholars who see it as taken at the cost of freedom, can also be seen as more complex in that these offered new modes of patriarchal power in a hegemonic relation to British culture.[26]

While Viswanathan focuses on English education only in terms of the discourses of the British, the effects on those colonized were complex and multiple. The levels of incorporation and influence of this education are also complex and different for those directly educated by them, and for those for whom the influence is indirect but no less significant. Furthermore, another question remains as to how these influences interact with local cultural formations and practices to reconstitute colonialism for colonial hegemony and new subject positions that become available to the Indian middle classes.[27] The process of creating history in relation to emerging concepts of communities cannot be seen as totally indebted to modernity or even to the orientalist narratives about India, for oral and written narratives of heroes and legends dealing with love and adventure existed, as did the episodes from the epics and the Puranas. As Meenakshi Mukherjee argues, these genres joined with the Romantic novel from England to create a new kind of historical novel.[28] These novels created a golden past that had to be regained from the colonizers. Within the narratives of travel analyzed in this chapter, instead of a directly anticolonial rhetoric there is the notion of this lost past, indicating the emerging process of self-definition as emergent historical consciousness at work. Indian novelists who used history to write historical novels, for instance, utilized far more explicitly many notions of history, chronicle, and fiction to reach an Indian audience, as Meenakshi Mukherjee reveals in her work.[29] Yet writing as travel writers rather than as novelists, as Behramji Malabari and Bholanath Chandra did, reveals a rather different focus and subject position that argues that European epistemology's effect was the focus not on the family or familial relation but rather on the description of a culture and society as one that was mappable and knowable through authorial mobility, distance, and comparative skills.

In narratives of travel, subjects of colonial modernity such as Malabari and Chandra appear most clearly in their complexity. In works such as Behramji Malabari's *The Indian Eye on English Life* (1893) and *Gujarat and the Gujaratis* (1882), Bholanath Chandra's *Travels of a Hindoo* (1867), and Devendra N. Das's *Sketches of Hindoo Life* (1887) such colonized and gendered subjects formed out of English education are visible in their complex relation to the colonial episteme and to their own land soon to be conceived in nationalist terms.[30] Malabari, a fervent supporter of colonial rule, saw modernity not only in terms of progress and reform of tradition, but also as a past and a present that was being lost, literally and metaphorically, through lack of appreciation (i.e., through a nonappreciation of history) as well as through colonization. Travel, as a mode of understanding and as a discourse of power that constructs authenticity through separation and alienation from what is traditional, was a means to regain that land, and it created subjects such as Malabari with complex modes of connection to European constructs as well as to an emerging notion of Self and community.

Malabari and Reform:
An Emerging Male Public Sphere

Behramji Malabari saw himself as a traveler and reformer in the mode of English writers such as Addison and Steele, who utilized the periodical press in order to address concerns within England. This model of the periodical essay became widespread among many Indians to attack colonial rule or questions of reform,[31] showing the operation of that complex process often seen by scholars such as Homi Bhabha as "colonial mimicry" but which an attention to class and a rejection of authenticity can enable us to understand as the preoccupation and power of a particular class reconstructed through local and specific hegemonic formations.[32] While Bhabha's work is useful in pointing out that such mimicry is not merely a slavish following of English models, his notion of the ambivalence of colonial authority and its excess does not address the multiplicity of responses that constitute available subject positions for the colonized. Nor does this account for class differences that are fostered by colonialism and its international divisions of labor through notions of copying, inauthenticity, or provincialism as Roberto Schwartz had pointed out in the case of Brazil.[33] Instead of looking at Malabari's writings as simply colonial mimicry, his subject positions can be understood rather through carefully accounting for his diverse audiences, the tasks Malabari has at hand, his own position in terms of gender and class, as well as his approval of colonial rule as necessary for progress. It would be necessary to unpack all of these elements in order to analyze the effect of colonialism and English education on middle- and upper-class Indians in the nineteenth century as they are differently positioned in terms of gen-

der, religion, caste, and class. Malabari's complex positionality becomes apparent especially in his understanding and utilization of
travel. While travel conveys to Malabari the "real India" in terms of
its distinction from what is English, the reforming imperative then
utilizes modernist ideas to construct difference within European notions of history. The distinctions between Self and Other, "home"
and "abroad," modern and traditional all constitute forms of distancing within colonial modernity that come from the Western epistemological tradition, and specifically in Malabari of history as an unbiased
and objective construct. This utilization of difference works also in
anticolonial nationalism as it utilizes modernity.[34]

Malabari called himself the "Indian Spectator" and worked for
reform of Indian society, supporting widow remarriage and against
"traditions" such as child marriage. He worked with the colonial
government in order to create legislation to enable reforms in the
condition of Indian women, even to the extent of going to England to
get the support of the English public for his cause. This is most visible
in his initiating and championing of the Age of Consent Bill, which
was to cause tremendous controversy among reformers and orthodox
groups of Indians in India, and for which Malabari obtained support
from prominent Englishmen as well as women such as Millicent Fawcett.[35] He was supportive of British rule, writing poems dedicated to
the British royal family in addition to those that were composed on
reformist themes. His poetry revealed the influence of writers such as
Alexander Pope in addition to the folk poetry of the Khailis of Surat,
which consisted of spontaneous poetry sung satirically in singing
contests. It is suggested that his taste for the English satirical poets
came from his participation among the Khailis.[36]

As a reformist leader, he articulated the problems of Hindu customs
and represented these to the British in both India and England. As
reformer and periodical essayist, he revealed in his writings and position an emerging public sphere in which he participated and helped
construct. In this sphere the newspaper columnist as a didactic and
detached observer of mores came to play an important role. Malabari's writings suggest the emergence of a class, predominantly male
(since few women knew English or were literate), that knew English
and was used to buying the newspaper to learn about current affairs
and news (and therefore possessed an emerging modern relation to

time). These periodicals were also read by the English, so that Malabari saw as his audience colonial bureaucrats, benevolent English reformers, the Indian reformers, and "leaders of society." In Malabari's accounts, those responsible for the so-called decline of Indian society were not the colonial rulers, but a lack of historical consciousness and a decontextualized "tradition." For instance, he sees in the practice of child marriage the "cause of many of our social grievances, including enforced widowhood" leading to sickly children, "poverty and dependence."[37] He believed that child marriage had no religious sanction in the shastras and that "tradition" was a problem for such practices, so that, in fact, absent religious sanction, the British government could prohibit it. The problem was religion, the solution was the colonial state.

Furthermore, writings such as Malabari's created masculine subjects by articulating a gendered authority relative to Indian women. In the Age of Consent Bill issue, for instance, his appeal in England was entitled "An Appeal from the Daughters of India," thus speaking for women of India.[38] In his columns he argued for greater knowledge and understanding of India by Indians and regretted that educated Indians "own to no concern in the fortunes of the vulgar herd."[39] Since the column would only be read by "educated" (which meant English-educated) men, that is, the upper classes, the existence of this new voice revealed the creation of an opposition between the "vulgar herd," that is, the masses, which included women of all classes and castes (though not seen monolithically), and a paternalistic elite, a discourse that maintained class distinctions over those of caste, religion, region, and language. The process of civilizing the "herd" becomes therefore the concern of an Indian male elite, which sees itself as educated, modern, and paternalistic. An issue such as the Age of Consent Bill was argued through the construction of a public sphere conceptualized by his close associate, Dayaram Gidumal, who put together an ambitious symposium of "Hindu domestic reformers and anti-reformers," who were all men, from various parts of India, the deliberations of which were published in 1889.[40] The colonial government collaborated with this masculinization of authority in various ways. In this instance, the government instituted in 1884 a process of consultation of the public that involved "such officials or non-officials as were considered to be well-acquainted with native feeling on the question." Not one woman was asked, even though Pandita Ramabai had given testimony to the Hunter Commission in 1882 and was well qualified to give her opinion. Unsurprisingly, "native" opinion was found to be against raising the age of consent and the issue was dropped by the government.

When Malabari called for consideration of child widows and the illiterate and the poor, his mode of relating to them seemed to be within Romantic notions of "rural folk" or the "poor" in relation to the poet as Self (as in Wordsworth, though different in content), a position that connects him with the English men and women who see themselves as benevolent to Indians. Thus the reformist position on widow remarriage and against child marriage is viewed by him as a process of mediation between the "leaders of society and the State," as his biographer hagiographically puts it. His position did not earn him much approval with the group of people seen as "educated natives."[41] Despite such opposition, this "benevolent" colonial community along with those Indians interested in reform became a community in which he saw himself as an equal, not only in class but also in race since he subscribed to Max Muller's constructions of a common Aryan ancestry for Europeans and Indians. This belief in the benevolent colonial state is clearly obvious in *The Indian Eye on English Life*, which is subtitled *Rambles of a Pilgrim Reformer*, in his description of colonial bureaucrats such as a Mr. Patrick Ryan, whom he describes in the following words: "As a magistrate he was more humane, perhaps, than just, always siding with the helpless and the ignorant, as against the powerful police or the unscrupulous limbs of the law." When Malabari mentions that Ryan "put me straight on the Home Rule and other political problems," the magistrate is presented as more in tune with Indian nationalism than Malabari himself.[42]

Other English men and women in his community are those who responded to his poetry and writings on reform. Thus, he mentioned, in a speech on Max Muller, that his book on English verse enabled him to be acquainted with the "noblest of Englishmen and Englishwomen . . . ," namely "The Earl of Shaftesbury, Miss Nightingale, Tennyson, Gladstone, Max Muller," and so on.[43] No doubt this list of names is influenced by an audience consisting of English military officers from whom he solicited donations, in this case, for translations of Muller's Hibbert Lectures. Believing that English rule was necessary to the progress of India was thus not unsurprising in a writer who worked on reform and education while believing that greatness was to be the equal of English politicians and writers. Thus, paradoxically, when he complained that the system of education was not teaching Indians empathy with the poor, he wrote: "Will it [English education] even give us a Shaftesbury or a Stansfeld, a Howard or a Penn, a Nightingale or a Fry?"[44] His understanding of India was marked by a belief in an emergent "native" community, of which he was a part, that aimed at equality with English models of greatness who were, however, clearly superior. It was therefore not surprising that after the symposium on the Age of Consent Bill created much controversy, Malabari went to England to get sympathy from the British public to get the bill passed. The English committee for the Age of Consent Bill was composed of many of the British elite.[45]

The Indian Spectator and the Colonial Gaze: Malabari and Nightingale

Yet, while Malabari participates in colonial modernity as a traveling subject, his position is by no means continuous with that of the English who insert him into a different location in their self-construction as Euroimperial traveling subjects precisely by seeing Malabari as the object of their gaze. This inequality also marks the fractures in the public sphere of colonial India consisting of benevolent British and reformist Indian men that Malabari attempts to constitute through his columns. Thus, at one point, while he sees Florence Nightingale as a model of compassion for the poor, Florence Nightingale sees him as a "native" who needs to be helped. Her views on Malabari and her relation to India are clear in the introduction she wrote to a book on Malabari's life and works, *Behramji M. Malabari: A Biographical Sketch*. In the introduction, the very inequality that Malabari is conscious of in relation to the poor of India is directed at him, whereas he has constructed himself as part of a community within which Nightingale was included. Nightingale, who had never been to India but thought herself an authority on matters of hygiene in India,[46] begins: "The most interesting portions of this book are those which give us a peep into an Indian home—that of Mr. Malabari and his family...."[47]

This is also where Malabari's account of those he sees as needing help from English-educated Indians is markedly different from Nightingale's account of Malabari as the "native." Whereas Nightingale seems intent on "unveiling" the "native," as it were, and structures her position as an outsider/traveler concerned with comprehending another culture through a brief "peep" as she moves along, Malabari sees the child widows and the Indian poor as persons to be brought into progress, as did the other Indian reformers, a progress which inserted him, along with those he could reform, into modernity. Nightingale's voyeurism, her need to uncover and to obtain knowledge, and her assumption of her own modernity, is to be contrasted with Malabari's desire to *become* modern that is revealed in his patriarchal notion of Indian culture and its unfortunates who need the paternalism of Indian reformers and of British rule.

Consequently, the relations between Nightingale and Malabari and between Malabari and the objects of reform are not quite the same, even though Malabari assumes that they are. For Nightingale, the view of Malabari's house constitutes a "peep" into the workings of a monolithic category termed the "Indian family," in which Malabari's mother exerted the supposed influence that made Malabari an exemplary native. Thus, to understand the workings of this house is, for Nightingale, the key to knowledge of Indian women that is vital to the project of "civilizing" the colonized. Nightingale's "peep" into the Malabari household is, we are told, in the service of that laudable goal. In the introduction to Malabari's biography, Nightingale sees Indian women as the "moral strongholds" who exert an "unbounded" influence and thus need to be utilized for "social" progress, at the same time as she says that she knows little about them: "We Englishwomen understand as little the lives and circumstances, the ideas and feelings, of these hundred millions of women of India as if they lived in another Planet."[48]

A further difference between Malabari and Nightingale in their perceptions of India is the reason for travel and for gaining knowledge. In the year 1892, when colonial power was at its height, Nightingale revealed little of the Romantic notion of merging with a more natural Other. Romantic relations between colonizer and colonized were no longer evident; instead there was a functional approach that was bent on continued colonial rule. Malabari, however, operated through Romanticized ideas of the poor that positioned them within Indian idylls of rural life and called on a glorious past of perfect harmony. That Malabari admired Max Muller and wanted to translate some of Muller's lectures into the vernacular is indicative of his use of an Indian and Aryan past. Uma Chakravarty points out that Muller "vastly popularized a racist version of the Orientalist Hindu golden age and it was this newly formulated golden age that became so influential in later Indian thought."[49] What is clear, however, is that while English men and women see India in functional terms, the utilization by the colonized of Romantic constructs enables knowledges of India that are seen in terms of progress into modernity.

Travel, Comparative Knowledge, and Modernity

Such differences between English travelers such as Nightingale and Indian traveling subjects are to be noted even while it is clear that Malabari's construction of Self as traveler follows upon European forms of travel, within which notions such as progress, historical consciousness, the comparative nature of cultures, and objectivity and authenticity are evident. For these notions, as Viswanathan points out, were the result of English education.[50] Yet when Malabari presents himself in the opening pages of *The Indian Eye on English Life: Rambles of a Pilgrim Reformer* as a "pilgrim in search of the truths of life," adding that "there is so much to learn and to unlearn from contact with a different civilization," we see travel as a pilgrimage, so much a part of the experience of many in India, becoming reconstituted into the reformist method of comparative study that aims, not at personal salvation, but at a secular salvation of a group of people being identified as Indians or "natives" who belong to the East as the English belong to the West.[51]

In an essay in *The Indian Spectator* that explains his methodology in works such as *Gujarat and the Gujaratis* and *The Indian Eye on English Life*, Malabari writes that he has not absorbed European notions of travel and that he has never been to Europe. Yet even without traveling to Europe, his English education taught him how to be a traveling subject, that is, to utilize a binary epistemology for the construction of the Self. Thus he maps his "home" within a framework of colonial modernity that is particular to upper-class and caste Indian men. In writings before and after the tour of England that he records in *The Indian Eye on English Life*, it is apparent that Malabari's masculine modernity includes the utilization of a comparative method that enables both a new appreciation of "home" and a critique of "abroad"/ England for its dirt, poverty, and lack of interest in India. Thus the comparative method enables not only a construction of home but also a critical view of England as one that does not fulfill the rhetoric of the colonizers.

The movement to understand a category of persons that Malabari calls "Indians," "natives," at "home" is part of the process that ends in nationalism, although Malabari had no part in that since he was interested in reforming India within continued British rule. Yet his modernity consists in the mapping of the characteristics of this group termed "Indians," thus taking on the categorizing and mapmaking power of imperialist geography. The ability to map his surroundings emerges in Malabari's way of looking at India and is elucidated in an essay on travel in his column in *The Indian Spectator* in July 1888. What is apparent in this essay is his mode of travel, which is presented as a series of concentric and methodical movements that enable him to map his surroundings, with digressions that construct nodes of authenticity: "The first tour I remember having made was round grandmother's kitchen. Thence I transferred my attention to the front yard of the house, thence to the street, the neighboring street, the whole suburb of Nampura, and the surrounding suburbs. . . . The climbing of trees and roofs in search of paper kites was another round of useful tours. (Kiteflying is one of the best Indian sports, and I am sorry to find it discouraged . . .)"[52]

It is this systematic mapping, intermingled with the digression on kite flying that creates a narrative voice concerned with the Indian past and its particular and quirky forms found nowhere else, that marks this traveler's difference from the Europeans writing about India. In Malabari's accounts, alongside this emerging appreciation of India as a lost past is its construction as a disappearing present. Thus there are two kinds of historical consciousness visible here: one is of the golden past that is compared to a degenerate present, and the other is what Renato Rosaldo has termed "imperialist nostalgia" and which he describes as a hegemonic relation to disappearing cultural forms.[53]

Such a relation is not only fundamental to anthropology but also to tourism, so that both forms of movement and knowledge are deeply implicated in the experience of modernity. Dean MacCannell has argued that tourism is the attempt to create a totality out of the fragmentation that all moderns experience.[54] Thus a tourist attempts to historicize culture and to museumize the past in order to achieve this totality and ordering. In the context of colonialism, and in the attempts of colonized people to see themselves as subjects, the fragmentation of modernity implies something else—a sense of distancing brought about by alien others that is different from the experience of modernity among people in the West. This is the specificity of colonial modernity.

Yet Malabari, unlike those who held either Muslim rule or British colonialism responsible for the loss of the golden age, never mentions who or what is responsible for the disappearance of kite flying; like Wordsworth naturalizing the poverty of rural folk, Malabari naturalizes problematic formations, or he presumes, as did the British, that they were "traditions" that were the result of degenerate religions and political norms. Here lies his difference from the anticolonialists or the nationalists even though his comparative framework is similar to theirs.

In addition, there is the relativist notion of culture in the comparative model, one that Malabari sees as acquired by first knowing about an entity called "home," seen as the domestic space that then becomes encircled by the larger entity of India and the "East" before one ventures out. Such a method also erases knowledge of power relations in the understanding of relations between cultures; incorporation of this method becomes a sign of colonial modernity that can compare "East" and "West." Thus he says, "No study is so absorbing for man as a study of human progress; no method so successful for it as the comparative method."[55] For Malabari, therefore, the comparative method enables one to admire foreign lands and monuments without being "ashamed of your own." Thus in the essay on travel he writes, "I honour you for your desire to examine the arts, sciences and philosophies of the West: but you cannot do this with advantage to yourself and the world unless you have already made yourself familiar with the *national* systems" (my emphasis).[56] For Malabari, travel in India is essential before travel abroad; and travel is seen as the acquiring of knowledge that enables one to "see or see through them" rather than merely "look at things."[57] Furthermore, travel enables the comparisons between "nations" which have a "system" that is apparent to scientific rationality; India is seen as a "nation" at this point through a quasi-scientific discourse that is authorized by traveling. Malabari's identity is a national one rather than one that suggests caste, religious, or regional affiliation. Perhaps being a Parsi, he could position himself more easily within a nation in speaking of reform of Hindu customs.

Paradoxically, even when, in a different context, Malabari had constructed English men and women as models of greatness that seem to have no parallels among Indians, he argues here that Indian cultural forms are quite comparable to European ones: "it makes me sick to hear a man rave about this thing or that 10,000 miles away, when a much better, perhaps the original thing, is lying unnoticed in his own land. Bah! I hate our Anglicised Aryan."[58] Here the problem of colonial education is attacked as creating subjects who appreciate English objects while they have no appreciation for their own; objects seen as English and Indian are not only equivalent, since they are both Aryan, but Indian ones are seen as originary, as authentic in a way that English ones are not. The reliance on Max Muller's ideas, whose essays he had helped to translate into the vernacular and which came out in 1882, are obvious here.[59] The discourse of alienation from an originary and authentic past is available through the Romantic discourse of travel. Such a form of colonial modernity is seen as distinct from an unauthentic condemnation of India by those educated through Indian education. Thus there are seen to be two forms of modernity: one that embraces an authentic Indian past and one that despises everything Indian. The former is valorized while the latter is often ridiculed by both English and Indians.

Yet in Malabari's discursive practices, along with the understanding of loss, there is also a desire for modernity, one that becomes embodied by England and which is available only in England. In this form of colonial modernity, Malabari constructs England as the destination for pilgrimage and where salvation is to be found. This notion of England, which I address more extensively in looking at the writings of Toru Dutt, is a gendered one that in Malabari becomes a site of learning and enlightenment instead of one of freedom as it is for Indian women. For Malabari, this destination is one of a pilgrimage that is to resolve the condition of colonial modernity that leads to being perplexed or ambivalent. England becomes the place where the potential and the failure of "humanity" is visible; what is clear is that these are notions adjudicated with the help of colonial epistemology. Thus Malabari writes that London is "pulsating with the highest aspirations and the lowest passions of humanity. With all its unattractiveness, London is still a Mecca for the traveler in search of truth, a Medina of rest for the persecuted or perplexed in spirit. . . . To the searcher after enlightenment it is a Budh-gaya; a Benaras for the sinner in search of emancipation."[60] Since Malabari elsewhere writes about the injustices of colonial rule even though he supports it, such a view of London must be read as a condition of travel in England that resulted from colonial education, from reformist views, and from the construction of a bourgeois male elite that based its power on utilization of colonial knowledge. The Indian notion of pilgrimage as a search for spiritual salvation is reconstituted into a search for an unalienated and authentic Self.

A Brief Aside on Bankim and Colonial Modernity

Yet comparative frameworks of knowledge work somewhat differently for a writer such as Bankimchandra Chattopadhya, whose acceptance of English rationalist philosophy later enabled his ideas about the superiority of Hinduism. Here the comparative knowledge can be turned around to an ironic look at the British themselves and to deny English claims of superiority. Thus in his letters on Hinduism, Bankim writes:

> Suppose a Hindu, ignorant of European languages, travelled through Europe, and like most Europeans in his situation, set about writing an account of his travels? What would be his account of Christianity? Observing the worship of the Virgin and the Saints in Catholic countries, he would take Christianity to be a polytheism. The worship of images would lead him to believe that Christianity was an idolatry too, and the reverence to the crucifix would induce him to think that there was also a leaven of fetishism in it.[61]

This anticolonial possibility of travel as a way to deconstruct difference, while retaining an Indian masculinist authority, is markedly different from the utilization of travel by Malabari. Malabari's view of England, different from that of the British in India, was that it needed reform too, especially in regard to women and the working classes, while Bankim's turns colonial discourse on itself to create discursive knowledges of Britain as were those created by the British about India. Furthermore, Bankim's understanding of the Self and community, more a notion of Bengali and Hindu identity rather than one that spoke of other communities in British India, came from what Partha Chatterjee calls a masculinist belief in rationally creating a glorious history that was distinct from histories created by Muslims. Chatterjee calls this belief one that "sought to create a national leadership in the image of ideal masculinity—strong, proud, just, wise, a protector of the righteous, and a terror to the mischievous."[62] Thus Bankim's travels become a way to understand and wield discourse as a political tool for a Bengali middle class that was employed by the British government, the awareness of which is not visible in Malabari's writings.

Bholanath Chandra:
Subjection and Modernity

Bholanath Chandra's *Travels of a Hindoo* (1869) suggests another related traveling subject created out of English education, whose travelogue maps an emerging sense of what it means to be an authentic "native." Chandra's work constructs him as the authentic "native" who is able to mediate between the English and an "authentic" India, but whose sense of Self, authenticity, and India is also partly indebted to Romantic notions of place and landscape. Such Romanticism, in the context of colonization, provides a means to articulate a new form of alienation that constructs a home and a Self intimate with and emotionally connected to that home as well as having the masculine authority to represent it, at the same time as it feels alienated from it. The cause of this alienation differs among these writers, as they are not always anticolonial or even nationalist. In the case of Chandra, the cause of this alienation is often ambiguous, sometimes represented as the passing of time and sometimes as progress.

The text begins with a letter to the viceroy of India, thanking him for permission to publish the book, which is presented as the result of

English education. The book, he says, contains the impressions produced by a journey undertaken by one "who is indebted for his education to the paternal government of the British in India," mentioning that he wishes colonial rule to continue for the benefit of the Indians.[63] It is clear that the subject position that Chandra inhabits in order to write and publish his travelogue to an English audience is that of a faithful Indian subject as the "native." Moreover, it is as a modern subject, because he begins by invoking the lost past of India — by saying that modes of travel were different twenty years ago and that travel is much faster now. Such notations of changes under colonial rule (in the name of a progress not unmixed with nostalgia) become a mark of travel narratives written by an English-educated Indian. Furthermore, despite Chandra's prefatory inaugural eulogy to the viceroy and to colonial rule, there are also indications that the writer is aware that the British see the Indians as inferior: "Ethnologically, he (the Hindoo) is the same with an Englishmen — both being of the Aryan-house. Morally and intellectually, he can easily Anglicize himself. Politically, he may, sooner or later, be raised to an equality."[64] While Chandra sees himself as belonging to the same *race* as the British, the statement about equality seems somewhat ambiguous in terms of the agency that will bring about political equality. Even though Chandra hesitates to blame colonial rulers for their prejudices, he clearly feels that his modernity has made him an equal, as will be all Indians once they begin to progress.

Once again, a comparative framework that organizes past and present structures this narrative, inserting Chandra into modernity in the process of mapping and representing the landscape of "home," one that later writers would build upon as an emotional connection to Self and nation. Chandra's narrative itself works in two different registers to reveal the violence of the colonial episteme as it constructs its subjects. On the one hand it makes the Indian landscape picturesque, thus inserting it into a Western aesthetic and mode of observation that eliminates social problems and conflicts. For instance, one passage describes an area in Bengal in the following way: "The banks of the Hoogly, for miles, present the most gay and picturesque scenery. On either hand are gardens and orchards decked in an eternal verdure, and the eyes revel upon landscapes of the richest luxuriance. From the groves shire out the white villas of most tasteful and variegated architecture.... No part of Bengal exhibits such a high degree of populousness, and wealth, and civilization, as the valley of the Hoogly."[65] On the other hand, the narrative authenticates itself through its invocation of the past, depicting places as the former dwellings of sages and writers and as sites of famous incidents in religious and oral tradition. Here again, the traveler/narrator is seen as knowledgeable in ways that English readers would appreciate, indicating the creation of a class of persons, predominantly male, who mediate between Indian cultures and the British by reconstituting knowledge of India through colonial epistemology. Thus, in this genre, combined with the knowledge about Indian practices are motives of travel that are clearly inculcated from English education. For instance, in describing the hills of Byjnath (Baijnath), Chandra says they are a welcome sight to "him 'who long hath been in populous cities pent,'" thus revealing that this is not a pilgrimage that is motivated by religious salvation but a Romantic need for nature for one who is living in urban spaces.[66]

Chandra's narrative brings together religious and folk history expressed in the appreciation and knowledge of places of pilgrimage with a Romantic sensibility derived from English education. This combination is a specific form of colonial modernity, which sees itself as alienated from ancient and valorized forms and traditions. Thus he writes, "The palace of the Sultan is traced in the altered building that is now occupied as the shop of Thomas and Co., and where we saw a Mussulman gent come and buy an English spelling-book."[67] There is an ambivalence built into this narrative, where the changes that can be seen by later readers as an erasure of an Indian past by a colonial occupation can only come into play through English education as well, revealing the problematic of colonial hegemony in which opposition can only take place through colonial paradigms. The narrative of "tradition" is created through a juxtaposition with changes brought about that are conceived of as "modernity." The headings of sections in Chandra's text reveal such a juxtaposition: *Nana and his council*; *Miss Wheeler*; *The House of Massacre*; ... *Ancient Khetreyas and modern Sepoy*; ... *Idolatry in Hindoostan and Bengal*; ... *Former insecurity and present security of travelling in the Doab*; *European fugitives during the mutiny*; *Ferozabad*; *Field of the Wreck of Hindoo independence*; *Approach to Agra*. The fact that this text is aimed at European readers is evident in its viewpoint about colonial rule; however, this text would also be read by English-educated Indians interested in learning about their own country, thus articulating an understanding of "home" in time and space. Chandra's text reveals that knowing about India for the English-educated Indians meant reading texts that presented the colonial hegemonic even if the content included more "native" knowledges about India.

While forms of travel as pilgrimage are clearly present in Chandra's attention to a mapping of India within a religious itinerary, his narrative utilizes also the genre of the European travelogue. The difference between the pilgrimages and Chandra's own narrative is evident in both the attention to places to stay, forms of transportation, and the evaluation of these in terms of efficiency and comfort in the Western or Indian style. In fact, it is clear that Chandra's narrative is similar to English travelogues, taking as its audience the armchair traveler as well as the actual traveler; as with guidebooks, descriptions of India are not only for those who like to read about it but for those who intend to visit.

If colonial paradigms are evident in this presentation of "authentic" India, what is particularly pertinent to the forms of Western travel is this focus on authenticity. As Dean MacCannell argues, for European travelers/tourists to go in search of what is authentic and natural marks their modernity.[68] Authenticity is not only presented through knowledges that are seen as "native" but also, more specifically, through an introduction by an Englishman that suggests the ideal kinds of colonial subjects that were to be created through English education:

That the author was a Hindoo seemed scarcely open to question. His thoughts and expressions respecting family and social life were evidently moulded by a Hindoo training; whilst his observations and opinions, especially as regards places of pilgrimage and other matters connected with religion, were eminently Hindoo. At the same time however, his thorough mastery of the English language, and his wonderful familiarity with English ideas and turns of thought, which could only have been obtained by an extensive course of English reading, appear to have led some to suspect that after all the real knight-errant might prove to be a European in the disguise of a Hindoo.[69]

What is evident is that where the colonial subjects remain Hindoo is in the areas of family, "social life," and religion—these are supposedly unchanged by English education as was believed proper for colonial rule. Colonial rule in India presented itself as not interfering with Indian customs. This colonial belief in an unchanging "Indian" family and religious life is taken by the English writer of this introduction, J. Talboys Wheeler, to authorize Chandra to write his book of travels; in contrast, it is the ability of European travelers to perform being "native" that often authorizes their travel narratives.[70] Where English education has an impact, according to Talboys, also the author of *A History of India*, is in language and a "familiarity" with "English ideas and turns of thought," none of which are believed to have encroached on family and "social life." This denial of the effect of colonial education on the private spheres was also utilized by Indian nationalists for a masculinist discourse maintaining that, according to Partha Chatterjee, the home as the spiritual element had been kept sacrosanct from colonial intervention.[71] Thus the colonized, English-educated, reformist male subject, as he appears to the English, is one that uses English language and ideas to express and reveal an unchanging religious and familial social existence. Yet the Indian traveler created by English education was one whose epistemology reflected social conditions altered by colonial rule, but one whose subject positions reflected these changes through new relations to religion, land, caste, class, and family. Authenticity, therefore, is utilized for divergent purposes by both English and Indians who see it as a means to articulate an emerging sense of a "native" identity.

Indian Women and Travel under Colonization

Although by the middle of the nineteenth century caste restrictions had weakened for Hindu men, they had changed in different ways for Indian women as well. Travel for women was undertaken for visiting relatives or for pilgrimages; travel to visit strange and unknown lands or for direct or indirect educational purposes was unknown, particularly since women were not supposed to have any formal education. For instance, when Sasipada Bannerjee proposed to take his wife,

Rajkumari, with him to England in 1871, they were stoned by Hindus of his caste when he went to pay a farewell visit to his ancestral home.[72] There was less of an outcry when Debendranath Tagore's wife went to England with her two children in 1877. Yet these journeys by women were still considered to be extremely reprehensible and, as Ghulam Mushid points out, they not only changed the women considerably but also had a tremendous impact on many Bengali men.[73]

Furthermore, by the end of the century, people from many regions of India were getting used to the idea of travel for secular reasons, particularly the desire for professional advancement and employment. The colonial structure of India led to greater mobility for Indians because middle-class Indian men began to pursue career opportunities in the government service all over India, which often necessitated their taking wife and children with them.[74] This was the case with the Bengali middle class or Bhadralok, that is, the professional class who were English-educated. As Meredith Borthwick suggests, one consequence of this mobility was that such women were "brought into direct contact with the larger, impersonal society beyond the normal narrow scope of the antahpur [women's part of the house] and its immediate locality."[75] While this version of "broadening of the horizons" can be seen as the educational aspect of travel, which derived from European travel's participation in scientific and anthropological discourses, it also subverted colonial power by empowering Indian women in many ways. Such empowerment violated the object status and the silence that colonial rule and local patriarchies had imposed on Indian women.

It must be noted, however, that for the purpose of both "Indian" identity and Selfhood, the group of people who took on the idea of travel as a process of becoming modern were predominantly of the upper classes and had been influenced by English education. Yet there were many for whom such a culture of travel was meaningless since they were not concerned with constructing a Self or a history and who were also outside the framework of either anticolonial, reformist, or nationalist discourse. These were migrant labor who from 1807, when slavery ended in the British empire, were taken to various parts of the world as contract labor. Ships' records, as examined by Surendra Bhana, show that by 1836, out of twenty-six thousand laborers to

Mauritious, one thousand were women. Legislation set in 1850 allowed that 25 percent of migrant labor were women. Indian migrant labor were sent to Mauritious, Fiji, West Indies, and Africa. In the second half of the nineteenth century, colonial policies combined with natural disasters had created many landless peasants and the goods from England had taken away the livelihood of many craftsmen and craftswomen. Internal migration and migration abroad came out of these socioeconomic groups and from the need for labor on colonial plantations after the abolition of slavery.[76] These indentured women became objects in the discourse of nationalism and of colonialism. For the colonizers they were seen, as with migrant women in Fiji, as sexually promiscuous, and the terrible conditions under which they lived were ascribed to their promiscuity rather than to conditions on the plantations. For nationalists in the early part of the century, they became symbols of the bravery and patience ascribed to Indian women.[77] Questions of authenticity or modernity were not relevant to the lives of the laborers, even though their conditions of existence were impacted by colonial and nationalist agendas.

If conditions for female indentured laborers were dangerous and difficult, since they were exploited both for sexual services and for their labor by both English and the Indian male laborers, conditions for upper-class women to travel within India were not encouraging. Travel within India by rail was often described as fraught with dangers; and loss of modesty or purdah, the threat of rape, and caste violations were implicit in this control of Indian women. For instance, Rokeya Sakhawat Hossain, in writing of the problems of purdah among Muslim women, recounts many anecdotes of railway travel.[78] She tells of women separated on the train from their husbands who cannot mention their names, and of the trouble and difficulty of trying to maintain purdah during travel by rail. Here new modes of travel as well as new ways in which women come into contact with strangers in railway stations and trains are seen as incommensurable with the practice of purdah. Hossain focuses on purdah as a problem, which it most certainly was, rather than on the ways in which modern modes of living were changing conditions for women. Because men's modernization was not seen to be the problem that women's modernization was, railway travel was not the issue for men that it became for women. This discourse of women's problematic insertion into modernity as a problem more threatening than that of men remained powerful even when women became used to accompanying husbands and families to places of employment.[79]

Yet, there were many in the upper classes and castes for whom travel was suggested by English education as a mode of broadening the mind, as an educational experience that taught about other parts of India and was necessary for the formation of the Self, as it was in European culture. One can assume that this was the materialist version of travel that complemented the binary of pilgrimage that would occur for spiritual reasons. The former also gained through incorporating notions of pilgrimage, as it had done in European culture, as is evident even in the titles of narratives such as Richard Burton's *Narrative of a Pilgrimage to Mecca and Al-Madinah.*[80]

This European version of travel fostered, as Borthwick suggests, a notion of India as one country, a consciousness that had not been there before. Such movement and understanding contributed to the belief that women across India had much in common and contributed to a discourse of "Indian womanhood" that erased regional differences and constructed the "Indian woman," a model that Uma Chakravarty argues was taken from the Sanskrit tradition of a "traditional Hindu woman."[81] Bengali women, for instance, became conscious that "their own region was but a small part of a much larger entity."[82] According to Borthwick, women's lives in one part of the country were compared with those of other parts of India as well as those abroad.[83]

Most Indian women who traveled abroad in the nineteenth century went either to obtain an education or to accompany their husbands. One instance of a woman who went to further her studies was Kadambini Ganguly, the first Indian woman to become qualified as a medical doctor in 1886, who left her husband and family and went to England in 1893. She returned with qualifications from Edinburgh, Glasgow, and Dublin. Jamini Sen became a doctor in 1897 and went to Glasgow and England for further studies. Anandibai Joshi went to the United States in 1883, leaving her husband in India, to obtain a medical degree.

Yet there were some who traveled because they combined many Indian cultural norms with an acceptance of modernity and British values. The Dutt family of Calcutta was one upper-class family that converted to Christianity and adopted many English customs, including mode of dress, education, and culture. The family went to Europe in 1869, so Govind Chunder Dutt's wife and daughters, Aru and Toru, became the first Bengali women to travel abroad for reasons of pleasure and education. Since they had converted to Christianity, they were not in danger of losing caste by taking a sea voyage.

The Dutt Family and the Gendering of English Education

Though Govind Chunder Dutt's desire to educate his daughters through travel to Europe was the first such effort, in this period the education of Bengali women was not unusual. The first regular girls' school open to all Bengali girls opened in 1819, and schools opened by Christian missionaries followed.[84] The first secular Bengali school was the Bethune School, which opened in 1847. With the formation of the Brahmo Samaj movement by reformist Hindus, other schools were opened and the idea of the education of women took strong hold among the upper-class Bengalis. Many girls, including Aru and Toru Dutt, were educated at home as zenana (the women's quarters) education became the mode for those who would not send their girls to school but were wealthy enough to hire tutors. Toru and Aru Dutt were similarly educated at home. Although some Hindu families disregarded the belief that education of women was sinful or that an educated woman was destined to become a widow, there were many Christian converts who were educated, so that a Bengali Christian woman was one of the first two women to sit for the Calcutta University exam in 1878.[85]

While most education for women was given so that they could be good wives and mothers, the Dutt sisters were unusual in that their scholarship and the knowledge of Western literature and culture was pursued for no domestic or professional end. While ideas of wifehood or motherhood as structured within Bengali Bhadralok society may certainly have entered their thoughts, what was most unusual was that English education would become a means for them to be writers. Even though many men were writing and publishing works that were negotiating with English genres and traditions of literature, women writing in English were still unusual. There were women who were writing, and one estimate tells us that from 1856 to 1910 about 190-odd women authors produced about four hundred works.[86] Yet writing in English placed Toru Dutt in a community of male writers from whom she was isolated by her gender. For the English, she was among a group of nonnative English writers writing in English for whom appreciation was to be given for their ability to write in English[87] and who were claimed by the English as part of the empire and as evidence of its benevolence. Edmund Gosse, the English critic responsible in some part for Toru's fame in English circles, said of Toru Dutt, "when the history of the literature of our country comes to be written, there is sure to be a page in it dedicated to this fragile blossom of song."[88] For Toru to write romances in English such as "Bianca" (1878) and *Le Journal de Mademoiselle d'Arvers* (1879)[89] was quite unprecedented, and this could be one reason why the protagonists of these works were clearly derived from English and French romances. These narratives were also similar to European romances of the time, with chance meetings and misunderstandings, rather than the very different mode of marriage relations belonging to the Bengali middle class or to the oral romance traditions of India. European-style travel, with its possibilities of adventure, meetings, and romances, influenced the choice of genre and style for Toru.

Aru and Toru had developed a love for European literature from their father, and for them, education was the pursuit of what in Arnoldian terms would be called "culture." Such a consequence was not unthinkable after the publication of Macaulay's famous "Minute" on education in 1835, in which he advised the use of English rather than Sanskrit for higher education in colonial India. The need to educate middle- and upper-class Bengalis to assist in trade and administration was also acknowledged by the government in India. Rasamoy Dutt, Toru and Aru's grandfather, was one of the first upper-class Bengalis to become familiar with English culture and literature. He was influential in spreading English education and possessed a large collection of English books. His son, Govind Chunder Dutt, loved English Romantic poetry, and he passed on this love to his daughter, Toru.

Toru's writing and poetry reveals the extent to which the Indian middle-class men in Bengal had participated in this discourse of the Enlightenment through English education. The lineage of English education at that point in colonial history is male. Thus in a later letter to Miss Martin, a friend she made in England, Toru writes, "Without Papa I should never have known good poetry from bad. . . . He has himself a most discriminating mind, and is an excellent judge of poetry. I wonder what I should have been without my father; nothing enviable or desirable, I know; without Papa we should never have learnt how to appreciate good books and good poetry."[90] Govind Chunder is a ubiquitous presence in Toru's letters, and it is within the Indian patriarchy that Romantic poetry has a place. More men than women had English education, since the education was aimed at creating employees of the English government, so that modernization as it derived from notions of education in Western culture became a patriarchal formation. In contrast to the frequent mention of her father, Toru's mother is largely absent in Toru's accounts of her education and studies; in fact, Toru's mother was not happy initially to be baptized to Christianity and did it out of obedience to her husband, though later she did develop a firm belief in Christianity. She does not figure at all in the narrative of Toru's English education.

Within the context of colonial modernity, the influence of the Romantics, Govind Chunder Dutt's favorite poets, translated into a yearning for change that initially was depoliticizing. Badri Raina argues that the influence of the English Romantics on the Young Bengal movement led by Henry Derozio, who taught at one of the first colleges for Bengali upper-class men, Hindu College, was to "produce patterns of behavior that effectively dissolved the possibility of any rigorous enquiry into Bohemia."[91] While for Raina the influence of the Romantics was mostly on this first generation of English-educated Bengalis, the example of Toru Dutt demonstrates that the modes of thought linked with the English Romantics continued through the nineteenth century in India to become part of a nationalist epistemology of the Self as nation. The politics of the Romantic movement in England, which was a critique of contemporary urban social values and a championing of an idealized working class, became negotiated in very different terms by English-educated Indians. Class conflict was neglected and instead, notions of home and Self, which were also the concerns of English Romantic poetry, were taken up as dominant forms.

Romanticism, Freedom, and Travel

Partha Chatterjee suggests that the nationalist subject that was interpellated by Indian nationalism was complicit with the subject of the
European Enlightenment.[92] More specifically, one could argue that
European Romanticism, with its stress on the formation of the Self,
both freedom loving and alienated, was responsible for the acceptance
of English culture and for the center/periphery division that structured the relations between the colonizers and the colonized. It was
also responsible for the resistance to this division, for it led to the
formation of the gendered Selves that could rebel against colonialism.
Thus the incorporation of the Romantic Self, with its recognitions of
the binary structure of freedom and unfreedom, underlay the recog-
nition by Indian women of their lives as unfree and that of Englishwomen as free.

It is important to examine the connection between this Bengali
upper-class notion of education, a learned appreciation for Romantic
poetry, and the gendering of colonial modernity. This nexus led to a
belief in progress for both individual and society and to the need for
educating women toward that end. It also inculcated two main ideas
among those who were colonized by the English: first, a belief that the
Enlightenment notions of freedom and equality, which were claimed
by the English as a sign of their superior civilization, were in fact to be
found in England, and second, that people in India had become alienated from a Self to which they had to be reconciled. Thus there
appears the belief that the freedom found in England in the nineteenth
century was to be found in ancient Hindu India. The reason for this
alienation was differently conceived by various writers, some blaming
a lack of modernity, some colonial rule, and some an unfocused and
general notion of degradation. These ideas were not unlinked to
colonial discourses but were combined with local and indigenous
social and religious articulations, as we have seen in the earlier sections of this chapter. Thus the problem of colonial modernity, deemed
"tragic" by Sudipta Kaviraj and a "torturous psycho-cultural situation" by Susie Tharu,[93] could be negotiated through Romanticism in
terms of alienation.

Yet what was ironic was that for the Romantic poets such as Wordsworth, the abode of freedom and liberty was not England but France, where the revolution had demanded equality, liberty, and fraternity. In the nineteenth century, for the Romantic poets, the hope that England would become like France was shattered, for these poets saw that oppression and the power of the monarchy and the upper classes seemed to have a stranglehold on the common folk. Wordsworth's poem, *The Prelude*, records both this hope and the death of this hope. The nineteenth century in England was a period of tremendous struggle for the rights of the working class and for women to obtain their freedoms and assert their equality to those who ruled them.

Consequently, it was paradoxical that this nonexistent equality was the basis of the claims of the colonizer about the superiority of English civilization and the inferiority of the Indian. As a result of such claims that were used to promulgate imperial rule as a positive development, for many of those upper-class Indians who were influenced by English education, freedom became a value available in England and not available in India. This became the case for many upper-class Indian women especially, women who were, as was often suggested by both English and Indians, "caged" in their homes; home here becomes a cage from which modernity would free women. Thus freedom, in colonial discourses, was interpreted in spatial terms. Amazingly enough, it was not colonialism that was seen as denying liberty, but rather Indian "tradition" that was seen as the problem. Indian women were unfree because women were in purdah in their *homes*; Englishwomen were free because they were not in purdah, could associate with men and women who were not necessarily their kin, and could move about *in the streets*. What was erased in these discourses were the constraints on Englishwomen, the domestic ideologies that regulated their lives, the fact that they did not have the vote, and the terrible conditions under which poor and working-class Englishwomen lived during the industrial age in the nineteenth century. Colonial writers such as James Mill participated in such colonial discourses on women by stating in *History of India*, published in 1817, that "among rude people the women are generally degraded; among civilized people they are exalted."[94]

What was important in Toru's work was the process of utilizing the Romantic aesthetic to fashion a Self through a poetry of landscape of "home" and the past that presents a heritage of freedom. In her work, the "home" as a cage and the "home" as a place of pastoral refuge are not synchronous but are formulations of particular and connected discourses, the former from ideas of liberty and natural rights that combine with reformist thinking and the latter from the Wordsworthian connection to a landscape of "home." Susie Tharu, in her essay, "Tracing Savitri's Pedigree," correctly identifies the signification of freedom in Dutt's poetry but does not connect it with the Romantic aesthetic. Such a connection is obvious in the poem "Savitri," where the narrative of the legend—"far-off primeval days / Fair India's daughters were not pent / In closed zenanas"—is placed against a backdrop of a quasi-English landscape of thatches, cornfield, and hedgerows. Dutt's poetics is later pressed into the service of nationalism, of which Toru had no part, for example in the work of Sarojini Naidu. However, Romanticism enables Toru Dutt to see herself as a Self to be brought into existence through poetry. The knowledge created by orientalists such as Max Muller is present here combined with Dutt's own studies of Sanskrit verses and legends. Her imagination utilizes what Uma Chakravarty argues was an "internalized notion of the 'golden' age of the Hindus, and of the highminded and Vedic qualities of Vedic women."[95] Chakravarty reveals that many women participated in this belief. Such a Hindu- and Vedic-idealized female freedom is believed available only in ancient India and recuperated in terms of Victorian morality—claiming for Savitri, for instance in Toru's poem of that name, "the very sexual refinement, the purity, . . . that the British insisted Hindu society lacked."[96]

Tharu argues that in this colonial context, comparative knowledge led those like Toru Dutt to refute British discourse on the Indian woman as unfree at all periods of history and to suggest that in the past Indian women were free. Thus in Dutt's poem "Savitri," which constructs a "free" past for Indian women that is clearly related to Victorian myths of sexual purity, "what has been so efficiently controlled are the very terms in which freedom may be imagined, not just by the writer but also by the reader."[97] One may say then, that freedom became hegemonic, in that it incorporated both consent to the forms of knowledge and intervention in its content. This discourse of freedom is examined by Gyan Prakash in relation to the history of bonded labor in India. Prakash argues that history itself, which was part of Enlightenment philosophy, was conceptualized as the movement from unfreedom to freedom. One could say that it was not only the reform of bonded labor but also women's freedom that had this common conceptual basis.

For the most part, however, the equation of freedom with mobility became widespread in a gender-specific way among many English-educated Indians. Freedom to move in the streets and outside the women's quarters became equated with a freedom that was seen in terms of a natural right. For many Indian women, since travel overseas meant breaking so many caste restrictions, and since women were seen as the repositories of tradition, the notion of travel to England became especially significant. To many, England and travel to England meant visiting the land of freedom, and the journey gave access to this freedom. For instance, Krishnabhabini Das writes in her account of her travels to England during the 1870s:

> For years I cherished the hope that one day I would go
> to England,
> the abode of liberty and freedom
> I would go to that country where there is freedom in
> every house,
> To that country where there is freedom in every house
> O Mother Bengal! Many of your sons go there in order
> to receive education,
> Why then, Mother, can't we, your daughters, go there?
> And illuminate our hearts with knowledge?
> We too are human beings, and have eyes;
> But we are blind and live in cages.
> With what difficulties have I come out of one of these
> cages!
> I have come out, Mother, to fill my heart with the nectar of
> knowledge.[98]

What is remarkable in the modernization of Indian women is the way in which such women began to think of their lives within their homes and the regulations under which they lived as restrictive, as a form of unfreedom. Though there cannot be any doubt that their lives were oppressive, restrictive, and extremely difficult, it is important to note that life in the zenana, considered normal before the British, was reconstituted as pathological in comparison with an abstract and idealized notion of English life, the patriarchal ideal of which became the norm for many English-educated Indians. Critiques of this discourse, negotiated in two different ways, are present in the travel narratives of Behramji Malabari and Bankimchandra Chatterji, as I have discussed earlier.

There may have been specific reasons why Toru Dutt began to see her home as a "cage" and England as a place of freedom, even though neither Toru nor Aru had experienced the oppressions, such as widowhood or child marriage, that colonial and reformist discourse stated had burdened Indian women's lives. One reason was that they had become isolated from their extended family. Though the Dutts became Christians, many of their extended family remained Hindu, so that the Dutt women were quite isolated at home. As Meredith Borthwick notes of Christian converts, "They alienated themselves from their own culture by doing so [i.e., converting], and as a result were left to fraternize mainly with each other or with British missionaries."[99] The women in these families may have been even more isolated, for they would not be able to "fraternize," as Borthwick puts it, with the missionaries. Toru's mother's resistance to her husband's conversion is understandable because she would have been cut off from her circle of women relatives, whereas her husband with his job and his English friends would not have been similarly affected.

Though Padmini Sengupta writes that Toru's life in Calcutta "was exciting and happy enough, with her parents, her pets, her numerous relations and illustrious friends, her books and her writing," and that the Bengali and English cultures blended together happily, this may not be an accurate reflection of the conflicts within Toru's life, short though it was (she died at the age of twenty-one).[100] From her letters and from an understanding of Bengali society of the time, we find out that she and her sister socialized with only some relatives, since those who were Hindus ostracized them not only for their conversion but because they disregarded many Hindu practices. For instance, many Hindu girls were married even before they were twelve, and Toru and Aru's not being married may have been considered reprehensible. In a letter to Mary Martin, Toru mentions the visit of a cousin who is younger than she (Toru would have been twenty then) and who has a boy of four and has lost her two younger children (78). During this visit, Toru reports playing with the children rather than conversing with the mother, with whom Toru may have had little in common. The incident indicates the ways in which, being unmarried, Toru did not have much in common with her married peers within her family who had different lives and interests; she played with the children instead. Since most women did not seek companionship with others outside of their homes and families, Toru and Aru saw few outsiders or even many of their relatives. Further, their education and interests in English literature and culture may have isolated them even more and also may have increased their absorption in their education. The feeling of restriction may have been augmented by this isolation.

When they went to Europe in 1869, they became the first Bengali family to visit England under their own impetus and finances. However, they did so not only to see Europe, but having absorbed English ideas on education and literature, also to be educated. On reaching Europe, their first stop was in France. In Nice, Toru and Aru stayed at a French pension, where they learned French. In 1870 they went to England, where they rented a house. Aru and Toru studied with private tutors and took music and singing lessons under a Mrs. Lawless, a "lady of birth," went to the theater, and had Indian dishes prepared by their cook. The family was involved in absorbing English culture and in social life with those interested in meeting an Indian family, for this was the first time any upper-class Indian women had visited England. They met many English who had Indian connections, and to those who visited them, their presence in England became a sign of the progress of India and of the value of English imperialism. The vice-chancellor of the University of London spoke of Aru and Toru as signs of "social progress" and said to Govind Chunder Dutt that "you have brought such evidence [of progress] with you, that I can hardly believe my own senses" (25–28).

Walking, Mobility, and Freedom

When the family moved to Cambridge, Toru and Aru attended the Higher Lectures for Women. They impressed people with their knowledge of English and of European life and thought. Mary Martin, who would later become Toru's friend, mentions that they became "a familiar sight in Cambridge, and the two sisters were often seen walking on the Trumpington Road and elsewhere" (39). It is important to note that they often went for walks, for this was part of the Romantic conjunction of mobility with freedom, and very much a part of the European discourse of travel and the construction of the Self through travel.[101] Going for walks had become an important aspect of English life, for it not only enabled the appreciation of nature that had become an integral part of English Romanticism, but also incorporated the movement and mobility that was required for such appreciation. The Romantic incorporation of the Self with nature was also accomplished by walking. As John Elder suggests, walking for Wordsworth was a "process of reconciliation" that provided the "dynamic unity of Wordsworth's life."[102] These walking tours were very distinct from the wanderings of the poor vagrants and pedlars who were seen as thieves and a threat to society, and were a way to reconcile the changes brought to the land by the enclosures. Thus, as Anne Wallace argues, Wordsworth's "peripatetic" was an answer to the changes brought about by the transport revolution and by the enclosures that made travel a form of "moving out into the world but continually returning to recover familiar ground."[103] By the middle of the nineteenth century, walking tours were an important pastime, and such tours occurred most often in the Lake District that Wordsworth had written about and publicized as a place where he had learned about nature.

For those who were influenced by English education, walking became an exercise both in connecting with the English landscape in England and with a "native" one that it claimed as the "home," as the place of return. Govind Chunder Dutt's favorite poet was Wordsworth, and so we can surmise that the experience of walking was an important element of the English experience through the incorporation of the Romantic traveling Self. Walks were important for Toru and Aru in that they enabled the experience of freedom that seemed denied to them in life in Bengal. Toru's letters, after her return to Calcutta, reveal the internalization of the discourse of freedom and unfreedom and the way in which this is connected to physical movements and travel outside the home. In one letter she writes, "We want so much to return to England. We miss the free life we led there; here we hardly go out of the limits of our Garden, but Baugmaree [their home outside Calcutta] happily is a pretty big place and we walk round our park as much as we like. If we can fulfill our wishes and return to England, I think we shall probably settle in some quiet country place. The English villages are so pretty" (64). And in another letter: "We see very few people here, except our own relatives and friends—indeed we seldom go out of our own house and garden. Oh, for the walks in Cambridge with you" (69).

What is evident here is the equating of "free life" with England and its walks and social circle. The appreciation of the English country villlage, mentioned in her letter above, also comes from an immersion in English Romantic poetry and paintings, from reading Wordsworth and seeing Constable paintings. City life in Calcutta is limiting but Baugmaree, because it is not in the city but in the country (the incorporation of the city / country divide is also in Romantic terms), where nature is closer and where walks are possible, is seen as less constraining, though the sisters may have been just as isolated as in Calcutta. It is also clear that since walking is not possible in Calcutta, it is not possible to have a Romantic connection to Calcutta, while this connection can occur in Baugmaree.

Free life becomes synonymous not only with mobility but with the ability to have a social life that is not limited to family and relatives, where men and women associate as friends and acquaintances. In comparison, the life of Bengali women is thought to be unfree because social life is mostly with neighbors and relatives, mostly with those of the same sex, and going for walks was not considered beneficial or important. Romantic notions of nature being tied mostly to the English countryside, to areas considered sublime, beautiful, or picturesque, it was not to be expected that the "dirty" streets of Calcutta, as Toru saw them, could be incorporated within the Romantic aesthetic. If the idea of the Picturesque could be used to describe Calcutta, it could only be so for Europeans, and not for those for whom the streets were familiar and were called home.

Furthermore, socioeconomic contexts in Bengal recuperated this binary division between urban and rural. Accounts of nineteenth-century Bengal present the country / city divide in colonial terms; that is, the city, Calcutta, is the place of employment and the country is the escape to "home" from this colonial state. While home as village and city as place of colonial alienation is the response of English-educated

Indians in middle-class Bengal to colonial contexts, those outside of this class also reconceptualized the city as a place where ties of kin were absent since many men could not bring their families to the city. For Bengali Hindu spiritual leaders such as Ramakrishna, the village remains the spiritual home.[104]

Yet even while Baugmaree becomes the true "home," where a limited "freedom" becomes possible, in contrast to Calcutta, where social norms may have been more constraining for women, movement outside Calcutta and to other parts of India is conceptualized in changing ways in this period. Outside of their own communities women were often more lax about cultural norms. For instance, they were less careful about the observance of the rules of purdah while away from their home locations. British notions of travel as a holiday also became incorporated into Bengali middle-class culture. For Bengali women, this holiday implied a change from the restriction of home into a relatively more mobile life. Borthwick mentions one Sarasibala Ray, who saw a trip to Murshidabad as an escape from the normal conventions of the antahpur.[105] Her community is Bengal rather than a larger India, so escape comes from being away from Bengal, which is seen as home.

This discourse of mobility and freedom translates not only into the country/city divide but also is seen as homologous to that of England/Calcutta in Toru Dutt's writings. This movement is apparent in another letter where Toru writes, "The free air of Europe and the free life there, are things not to be had here. We cannot stir out from our own garden without being stared at, of having a sun-stroke. And the streets are so dirty and narrow, that one feels suffocated in them" (67). Here Toru equates England with freedom and Calcutta with restriction for women. Calcutta is seen as restrictive because the Dutt sisters are anomalous to Bengali society (they wore Western clothes) as well as because of the weather. The colonial discourse of the detrimental effects of the Indian climate is visible here, as is the way in which Toru and Aru see themselves as anomalous in Calcutta but not in London, where they also stood out, as Mary Martin reveals in a letter to Toru. Furthermore, the weather affects them in ways different from other Bengali women who suffered the climate in closed and small rooms in the inner parts of their houses. Toru Dutt complains that the weather prevents her from going outside for walks.

While the rural landscape was being appreciated by a new aesthetics, this aesthetic was one of nostalgia. That is, the rural countryside was celebrated through its opposition to the industrial city, where
the problem of alienation from other human beings was to be felt.
However, this nostalgia took the form of celebrating nature because it
was a reminder of past connections and not for itself or for its importance in providing food and shelter. Instead, and this is visible in
Toru's poetry, nature is celebrated because it provides a reminder of
moments in which the poet was connected to some human being. Such
is the poetry of Wordsworth, and Wordsworthian influences are obvious in Toru's work. In her most celebrated poem, "Our Casuarina
Tree," the tree is remembered and celebrated because it reminds the
poet of childhood companions with whom she played under the tree
and who are now dead:

> But not because of its magnificence
> Dear is the Casuarina to my soul:
> Beneath it we have played; though years may roll,
> O sweet companions, loved with love intense,
> For your sakes, shall the tree be ever dear![106]

Such a relationship to nature is most visible in Wordsworth's *Prelude*.
Furthermore, the tree enables a poetics of place that constructs a Self
as "native" to a place where there is no alienation. Thus the tree
becomes a marker of a native place to which the speaker must be
reconciled:

> And every time the music rose, —before
> Mine inner vision rose a form sublime,
> Thy form, O Tree, as in my happy prime
> I saw thee, in my own loved native clime.

Within the context of colonialism, such a Romantic connection to
the Indian countryside becomes extremely significant. Since the English landscape becomes the originary landscape of alienation, English education left some Indians nostalgic for England. However,
and this is important for the emergence of nationalism, the elements
of which begin to emerge in Toru's work in the last years of her life, it
inculcated a consciousness of India, within which the Indian landscape, as it does in "Our Casuarina Tree," also becomes an element

for nostalgia. Under colonialism, this nostalgia enables a feeling of loss for an Indian landscape and nature that was being appreciated with the Romantic aesthetic. Thus the Casuarina tree can become a reminder of the lost past under colonialism, a reading that explains why this poem has been so popular since it was written and why it became a staple in anthologies of Indian poetry after independence.

Not surprisingly, in Toru's letters as in her poems, the landscape of Baugmaree enables the union with nature that was so much a part of the Romantic experience. To extend this appreciation of nature into the context of Bengal was what was remarkable about the poems of Toru Dutt that are even now interesting. While many of her translations of French and Sanskrit poems seem to us now written in tortuous style, the poems about Baugmaree seem more direct—perhaps because they convey the alienation of colonial modernity. Here the alienation that made her write in her diary that she was a "steadfast French woman" is absent.[107] The first paragraph of description of the Casuarina tree, in the poem of that name, which seems also derivative of Romantic poetry, is relieved by the description of the "kokilas." The use of Bengali words comes as a relief to the Romantic style and much of its pleasure comes from the contrast to that style as well as its incorporation within it. More of the contrast appears in her letters to Mary Martin, especially one in which she describes the fruits of summer: "I wish I could send you a basket of our fruits of the season. It would gladden your eyes! Yellow or vermilion mangoes, red leechies, white jumrools and deep violet 'jams'" (312). Sarojini Naidu's work later picks up this exotic landscape and its details to present a more nationalist notion of place as India. In Toru's poetry, her reconciliation with a "native" land cannot but be deemed "exotic" in the context of poetry written in English. If Toru sees herself as a "native" then she has to take on the "native's" task of representing herself and her land to the English, as she does in her letters to Mary Martin. In doing so, then, being "native" becomes a way of articulating a Self in colonial terms, even though these terms also exceed the intention for which they are created.

Romantic alienation, evident in Toru's relation to the Bengali countryside, is also evident in her representation of other Indians. Thus in Toru's letters to Mary Martin, we see her use of "native" to refer to "Bengalis" and "Indians." The European term "native" seems to come from readings of English literature, English (published by the English) and Indian newspapers in English, and other texts that were mainly for and by the English. Mary Martin took her to task for the use of this term and Toru acknowledges her error. However, she does use it again, revealing the extent to which colonial modernity is experienced as alienation. Gauri Viswanathan has pointed out that this phenomenon is evident in other Indian writers such as Nobinchunder Dass, who also refers to other Indians as "natives." Viswanathan sees this as the "identification of the subject with the ruler," that recreated the subject and reveals the "culminating moment of affirmation, the endorsement of the Macaulayean dream."[108] Yet more than the fulfilling of the colonial dream, such use of the term "native" suggests the excess that recasts colonized subjects. Identifying herself and other Indians as "natives" enables a conceptualizing of herself as one sympathetic to those suffering from the injustices of British rule. In her later letters to Mary Martin, Toru mentions incidents of British injustice, revealing an altering set of concerns about colonial rule. The colonized Romantic Self also becomes an oppositional one when Toru begins to learn Sanskrit and to protest about the practices and injustices of colonial rule during the last two years of her life.

It is of course difficult to write much about a woman who died at an early age, as did Toru. On the one hand, one cannot be too critical about the work of such a young woman, for no doubt she was changing and would have changed had she lived. On the other hand, the body of work she left behind has had a considerable influence; she is often taken as the first Indian woman to inaugurate what has been termed Indo-English literature. Thus we need to pay considerable attention to her. Furthermore, it is also important to see her as an Indian woman who accomplished something that few Indians or Europeans thought an Indian woman could do, and therefore to trace out the circumstances that made it possible for her to accomplish what she did. In the aftermath of Macaulay's "Minute" on Indian education in 1835, promoting English education among the Indian people, Toru Dutt became one of the few Indian women to take advantage of this education when only Bengali men were doing so.

The effect of colonial modernity was the gendered acceptance of colonial discourses by some Indians who had come to see themselves as belonging to an ancient culture that had degenerated from former glories while England had progressed. To accept this idea was to designate "native" customs as a problem and thus to accept one's own belonging to this unmodern and constraining culture. What the boundaries of this culture and community were changed from person to person; the process of delineating and articulating this community was also part of this emerging sense of Self constructed through a Romantic epistemology.

Many among the Bengali Bhadralok accepted these ideas of modernity as progress; Toru Dutt and her family reveal the acceptance of such discourses. Some Indians, such as Pandita Ramabai, did not; she accepted English education in certain ways and rejected it in others. Ramabai did not see her travel to England as the attainment of freedom that lay within English culture. She had traveled all over India for much of her life so that spatial mobility did not have a special significance. The effect of the European culture of travel on these women not educated by English education forms the topic of my next chapter.

Chapter 5

Pandita Ramabai and Parvati Athavale:
Homes for Women, Feminism,
and Nationalism

❦

The task of preparing *The High-Caste Hindu Woman* has not been for her a congenial one. She is not by nature an iconoclast. She loves her nation with a pure, strong love. But her love has reached the height where it is akin to the motive of the skillful surgeon: she dares to inflict pain because she regards pain as affording the only sure means of relief. She is satisfied, moreover, that India cannot arise and take her place among the nations of the earth until she, too, has mothers; *until the Hindu zenana is transformed into the Hindu home, where the united family can have "pleasant times together"* [my emphasis].[1]

In her essay on women in Western India and the writer Tarabai Shinde, Rosalind O'Hanlon argues that the process of gendering under colonial rule must be examined to understand the conditions and representations of women in the nineteenth century.[2] O'Hanlon suggests that such work also includes examining women's resistance to this gendering. For instance, she reveals that Tarabai Shinde, in her *Comparison Between Women and Men* (*Stri-Purusha-Tulana*), responded to recastings of Indian patriarchy under colonialism by a critique of the representation of women in contemporary discourse.[3] Shinde accomplished such a critique by breaking down the categories themselves through which gendering occurred, but she could not help reproducing them as well. O'Hanlon states that examples such as Shinde's show that "there could be no neutral spaces from which women could defy and hold themselves apart from Indian forms of patriarchy."[4]

The work of women such as Pandita Ramabai, almost the greatest champion of women's struggles in the nineteenth century in India, which may be seen as the early beginnings of feminism, reveals that there were indeed no neutral spaces; especially in articulating the problems and the oppressions of Hindu women, Ramabai was to rely on the discursive practices of colonial discourse on women in India, and therefore participated, as did the Indian reformers in their own ways, in the creation of the Hindu woman as an object of missionary and colonial benevolence. Yet it was her conflict with the nationalists, the colonial state, and the English missionaries that was to make her utilizations of such a discourse crucial for constructing her agency and for the emerging locations of feminism in India. Rama Joshi and Joanna Liddle have argued that the "woman question" in India was limited because it was caught between the political agendas of colonialists and nationalists.[5] Yet for feminism in India, this is also the condition of its possibility; both Ramabai and Parvati Athavale, the subjects of this chapter, find some possibilities in and are limited by these complex negotiations. Liddle and Joshi are correct in suggesting the limitations of such negotiations. I would suggest that these limitations extend to Indian feminism's normative heterosexuality, its silence on female sexuality, and its dominant Hindu ideology. All of these silences emerge in the struggles of women such as Ramabai and Parvati Athavale. Such a struggle created the Hindu woman as the subject of feminist struggle in India, rather than a more heterogeneous figure, but did so against Brahmin orthodoxy and colonial commodification.

In this chapter, I look at two women, both from Western India and both reformists, who traveled to England and the United States. Both devoted their lives to ameliorating the condition of Hindu women in India, though Ramabai started her work in India in 1889 and Athavale in 1902. The two are connected as well because Athavale's sister was one of the first two pupils of Ramabai at her first widows' home in Bombay, Sharada Sadan. The pupil Godubai, a child widow, later married the famous reformer D. K. Karve, and Athavale came to work at the widows' home that Karve established. Karve became a champion of women's education, for he went on to establish also the first women's college and university, the SNDT University in Bombay.

Pandita Ramabai and Parvati Athavale traveled to the West to learn English and to educate themselves about the condition of European and U.S. women. They did so in terms very different from those of

Toru Dutt or Behramji Malabari. Being reformers at the end of the nineteenth century, when historians tell us the "woman question" had been "resolved" by the male nationalists as the spiritual and sacred center of Indian identity, these women show us that this "resolution" was done through terms opposed by these women or "resolved" by them in very different ways.[6] If the nationalists suggested that woman / home / nation were synonymous and metaphors for each other against a colonial state that attempted to supersede the authority of patriarchal family and kin,[7] then the women reformers in this period worked to disentangle these terms from each other through their discourse of reform as well as their own position within and outside it. In doing so, however, their negotiation with colonial rule and with the nationalists was a complex matter of religious and racial affiliation and disaffiliation. Working within various patriarchal formations, Pandita Ramabai converted to Christianity and Parvati Athavale retained a belief in a reformist and modernized notion of Hindu religion and custom. Notions of family and nation were central to their creating and negotiating spaces for themselves, and their reconstructions of "home" and domestic space can be seen within their narratives of travel and their relations with those they encountered.

Pandita Ramabai:
Wanderings with Her Family

Pandita Ramabai's endless travels had been the result of her father's resistance to Hindu orthodoxy in educating his wife and daughters and not marrying off Ramabai as a child.[8] Her parents had to leave their home and live in a remote area because of objections to her father's belief in educating his wife. When Ramabai was nine, they left this forest home and embarked on pilgrimages to many areas of India, in part because her father had spent all his money in hospitality to visiting disciples and friends and visitors. During these endless pilgrimages, the family earned a meager living by reciting the Puranas, though they gave away most of what they earned as alms to other Brahmins. Her parents died from starvation after many years of pilgrimage, an event mentioned with much anger and pain in Ramabai's *Testimony*, so that we know this was a crucial turning point in her life in terms of her attitude toward her religion. She continued to go from place to place around India with her brother for six years. We learn from later writing that those travels were full of hardship; they traveled on foot for they were too poor to use any conveyance and there was often hunger and exhaustion. At one point, they had to dig holes in the ground and cover themselves with dirt to protect themselves from the cold. They traveled about two thousand miles on foot.[9] In her *Testimony*, Ramabai writes: "I cannot describe all the sufferings of this terrible time. . . . We had fulfilled all the conditions laid down in the sacred books, and kept all the rules as far as our knowledge went, but the gods were not pleased with us and did not appear to us. After years of fruitless service, we began to lose our faith in them. . . . We still continued to keep caste rules, and worshipped and studied sacred literature as usual."[10] Clearly this period was testing Ramabai's faith, which seemed to be dwindling, so that her later conversion to Christianity was not too surprising.

From Ramabai's account, we learn as well that they were earning a sparse living by giving lectures on topics such as the education of women, indicating the influence of her parents. Other topics were female emancipation and "The Rise and Fall of the Aryan Race."[11] Since it was Ramabai's mother who had actually been responsible for teaching her Sanskrit and the scriptures, her belief in women's education was directly influenced by her own upbringing. Unlike Toru Dutt's English education, Ramabai's education came along with maternal nurturing and thus with a different lineage, even though she revered her father's memory all her life. Ramabai learned Sanskrit from her mother, Lakshmibai, to whom she dedicated her book, *The High-Caste Hindu Woman*. Mother and daughter were very close, and the lessons were taught early in the morning before her mother began her household chores. Ramabai cherished the memory of these early morning lessons all her life.[12] Thus giving lectures and teaching others may have been possible because she considered her mother as "the light and guide" of her life and she had seen her mother as a teacher.

When Ramabai and her brother reached Calcutta, they were given much adulation and respect. They debated the most scholarly priests and there Ramabai earned the title of Pandita. Keshab Chandra Sen, the Brahmo leader of the reformist Hindu movement, welcomed them to his home and gave her the Vedas to read, which was forbidden to women. During this time in Bengal and Assam, her brother died, and she married a man of her own choice, one who was of a lower caste and came from a very different region as well. Her age at her marriage was well beyond the norm for women of her community so that this marriage was considered scandalous. Both Ramabai and her husband were ostracized by the people around them in Bengal and Assam where they lived. After nineteen months of marriage, her husband died, leaving her with an infant daughter.

In 1882 the well-known reformers Ramabai Ranade and her husband, M. G. Ranade, invited her back to western India and Ramabai accepted the invitation. In Pune, she worked and studied with them to create the Arya Mahila Samaj, the women's Hindu reformist group, and started local women's groups called Mahila Samitis in other parts of India as well. The purpose was to improve the condition of women and provide education for them. By this time Ramabai was famous all over India and was giving many lectures on the topics of women's condition. She gave testimony before the Hunter Commission on Women's Education, and because of her testimony, became well known in England as well.[13] Ramabai's accomplishments and her life are extraordinary especially within the context of the condition of women in Western India at the time, which was quite restrictive, especially for Brahmin women, as Meera Kosambi reveals in her essay on Ramabai.[14]

Her testimony before the Hunter Commission is quite remarkable, revealing ideas of reform that at this point seem not to be directly influenced by Western missionaries or other English influences. In her testimony, she said that women's education should include knowledge of English, be given by women teachers, and include education in morals and character. She saw women doctors trained in Western medicine as a necessity since male doctors often were not allowed to attend women. Women teachers should be paid more, since they had to be of superior character and position, teaching students about character and morality as well. She suggested that the colonial government was not helping Indian women, arguing that it should be treating women with equal justice. Her testimony obviously had some effect because the Hunter Commission led to the movement by the countess of Dufferin, wife of the viceroy, to establish hospitals for women.[15] All of these ideas were acted upon during her life, since a moral education was carried out in all of the homes she established and the ideal of female sexual "purity" outside of a heterosexual marriage guided her work with women. Perhaps this testimony also influenced her cousin Anandibai Joshi's decision to go to the United States to become a doctor.

It is not clear in any of the accounts of her life when exactly she began to use the language of reform that enabled her to conceptualize all Hindu women in India as united in their oppression. We know that Ramabai and her family were acquainted with discussions in the press because she mentions in her memories of childhood that her father and mother were in the habit of reading newspapers and books in that language and that she picked up this habit from them.[16] During the period she was in Calcutta, she was in contact with the Brahmos and there must have read and learned their ideas. Yet we also know that when she arrived in Calcutta, she was giving lectures on women's emancipation, so that her father's and mother's influences, all of the reading they did in the wandering period, as well as their contacts with many reformers may have led her to use the vocabulary of the reform movement even before she reached Calcutta, met missionaries in Assam or Bengal, or worked with any reformists on her return to Bombay.

As she relates later in a letter, what she learned during those years of wandering was that the condition of women in every part of India was the same under colonial rule and Hindu patriarchy. Like other reformers, she was creating her own "fuzzy" sense of community[17] since she saw women from different regions in India as connected by a common exploitation and thus as part of a group that would often be referred to as Indian "women," a category of persons that was seen not as wives, mothers, and sisters but as persons exploited because of their gender.[18] As she says, "We saw it [i.e., the hardship of women's lives] not only in one part of India but it was the same in the Madras presidency, Bombay presidency, Punjab, the Northwest Province, Bengal, Assam."[19] She also learned how little was being done by the English government for the education of women in India. Ramabai's consciousness of unity through oppression is directed only at the Hindus of India, and mostly those of the Brahmin caste. The unity, therefore, is that of a community of Hindu Brahmin men who are unified by the similarity in their treatment of the women, and Hindu

Brahmin women who are oppressed by Hindu religion and custom. It is evident that Ramabai's discourse of reform takes as its subject the high-caste Hindu woman, a figure later to become the title and subject of her book.

Ramabai's wanderings cannot be seen in terms of a Euroimperial travel as formation of a unified Self because it does not become consolidated through the voyage out and the return to home or nation. The lack of a home that marks this long pilgrimage and wandering suggests a vastly different subjectivity that cannot even be consolidated within the nationalist construct of home as nation. Without a point of return to this "home" space, one that is impossible for Ramabai because it is the Hindu family and its structures that inhabit this space, Ramabai has to create other homes and other family structures that depart radically from the normative upper-caste Hindu family. It is such a departure that takes shape as the homes for upper-caste widows that she establishes on her return from the United States and England.

If narratives about Ramabai continue to construct the trope of "travel" as central to her formation, they often do not include within them all that she read and the people she met on those travels. Furthermore, her description of the educational function of travel contained in her *Testimony* in 1917 comes at a period when she had already done an enormous amount of work with women and with missionaries and during the time of nationalist agitation all over India, so that these influences could have inflected the narrative constructed at the time.

It was not travel as a secular itinerary of Romantic sights but as a religious journey to places of interest only to Hindus that was central to Ramabai's notion of community. In these locations, she learned the difficulties of the lives of people under Hindu orthodoxics, as well as under the inaction of the British government, all of which she later recounts.

To suggest that Ramabai's agency is constructed through European travel erases her negotiations with nationalism and colonialism, which positioned her in a complex and liminal relation to these discourses. By claiming the importance of travel as the construction of the Self, even her conversion to Christianity is not seen in light of the scholarly debates with which she was engaged, but with the amorphous effect of travel as freedom and mobility. In a biography of Pandita Ramabai, Helen Dyer, for instance, writes that Ramabai's doubts about her religion came from her travels around India: "It was during these wanderings with her brother that Ramabai's faith in the Hindu religion was shaken, though until twenty years of age she worshipped the gods of brass and stone. The freedom of their lives had given to the brother and sister keen powers of observation, and they resolved to test the teachings of the sacred books whenever possible."[20] For Dyer, travel is associated with freedom in the tradition of European travel that I have been discussing in earlier chapters. In writing about Ramabai, Dyer must disregard the terrible tragedies in the wanderings of Ramabai and her family in order to construct this narrative. Dyer not only sees travel as freedom, but also connects Ramabai's reformist ideas to her "free" access to Hindu homes. Such an access is an orientalist formation that Ramabai simply did not deploy except in her attempts to "rescue" women from temples where she felt they were being prostituted. Even so, such an incident differs from orientalist fantasies of Euroimperial travel in that it is performed by an Indian woman who does not have the power of colonial rule behind her nor the masculine, colonial subject position. Yet since Ramabai converted to Christianity and practiced an evangelical form of it, the rescue does share in a "missionary" impetus of saving Indian women from lascivious and corrupt priests, in the emphasis on "sexual purity" and heterosexism, though in a vastly transformed version from that of the racism of most European missionaries.

A similar formulation of European travel is visible in Nicol Macnicol's biography of the Pandita, published in Calcutta in 1926 in the Builders of Modern India series. Macnicol states that Ramabai emerges from her years of pilgrimage with her family as a "graduate in Life, in its wisdom and calm judgment."[21] He states that what would in other countries be called a beggar or a tramp is in India a pilgrim, and Ramabai's family fell into this category. Even though Macnicol acknowledged that Ramabai's wanderings were more pilgrimage than travel, he goes on to see Ramabai as occupying the subject position of a European traveler when he claims that Ramabai's travels were an education in which "the panorama of India in all its mystery and variety passed before her eyes and she had eyes to see it."[22] A pilgrim, like a tourist, would have little interest in participating in the life of the region in which she was moving, yet the pilgrim would not have what John Urry calls the "tourist's gaze" either, so that to see Ramabai as viewing India's "panorama" argues for the subject position that Ramabai did not have as a pilgrim and as part of a family of Puranikas, those who read the Puranas aloud and get alms and gifts in return.[23] Ramabai was not a European traveler or tourist taking "peeks," like Florence Nightingale, at "native" life, nor mapping the region like Behramji Malabari or Bholanath Chandra, or even a pilgrim with faith, but a daughter in a family expelled by Brahmin orthodoxy. In addition, there was Ramabai's growing skepticism about Hinduism that came from the family's poverty, ostracism, hunger, and deprivation that could not be contained within the positions constructed either by more normative notions of pilgrimage within Hindu society or by European travel.

Ramabai's critique of Hinduism and colonial rule emerged not from a notion of travel as education but perhaps out of the empathy she may have felt with all outcasts, since her family had also been cast out from their own community of Chitpavan Brahmins and had taken the path of nonconformism unlike other members of their caste.[24] Her perceptions of the enormous injustices to lower castes and women no doubt also came out of her years of wandering. It was during her years with her brother that she was regularly speaking of the education of women and also showing her knowledge of Sanskrit and of Hindu religious philosophy.[25] Thus she says, "We were able to do nothing directly to help them but in the towns and villages we often addressed large audiences of people and urged upon them the education of the women and children."[26] It was during these lectures in Calcutta that she was questioned by some Brahmin pundits who gave her the title of Pandita Ramabai Saraswati, one that was extremely rare for women to have.

These experiences were different not only from those of European travelers but also from those of the wandering sadhus and pilgrims who usually comprised travelers who moved far distances within India. While for many Indian women, religious pilgrimage was the only reason for traveling long distances, Ramabai's experience is both part of that framework and separate from it in that she was more of a teacher than a pilgrim. She was traveling, first, because her parents or her brother and she were not allowed to stay in their own village, and second, because she and her brother continued in the life they had known with her parents, for they had no home to return to. She may not even have been particularly religious at this time of her life, though she could debate and discuss the shastras with any learned scholar.

Another tradition within which her wanderings could be conceptualized would be that of the Bhaktas and of Vaishnavite forms of worship. These movements had begun in the sixth century and influenced many religious formations in the subcontinent. Bypassing religious mediation by Brahmins and other priests, such movements in their various forms "asserted the equality of all souls before god, regardless of caste and status," so that self-realization became accessible to all castes and included both men and women as the Bhaktas.[27] While the relative importance of the male and female Bhaktas is up for discussion, most scholars agree on the influence of the Bhaktas on developing vernacular languages, and this is the tradition in which women's poetry and narratives have been available since the sixteenth century in oral tradition. KumKum Sangari, for instance, argues for the importance of this tradition in the formation of female agency for women Bhaktas such as Mirabai, who in the fifteenth century negotiated with patriarchies of the time to formulate "structures of feeling which can compensate for the absence of . . . freedoms."[28]

For many women Bhaktas, devotion implied leaving aside family and marriage constraints in order to pursue a life of wandering and teaching, while for others, such as the Marathi Bhakta, Bahinabai, it implied a conflict with a husband who wanted the attention she would rather have given to her devotions. Bahinabai's writings contain a narrative that was a record of marriage as difficult and full of terror and conflict since she was married at the age of three to a priest and astrologer who was thirty.[29] The women Bhaktas provide traditions of both a life of wandering and a critique of the marriage-family system of Hindu high castes, a combination that provides a context for Ramabai's later beliefs. Such contexts suggest also that Ramabai's idea of travel was not a direct result of influence of either the British reformers or the Indian reformists and nationalists who adapted Enlightenment ideals within local patriarchal power structures. The influence of the Bhakti tradition of homelessness and wandering came also because Ramabai's childhood pilgrimage had included Dwarka, a

Vaishnavite shrine. In addition, she was an admirer of Mirabai, the female Bhakta poet who, in the sixteenth century, left her husband and family and chose to live in wandering worship of Krishna.

Moreover, Ramabai's father, Anant Shastri, was a Vaishnavite, a follower of the Bhakti movement, adhering to religion as devotion to a divine personage. Ramabai's later renunciation of Hinduism for her own version of Christianity, which she saw as a religion with roots in Asia and which involved devotion to Christ as well as service to others seen as equals, must have been influenced by this tradition. Nicol Macnicol, in his biography of Pandita, states that Anant Shastri's religious faith involved a complete dependence upon the sovereign will of the Lord and was a lesson that Ramabai "never as a Christian had to unlearn."[30] Yet Macnicol ignores the influences that made Ramabai's Christianity a means for the freedom of exercising her own will as well, and which brought forth censure from many India-connected clergy in England.

Travel to England: Ramabai's Struggle for Liberty

While travel within India could take its forms and practices from pilgrimage and Bhakta practices, as well as the necessities arising from excommunication, poverty, and debt, travel to England and the United States could not but be influenced by European travel traditions. Travel to the West in the nineteenth century, especially for education, came with an apparatus of English education, the formation of elites under colonial rule, and the set of practices that had been formulated by Indians, especially Hindus, to negotiate with religious and social contamination. This Indian culture of travel was, as I have argued in the previous chapter, predominantly a male construct, interrupted by women who utilized it in very different ways. For Ramabai such a negotiation was done, not through English education and the Romantic language of freedom, but through a religious experience expressed as desire that is neither eroticized nor romanticized: "I felt a restless desire to go to England. I could not have done it unless I had felt that my faith in God had become strong."[31]

Ramabai went to England to become a doctor with the intention of working with Indian women on her return. Her cousin, Anandibai Joshi, had gone to America in 1883 (she sailed for America the same month that Ramabai left for England, though neither knew of the other's plans) and remained there until 1886 in order to obtain her medical education. Ramabai was concerned with the perception in India that education was only to be had by going to England. In response to hearing an Anglican bishop say that Indian women who came over to England were not much use to their country, she said that she had learned much in India and that it was only for a scientific education that she was visiting England: "people ought to remember that we Indians can be learned in our own country and can be useful too. We are anxious to come to England and to learn English because these two countries are so closely connected and also because the best scientific books are written in English."[32] Her anxiety to dissociate herself from English imperial notions and her critique of racial superiority are evident here, as is the belief in Western medicine as necessary for Indian women.

Accounts of reasons why she went to England are inflected by the agendas of biographers who refuse to acknowledge the complexity of the negotiations she made with hegemonic narratives. The account of her life published by the Christian Literature Society, for instance, claims that she was motivated solely by a spiritual desire that symbolically was a step to separate herself from the Hindu culture and people. This step was, in this account, undertaken by religious faith. Ramabai is quoted as saying, "I went forth as Abraham not knowing whither I went."[33] Another account, by Padmini Sengupta, positions itself within nationalist historiography by establishing Ramabai as one of the "pioneering" women of India, whose activities provided "the backbone of India's fight for social freedom."[34] This account suggests that Ramabai went to learn English and more current educational methods, without mentioning any spiritual or religious motivation. In her own *Testimony*, Ramabai simply says that she went to England "in order to study and fit myself for my life work,"[35] revealing little but her skill at negotiating powerful and contentious discourses.

Ramabai had some previous connections with the missionary society based in England that supported her. We know from her testimony to the Hunter Commission that she believed more Indian women were necessary as teachers and doctors, so that she may have felt that the missionaries were the best means outside the colonial government to provide her with resources for this goal. She was not to know that apart from some training in education and spirituality, neither the English church nor the British people would give her any money to begin the homes for widows that she aimed at establishing.

Ramabai left for England in 1883 and was baptized later that year. It must also be noted that Ramabai, most unusually, published a book, *Streedharm Neeti* (*The Duties of Women*), in order to obtain money to travel to England. In India she had contact with some Anglican Sisters and it was to them that she went in England. Sister Geraldine, whom she had met in India, took her under her protection at the nuns' residence in Wantage. On reaching England she was compelled to give up her idea of becoming a doctor because of her deafness, and instead devoted herself to learning as much as she could with a view to working on women's education and helping women in need.

There is no evidence that for Ramabai England became the land of freedom that it was for Toru Dutt. On the contrary, she found that having left Hinduism and taken on Christianity, she was expected to have unquestioning obedience to the latter. Much of her correspondence with Sister Geraldine during her stay in England is taken up with her often hurt and anguished assertions of her own belief and her refusal to accept unquestioning obedience to Anglican Church hierarchy. Other conflicts arose because she was determined to bring up her daughter in a way that she thought best without interference from Sister Geraldine and the other nuns who thought they, being British and belonging to a race with supposedly superior educational institutions, knew best how to bring up and educate a child. Thus for Ramabai, England became a place of restrictions rather than of freedom and liberty. What is clearly played out here is the racism of English missionaries that was central to the enterprise of the spread of Christianity.[36] It was against this Christianity and her experiences in England that she was to formulate her own version of it as an Asian religion with Asian roots.

In contrast to England, the United States, where she went after England, became a place where freedom could be found, for it was women and groups there who provided her with money that enabled her to open the homes for widows in Bombay and Pune. In fact, in one of her letters to Sister Geraldine, written from Boston, she writes that she does not think money can be raised for her work in England. She mentions that only seventy pounds have been collected in England, so that most of the seventy-five thousand dollars she needs will have to come from the United States. In contrast to the condescension and attitude of superiority of the English, she turns to America as a place of freedom and help.

In light of her conflicts with the English church, it is interesting to examine the way that her time in England is represented by British women who were her contemporaries. Mrs. E. F. Chapman in her book, *Sketches of Some Distinguished Indian Women*, writes that it was the sisters at St. Mary's in Wantage who taught her about Christianity with the consequence that Ramabai was baptized in 1883.[37] Chapman wishes to show the influence of the Sisters but has also to deal with the fact that Ramabai was baptized the very year she went to England so that the Sisters' influence could not have been all-important. Chapman claims that "in the Home of the Sisters of St. Mary at Wantage, the Hindu widow found a warm and loving welcome, as well as simple, earnest instruction in the Christian faith."[38] Chapman's narrative is instructive because it suggests the parameters of the colonial representation of a woman such as Ramabai. First of all she is presented within the imperialist discourse of reform as the "Hindu widow," and not as the many other identities she could have been presented under, such as "educated woman" or "woman scholar," for instance. Secondly, the very thorny nature of Ramabai's theological disagreements with the tenets of the Anglican Church and its patriarchal hierarchy is not even considered possible in regard to an Indian woman such as Ramabai. What can only be considered in relation to Indian women is what Chapman describes in her narrative as a "simple, earnest instruction in the Christian faith." This missionary construct is in accord with many Englishwomen's representations of Indian women as victims of Hindu religion who found help and friends in England and were objects of missionary benevolence. Yet from Ramabai's own narratives it is clear that one of the most important figures in her conversion was not Sister Geraldine but the Reverend Nilkant Nehemiah Goreh, a famous Marathi convert who had been born, like Ramabai, a Chitpavan Brahmin. Like her, he was a Sanskrit scholar, and he wrote a letter to her in England that supposedly made her decide to convert. In her later account of her life she would write, "I think no one would have had the power of turning me from the Brahmin religion but Father Goreh."[39]

Ramabai did think of many of the Englishwomen she met at Wantage and Cheltenham College, where she went to teach and learn, as friends, and she was grateful for their help. Yet her trip to England made her very aware of the power differentials between English and Indian women. All these complexities that could not be part of imperial discourse on India are left out of narratives such as Chapman's. Chapman presents Ramabai's trip to England in the following way: "like others of her race, her longing eyes turned to England, believing that there alone she could find the instruction and assistance she wanted."[40] What Ramabai saw as her need to acquire a specific medical knowledge to help other Indian women is represented here as the need to reach England and help. It is not surprising, therefore, that Ramabai found not much help in England to establish her home for widows, perhaps because the English would give to their own missionaries but not to an Indian woman.

The Pandita's correspondence with Sister Geraldine and Sister Geraldine's comments and notes on her reveal that the Pandita's struggle for the freedom to think and worship whatever form of Christianity she wished was waged against Geraldine's orientalist and racist assumptions about Indians, "natives," and Indian women and Geraldine's desire to validate her own form of Christianity to the detriment of other denominations. For instance, in one letter of disagreement with the opinion of church officials, Ramabai writes, "I am arguing with those people who give their opinion or decide anything for me without knowing my will, and above all, God's will" (25). Sister Geraldine believed that because Ramabai had asked for help from the sisters she had relinquished, like a child to a parent, all decision making about her actions, her future, and her beliefs. However, Ramabai was adamant about retaining her own choices and decisions, so that she often apologizes to Sister Geraldine for being obstinate or misunderstanding her, when it is clear that Ramabai understands her very well and chooses not to appear to disregard her opinion.

Sister Geraldine's assumptions about the Pandita, especially in face of the Pandita's life and achievements, are astonishing. How she could have thought of Ramabai as a child needing a parent is remarkable, especially since she knew the details of Ramabai's life. She knew that before going to England, Ramabai had given lectures all over India on female emancipation and education, debated the most learned scholars, married a lower-caste man at the age of twenty-two by her own choice (in an age of child marriages this was astonishing), written a book to finance her travels, left her own religion, and become notorious as a heretic. Ramabai had come to England because she had reached the conclusion that Indian women doctors and teachers were needed to help other women, for neither Indian men nor foreign women could have access to Indian women. Yet in the introduction to her collection of Ramabai's letters, Geraldine suggests that prior to Ramabai's time and education in England, Ramabai was "impulsive and energetic, and at the time undisciplined, she was swayed by every passing thought" (7). Sister Geraldine suggests that Ramabai was swayed in her faith by other people with whom she came in contact in England so that Ramabai was changed from her "simple, childlike self" (35). In a somewhat defensive gesture, Sister Geraldine writes that she is presenting Ramabai's faults only in order to make her life appear more "bracing and heartening." She goes on to claim that Ramabai was often lacking in "candor and sincerity." In her introduction, after stating that Indians were incapable of such perfection, Sister Geraldine claims that Ramabai often resorted to telling lies: "I should think at one time she was an exception to the generality of Hindus; truthfulness was one of the traits of character in which she was an exception to the generality of her countrywomen; but she has both, in word and in letter, proved that she can no longer be credited with this virtue" (115).

Such attitudes irked Ramabai, who had no intention of complying with the unquestioned obedience that the Wantage Sisters and the Anglican Church officials demanded of her. This denial of her understanding, her agency, and her free will seemed to her to be another way of oppressing women. She was especially upset when church officials thought she should not accept a professorship at Cheltenham, when in India she had been used to lecturing in order to earn her living. She disliked being financially dependent on the Sisters and wanted to earn money. Church officials, most of whom were men, decided this was wrong. Thus one bishop writes to Sister Geraldine that in his opinion Ramabai should not give lectures at Cheltenham, because "all who have experience of native Christians know that it is the rarest thing possible for one of them to return to India from this country without having been completely spoilt and upset by the notice they have received here" (39). Under the guise of saving Ramabai for her own countrywomen, the bishop suggests that publicity would ruin her. Again, this comment completely ignores that fact that Ramabai had been lecturing to men and women even in India. The bishop implies that since the English are supposedly superior, it would be elevating a woman from an inferior race to allow her to teach anything to Englishwomen. His fellow bishop of Lahore agreed somewhat, also believing that giving Ramabai a professorship at Cheltenham would go to her head, whereas giving her a "humbler title such as teacher-ship, making no demonstration in any way, would probably lessen the danger of elation of mind very considerably" (43).

Sister Geraldine agreed with this opinion, writing to Ramabai, "I do not feel that there is any course open to us but to accept the opinion of those who, from their knowledge of India and its people, are far better judges than ourselves in the matter" (53). Ramabai disagreed, feeling it to be a matter of principle to assert her own opinion and make her own decisions. Thus in response she asserts her connection to India, her knowledge of it, the insufficient knowledge of these bishops, their biases, and her refusal to submit to the authority of the church. She responds to Sister Geraldine by saying that she is pained by her letters: "It is plainly saying no less than that the people who are not of that country know India and its people far better than I do, who am born and brought up in it and that you or rather the people who are your advisers, do not trust me and my honour, that they have authority to decide anything for me, and that I ought not to have a voice of my own to say anything against that decision. . . . Your advisers, whoever they may be, have no right to decide anything for me" (5). She goes on to say that though she is grateful to the Sisters for giving her a home in England, "at the same time, I must tell you that when I find out that you or your friends have no trust in me, and they want whether directly or indirectly to interfere with my personal liberty, I must say 'goodbye' to you and go my own way" (5). Over and over she claims her right to her own life and to her own decisions: "I have long since taken all matters which concern me into my own hand and shall by no means let others lay hand on my liberty" (5). Freedom for Ramabai was the exercise of her free will.

It was incidents such as these, which were repeated many times during her stay in England, that made Ramabai distrust the Anglican Church and its hierarchy, so that in a later letter she would say, "the freedom of thought I honestly say I was not allowed to have by my Wantage friends" (73). In fact she developed a distrust of the English and England's supposed "freedom" and liberty, for she had found out that the English were racially biased against the Indians and that as colonizers they wanted to control India as much as Sister Geraldine's church wanted to control her.

In effect, she discovered that freedom and liberty meant obedience to another set of masters. This was clear to her when Sister Geraldine wrote to her saying that Ramabai had misunderstood what liberty meant, for liberty "in its corrupted sense . . . means license, lawlessness, and on the other hand, true liberty means obedience to law" (53). Ramabai gave this definition no credence, for in response she reserves the right to her own definitions: "If it pleases you to call my word liberty as lawlessness you may do so, but as far as I know I am not lawless." She goes on to explain her refusal to submit: "I have just with great efforts freed myself from the yoke of the Indian priestly tribe, so I am not at present willing to place myself under another similar yoke by accepting everything which comes from the priest as authorized command of the most high" (61). It was not surprising that she found support and help for starting her widows' home not in England but in the United States, where she was allowed to be an authority on Indian women and to give a series of lectures so she could earn money. In the United States too, support came not only from missionary groups but from women who had been involved with the Abolition and Temperance movements, which were more secular. She also published *The High-Caste Hindu Woman* in the United States, and the money from its sale along with money from lectures allowed her to repay some of the people who had helped her in England.

Ramabai had to argue against stereotypes of Hindu women, for she found that the pervasive belief in Britain was that all Hindu women were uniformly oppressed. To one such charge she responded, "You can call some of my countrywomen 'hedged' but you cannot apply this adjective to Marathi Brahmin women. You have seen yourself that

Marathi ladies are neither hedged nor kept behind thick curtains" (60). She also realized that this stereotype was being used to prohibit her from teaching men and speaking in mixed public forums. In opposition to such biases, she expresses her surprise that even in so-called free England, she is not to teach men: "It surprised me very much to think that neither my father nor my husband objected [to] my mother's or my teaching young men while some English people are doing so" (60).

In all these letters, where Ramabai insists over and over that she has a right to make her own decisions, which to her is the meaning of liberty and freedom, what is apparent is that England is not a place that gives her liberty. Her view of England is of a place where certain knowledge of science is available that she can use to help Indian women and where there are institutions of higher education for women that do not exist in India. England is not, as with Toru Dutt, seen through the mediation of Romantic literature and its ideological constructions. Ramabai's view of England is strictly functional: it can provide her some skills she needs. However, she finds that even obtaining these skills is difficult, for English racism toward Indians is an obstacle at every turn.

Ramabai in the United States: Benevolence, Sisterhood, and the Ramabai Circles

After her stay in England, Ramabai traveled to the United States to be present at the graduation from medical college of her cousin, Anandibai Joshi. She was invited for the occasion by Dr. Rachel Bodley, dean of the Women's Medical College of Pennsylvania, where in 1886 Joshi became the first Indian woman to become a medical doctor trained in Western medicine. Joshi had left for the United States at the same time that Ramabai had left for England. She, too, had tremendous difficulty adapting to American weather, food, and culture, and this difficulty affected her health such that six months after her return to India, she passed away. Unlike Ramabai, Joshi remained faithful to her religious beliefs and supported the Hindu marriage customs that both Indian and English reformers had attacked, confounding her liberal women supporters in the United States. Asked to give a speech on child marriage, she defended it rather than attack it, leaving her audience quite dissatisfied. Rachel Bodley was one of those disappointed, and in her introduction to Ramabai's *The High-Caste Hindu Woman* (published in Philadelphia) writes that Ramabai's book was both a relief from Anandibai's views as well as adequate explanation of why Anandibai would have such views. In this instance, Ramabai's reformist use of missionary discourse on matters relating to the woman question was more acceptable to the American women concerned with helping their "sisters" in India.

Ramabai occupied her time in America in learning about educational systems for girls, especially the kindergarten. She translated some textbooks into Marathi, in one of the first attempts to systematize an education for Indian girls. She was particularly admiring of the American women who devoted their time to social good, wishing, like Parvati Athavale after her, that Indian women could be like them: "I am deeply impressed by and interested in the work of Western women, who seem to have one common aim, namely the good of their fellow-beings. It is my dream, some day to tell my country-women, in their own language, this wonderful story, in the hope that the recital may awaken in their hearts a desire to do likewise."[41]

In contrast, in her book *The Peoples of the United States*, published in the Marathi language in 1899, Ramabai criticizes American customs and manners while appreciating the impetus in the United States to build a new society through good citizenship and social concern.[42] She praises the American flag and the local administrations, admiring the notion of a democracy for the people, by the people, and of the people. This must have been a response to the colonial rule within India, to the power relations within the caste system in India, and to the social and racial hierarchies in England and English rule. She contrasts this with what she sees as a valuing of people for their intrinsic merit and worth in the United States. She praises the citizenry for being interested in learning and art, as well as for the equal worth given to boys and girls. Compared to the illiteracy of peasants in India, which British rule had not changed, she saw that in America even the laboring classes could read and write and were interested in literature and philosophy. It is apparent that Ramabai saw the United States as a democratic experiment that had much to commend it, especially in comparison with what she saw in England and with the condition of Indian women under British rule. Yet at a Methodist meeting in New York, Ramabai also noticed that even in a supposedly egalitarian society like the United States, women were not seen as the equals of men.

Ramabai was critical of practices such as slavery, racism, and segregation. She pointed out that such institutions showed that white Americans needed to be better in many ways. Consequently, she believed the end of slavery was a good sign. She met Harriet Tubman and narrated Tubman's story in a long letter to her daughter Manorama, adding that there were many children and women in India who were being treated like the slaves were in the past in the United States. The treatment of Native Americans was also deplored, but she praised the benevolent gesture by the government of giving them American citizenship. She saw racism as a form of caste system but did not think it was as exaggerated as in India. She thought the Mormon sect had practices worse than Indian religious sects, particularly in their treatment of women (183). She frowned upon women's use of the corset, criticizing the slavish devotion to fashion among many women. Anything that involved the killing of animals, whether for food or for feathers for hats, disturbed Ramabai, even though she thought that most Americans were honest and religious.

With such a belief in the generosity and goodness of American women and with a book such as *The High-Caste Hindu Woman*, Ramabai was successful in getting money to start widows' homes in India. Arriving in March 1886, by October 1888 she was working with sympathetic women and men headed by Unitarians to establish a multidenominational Ramabai Association with over sixty-three Ramabai Circles in various cities giving about five thousand dollars each in annual subscriptions. The goal was a home for child widows that was to be secular in order to attract Hindus. Though the setting up of such organizations must have taken much time and effort, all the while she was giving talks and lectures wherever she went, as well as doing a lot of translations and writing.

Attitudes toward Ramabai in America were also imbued with colonial and missionary discourse, yet she seems not to have found this irksome. Whereas in England she was not accepted as an authoritative source on the condition of Indian women, since the English with whom she came in contact felt they, as colonialists, understood India and the Indians so much better than she, in the United States she was feted and honored. Such contrasts with her experiences in England and with the hierarchies of colonial and British society probably led to Ramabai's appreciation of the United States. Furthermore, absent direct colonial ties with India, U.S. attitudes toward the people of India could remain within missionary forms of benevolence rather than the strategies of colonial state domination. Ramabai would also have been receptive to the notion of the United States as a democratic experiment because it was a Christian nation that supposedly was creating an egalitarian society.

Newspaper accounts of her travels express amazement at and appreciation of her articulate and measured responses to the large audiences she drew wherever she went. Within these responses, she is seen as an anomalous Indian woman who will save other Indian women with the help of American women. One poem on Ramabai included among the papers collected by the San Francisco Ramabai Circle records the kind of discursive practices that made her available to them.[43] Such practices seem imbued with colonial discourses in a way that is different from the response to her in England. Whereas in England she seemed threatening to colonial and missionary discourses about Indian women, in the United States she was seen as a Christian savior of non-Christian Hindu women.

This poem, entitled "Ramabai," describes her as a "little Hindu maiden" looking for truth and freedom. Her father is erroneously believed to have renounced caste in order to "give his fledglings liberty" from "man's close, cage-like code allowed." Such a father, according to this narrative, which ignores Ramabai's mother's influence, enabled Ramabai to be an anomalous and unusual woman. The poem goes on to suggest that Ramabai was unusual also because she was not brought up in a zenana, the space that within European colonial discourse signified female incarceration: "so the maiden grew / To reach of thought and insight clear and no dim zenana knew." This panegyric sees Indian women as "dumb," "blindly grop-[ing]," "immured in dungeons," and requiring to be rescued by Ramabai with the help of American women. Indian women are trapped in this dungeon blocked by a stone, and the power of Christ, mediated through Ramabai and American women, can move the stone and free these "sisters."

If Indian women are incarcerated by "man's close, cage-like code," then American women are enslaved by their lack of desire to save Indian women:

Bravest of Hindu widows! how dare we look at thee
So fearless in love's liberty, and say that we are free?
We, who have heard the voice of Christ, and yet remain the slaves
Of indolence and selfishness inurned in living graves?

Yet here Ramabai is also the force that will take Christian American women out of their indolence to share in Christ's work. The "freedom" that they assume they have is shown to be a slavery of indolence by Ramabai's example. Ramabai is believed to be more free, being "fearless in love's liberty." Even though the language is imbued with British colonialism's discursive practices that once again contrast the Western woman's "burden" with the complete subjugation of Indian "sisters," here Ramabai is more "free" because freedom is presumed to be a spiritual and Christian liberty. Such a liberty is available through service to others that "indolent" U.S. Christian women cannot get unless they perform missionary service for their less fortunate sisters.

Ramabai's representations of Indian women's lives, as revealed in her writings and ideas, could be accommodated because to some extent they too represented the "Hindu" woman as an essentialized and oppressed category, subjugated by religious custom and rule. She herself could only function as an anomaly in such a representation, and her conversion to Christianity would make her available both as an exception and as one who "freed" herself from such an oppressive religious custom. Lata Mani's work on the discourse of sati has shown that missionary and reformist discourses utilized such a construct of the "Indian woman" in complementary ways that left unchanged the notion that social lives in India were wholly governed by religion.[44] The figure of the "High-caste Hindu woman" both fits into this framework and departs from it in its attack on the Hindu patriarchy and British rule.

While Ramabai was only able to get money for her work from the United States, it is clear that the discursive practices within which such assistance became possible were imbued with colonial discourses dependent on an unequal "sisterhood" between Indian women and

Western women. Ramabai's Christianity would have also enabled a missionary discourse to be mobilized in which Ramabai was the missionary, since she was after all an anomalous Indian woman unlike her "dumb" sisters. Furthermore, such participation in Ramabai's cause enabled the construction of American women as liberated subjects who have a "home" in opposition to the Indian zenana. Rachel Bodley, in her introduction to *The High-Caste Hindu Woman*, reveals a more secular influence within such a missionary form of benevolence, one that does not depend on spiritual enslavement and freedom but on the notion of "home" as that ideal domestic space of heterosexual companionate marriage. Such a home is possible only in the West and constructed through its other, the zenana, the Hindu variation on harem as a space of incarceration for women.[45]

Rachel Bodley's introduction is a classic illustration of the female domestic subject as catachresis, a subject that even Ramabai utilizes and shares though she can only do so in conditions dissimilar to those of Euro-American women. In narrating the account of Ramabai's childhood, Bodley contrasts Ramabai's lack of a home with U.S. women's idealized domestic location within a home. Bodley describes Ramabai's account of her parents' deaths from starvation in the famines of 1873–1877[46] by saying, "we American women in our homes have never before looked into the face of one upon whom a ministry of sorrow so overwhelming as this has been laid and we need, in our prosperity, to realize that God hath made of one blood all nations of men."[47] The discourse of slavery, freedom, and the "home" is pervasive in the descriptions of Ramabai in the United States also because the women who supported Ramabai and worked in her Ramabai Circles had participated in the cause of Abolition.[48]

While most of her American supporters remained loyal when Ramabai's first home for widows almost shut down because of allegations that the supposedly secular nature of the home was a falsehood and that girls were being converted to Christianity, she did lose some support. Most of her supporters accepted Ramabai's decision to create an openly Christian organization, yet the person sent out by the Ramabai Association sympathized with Sister Geraldine's race-based prejudices against Ramabai. This Sarah Hamlin, who came out to India to oversee Ramabai's work on behalf of the funders, for instance, complained to Sister Geraldine that Ramabai had spoilt her daughter, was irresponsible, and was not competent.[49] Hamlin seems to have had problems with Ramabai, and Ramabai certainly had problems with her, for Hamlin's interference with the board of Sharada Sadan exacerbated the conflict and almost shut it down.

Conversion to Christianity:
Conflicts with Nationalists

It is very likely that Ramabai's difficult life and her dissatisfaction with Hindu religious textual representations of women as well as its customs and practices had led her to Christianity. Even in the Hindu reform movements such as the Brahmo Samaj she saw that women were just as oppressed and that some leaders were hypocritical in not practicing what they preached. Furthermore, as A. B. Shah comments in the introduction to *The Letters and Correspondence of Pandita Ramabai*, Ramabai was impressed by the selflessness and dedication of Christian nuns in India as well as with the concept of a personal God as the God of love (xv). She could also, as a Christian, though a widow with a small child, escape many of the very harsh restrictions that operated on the lives of Brahmin widows. Some of these restrictions did not apply to her even in India, for she had become an iconoclast and broken many customary practices that applied to Hindu Brahmin widows. Her conversion aroused much anger among the Hindu reformers who had worked with her or known her; since Christianity was the religion of the British colonial rulers, her conversion was seen as a traitorous act among all those who called themselves anticolonial or nationalist. Yet given her family history, her years of wandering, and her aim of helping Hindu women, her conversion must be seen in terms of the only position available to her to accomplish her goals. Furthermore, responses to her conversion came not only from anticolonial agendas but also from the history of Christianity and conversions in Western India at the time.

While Christianity did not take hold in India to become a dominant religion, it did function as an escape from oppressive religious Hindu practices and therefore as a threat to Hinduism. The Marathi writer Baba Padmaji, in a Marathi novel published in 1857, represented Christianity as a means of escape for a Hindu widow; Baba Padmaji himself had converted to Christianity, influenced by the famous convert Narayan Sheshadri, who had been at the center of a controversy relating to his brother's readmittance to caste after he had lived with Narayan.[50] Padmaji had gone on to edit a newspaper called *Satyapadika* and later wrote the Marathi tract, *What Is in the Veda?* which was published in 1880. His writings show the influence of the missionaries as well as the European religious radicals.[51] Conversion to Christianity in this region was not a pervasive practice though there is mention in other works of literature that this was seen as a possibility.[52] While we do not know if Ramabai knew of such work, it certainly prefigures her experience and reveals that conversion to Christianity was available, even if proscribed, as an escape for caste Hindus from Hindu orthodoxy and for those outside caste who were considered untouchables.

Some part of the hostility to her came from the history of the missionaries in Western India. In the 1830s and 1840s the missionaries had attacked local customs and religious observances of Bombay's three major religious communities, Muslim, Parsi, and Hindu, through vernacular pamphlets, articles in the press, street lectures, and debates. This campaign created so much anger that missionaries were debated by students and even pelted with stones. The missionaries were disappointed that English education resulted in a questioning of customs and practices but few converts. In 1843, out of ten vernacular newspapers, all were anti-Christian though not antirationalist.[53] Hindu social reformers rejected Christian doctrine to argue for a notion of a Creator who was the standard of goodness and justice and saw everyone as equal.[54] Even though reform societies such as the Marathi Dhyan Prasarak Sabha (Marathi Society for the Spread of Knowledge) saw Hindu doctrine as the reason for the degeneration of Hindu society and the cause of India's decline and praised the British legal system, it nowhere suggested Christianity as a recourse. Western scientific knowledge was often discussed as beneficial and necessary to India,[55] whereas Western religious tradition was neither widely accepted nor welcomed.

Within such a context, it was not surprising that despite her adherence to certain caste rules and to leading an ascetic and "moral" life that would have won approbation in both Victorian and Indian patriarchal social circles, Ramabai was attacked for her conversion not only in the orthodox Hindu press but also in some of the reformist press. The *Induprakash* had been set up in 1862 by the reformer M. G. Ranade, who had, along with his wife Ramabai Ranade, befriended Ramabai and set up the Arya Mahila Samaj; the November 19, 1883, issue contained the following: "Pandita Ramabai was in the first instance a Hindu, then she became a Brahmo, now she has become a Christian. This shows and proves she is of an unstable mind. We should not be surprised if she becomes a Muslim soon. She has only to meet a Muslim Kazi who will convince her that his religion will give her peace and salvation."[56] Yet there were other sections of the reformist movement that supported her. For instance, the *Subodha Patrika*, the weekly newspaper of the theistic reform movement, proclaimed that the history of Ramabai "may well deserve to be written in gold."[57]

The orthodox of the educated Hindu community were unalterably opposed to Ramabai because of her conversion. Bal Gangadhar Tilak, the conservative nationalist leader, was one of them. Tilak's biographers echo some of the complicated and mixed reactions to Ramabai that must have been endemic at the time. One hagiographical narrative of Tilak's life is torn between praise for her intellect and her abilities and condemnation for what she did with them. Yet, as Uma Chakravarty points out, Tilak took such positions that constructed certain orthodox men as "patriots" and others as "traitors" if they opposed Brahminical patriarchy's caste and gender conservatism as a way to neutralize opposition and gain political power.[58]

It was not only her conversion but the belief that the young widows in her care were being converted to Christianity that increased hostility toward her. When Ramabai set up her first widows' home in Bombay, Sharada Sadan, she did so with money from the U.S. Ramabai Association and with the agreement that it was to be a secular institution. However, when a Christian weekly of December 21, 1889, published the news that out of seven widows at Ramabai's Sharada Sadan, two had wanted conversion to Christianity, the publication *Kesari*, Tilak's mouthpiece, attacked Ramabai as traitor to her own society, an enemy of Hinduism, and betrayer of female education.[59] Even though Ramabai argued that she had to ask Christians and those abroad for funds because none in the Hindu community would give her any, the *Kesari* mounted a campaign against her so that even her reformist Hindu supporters such as M. G. Ranade broke their connection with her. As a result, Ramabai chose then to move out of the limelight in Pune and Bombay and start out on her own without the support of the reformers.

In describing this incident, Tilak's biographer does mention that Ramabai later did good work in the famine and that she opposed the British authorities with a "fearlessness before which not only the fair sex but some even of the unfair sex must hide their diminished heads in shame." Defending Tilak as being open to female education and denouncing as a lie the fact that Tilak was opposed to it, which he was to all intents and purposes, this account states that in her conversion Ramabai committed a "grave and unpardonable sin against Hindu society."[60]

It is clear here that because of her conversion, many could not acknowledge her accomplishments as a testimony to the abilities of Hindu women. Since Tilak's nationalism was dominantly upper-caste Hindu in its ethos, it was difficult for him to accept Ramabai as a nationalist when she was a Christian not by birth but by choice. Her rejection of Hinduism would probably have registered as a rejection of the basis upon which nationalist struggle, for those like Tilak, could have been founded. Furthermore, opposition to a woman such as Ramabai would have been one way to gain an easy popularity as a defender of Hindu tradition. Here what Uma Chakravarty reveals as Ramabai's rejection of a Hindu past with greater freedoms for women, a past that served as the foundation for cultural nationalism, would have led to her conflicts with Hindu nationalists.[61]

Even though Ramabai's thinking and work had reformist influences, she did not agree with the attempts of either reformists or nationalists to control her. Furthermore, her reformist framework became a contentious issue because it was utilized by a woman, for she challenged the patriarchal frameworks of both the reformist and the nationalist agendas, frameworks that suggest a continuity between them.[62]

Despite such hostility, the Sharada Sadan kept attracting more widows and moved to Pune for reasons of economy. The famine of 1896–1897 found Ramabai rescuing women and children and bringing them to her newly opened Mukti Mission near Kedgaon, which was conceived as a Christian institution where revivals and missionary activity were central. Ramabai had to find a space for herself outside the urban centers where a patriarchal nationalist struggle was being waged in Western India, a space where her actions and movements were not under intense scrutiny. Such a place became the Mukti Mission, where she created a community of women who tried to be independent in feeding and clothing themselves and were able to be literate, morally pure, and free of the proscriptions of caste. This "home" that she would create would be one whose ideal of female purity came from the Western companionate marriage and from Brahmanical laws, with emphasis on a heterosexual union and the common erasure of female sexuality, but was outside the norms of the nuclear family since it comprised only women. Within this space that altered Western formations by collapsing "home" and "community" outside the family, she functioned, paradoxically, as a Christian evangelist, a role that she came to feel was her calling. Church services were regular, missionaries worked there as well, and the money from the United States continued to make Kedgaon's community possible. Yet for Ramabai, all of this was not incompatible with her own version of nationalist goals that were not synchronous with those of the dominant nationalist leaders at the time.

Ramabai's hope was for many Indian converts to Christianity to create what she called "a great army of Christian apostles" who she believed would "eventually regenerate the whole Hindu nation through their lives and their teachings."[63] Believing that Christianity was originally an Eastern religion, she saw it as particularly suited to the Indian way of life. Ramabai's notion of the Hindu nation was more a community defined by caste and race as well as by religion. Her goal for regenerating the Hindu nation by conversion to Christianity was a contradiction unless we understand that by "Hindu nation" she meant a community conceptualized through the religious itinerary of her youth and outside the misogyny that she saw pervading this community. Perhaps this fuzzy notion of the Hindu nation, along with her opposition to British rule, indicates why she remained a vegetarian and wore a sari unlike other converts.

Uma Chakravarty has argued quite powerfully that nationalist notions of women constructed an upper-caste and Aryan identity for "Indian womanhood."[64] She argues that Ramabai was outside this nationalist construct of women because she did not consolidate an Aryan and golden past for women. While this indeed seems to be correct, Ramabai's understandings of women are, however, upper caste and Hindu, so that in some areas she does utilize the constructs of a dominant Hindu nationalism. Where she differed was in her refusal to valorize Hindu religion and culture and her opposition to it by using some of the discourses of reform in its missionary and evangelizing form in regard to Hindu women.

Home and Harem:
Ramabai's Resolution of the Woman Question

It has been argued that Ramabai was disliked by the nationalists not only because of her conversion but because her critique of Hindu domestic life attacked the home that had been seen as a sacred space and a sacrosanct domain for the innermost "spiritual values."[65] Her preoccupation with turning the Hindu house into a home also extends to a denunciation of the joint family system, in which the women's area, the zenana, was the darkest section of the house and in which Ramabai says in *The High-Caste Hindu Woman*, "the child-bride is brought to be forever confined." The hierarchical joint family seemed to her to be inimical to fostering affection between husband and wife, banishing the wife to the "confinement" of the women's section. Thus she says, the bride "does not enter her husband's house to be the head of a new home, but rather enters the house of the father-in-law to become the lowest of its members. . . . Breaking the young bride's spirits is an essential part of the discipline of the new abode."[66] Within such a house, Ramabai revealed, the rule of the mother-in-law was often harsh, there was no form of consent involved in the marriage, and display of mutual affection between husband and wife was prohibited. Ramabai condemned the separate and gendered spheres of existence since they did not create a "home." She believed that even where there was a happy union, there was "no such thing as the family having pleasant times together."[67] This ideal of the Western companionate marriage and the nuclear family, pervasive in the missionary discourse as well as the discourses of the family in both England and the United States, is also powerful in Ramabai's opposition to Hindu custom. Visible too is the notion of home as the site of the companionate marriage that enables freedom for women.

The critique of "home" as impossible for a Hindu family with its joint family system must have been seen as unforgivable by Hindu reformers and conservative men alike, since it argued that only a nuclear family with a companionate marriage could become a "home." Her setting up of her own "homes" for women, initially secular and later Christian, thus would be problematic. In her "homes," Mukti Mission for instance, there were few men; sometimes Ramabai would not allow entry into her homes to male visitors unless they were accompanied by women, thus removing the access to the domestic space that functioned as a sign of patriarchal power for men. In Kedgaon, she also had a home for boys whom she had rescued during the famine. She had found that some of the industries at Mukti Mission needed male labor to do heavy work at the printing press and in the fields, to garden and do carpentry work.[68] She even set up a "home" for "fallen women" whom she had rescued from brothels or from the famine, women who would have been expelled from the sacred sphere of the family. While initially she had set up a home for high-caste widows, she had separate homes at Kedgaon for prostitutes and for the child widows, reinforcing some of the patriarchal binaries that created gendered, heterosexualized inequalities and which would use "woman" as a sign of domesticity, controlled sexuality, and purity.[69]

Ramabai's practices of resistance to Hindu custom were complex because they recuperated the ideology of the Western companionate marriage and its problematic construction of domestic space in a context that was "harem"-like in that it was a community of women without men. Ramabai's "home" did not go so far as to deconstruct the sexual binaries of the marriage-family system that in India became a recasting of Victorian morality. Her notion of "home" depended on its distinction from the "harem," as it did in colonial discourses, depending upon a representation of incarcerated Indian women, who in the Indian context were presented as pathetic victims rather than promiscuous and devious women, as were the representations of the harem in nineteenth-century European depictions of the Middle East. For instance, when Judith Andrews, president of the Executive Committee of the American Ramabai Association, visited India in 1893, she took Ramabai as tour guide to the tombs and palaces of North India. Ramabai took Andrews to see the dungeons under the beautiful palaces. Asking the guide at the palace to show them the places where women were imprisoned and hanged, instead of merely the "outside beauty of the 'poems in marble,'" Ramabai exclaimed: "I beg of my Western sisters not to be satisfied with looking on the outside beauty of the grand philosophies and not to be charmed with hearing the loud and interesting discourses of our educated men; but to open the trap-door of the great monuments of ancient Hindu intellect and enter into the dark cellars, where they will see the real working of the philosophies which they admire so much."[70] Probably the last part of her sentence was a reference to Swami Vivekananda's speeches in the United States on Hindu religion's greatness and his attack on Ramabai for her opposition to Hinduism. Here the European travel discourse of oriental despotism and the "harem" is utilized by Ramabai to address the oppression of women in India. Such a representation of history, though problematic, would be counter to the nationalist practice of the construction of a glorious past of India. The discourse of rescue reveals the influence of works such as *The Story of China's Inland Mission, The Lord's Dealings with George Muller,* and an account of the life of John G. Paton, founder of the New Hebrides Mission, texts that Ramabai claimed in her *Testimony* had vitally influenced her missionary work.[71]

Reform in a Nationalist Period: *Ramabai and Athavale*

Because of her gender and politics, all of Ramabai's practices were complex negotiations with existing and contentious discourses. This is apparent in her use of the category of "woman" as a basis for struggle. Within the discourse of reform, which prefigured the feminist movement, the category called "woman" came into conflict with others such as wife, mother, sister, but it negotiated this conflict by retaining both: that is, exploitation of "woman" was utilized in reformist literature by addressing, as did Ramabai, the plight of the "widow," so that the roles of female persons in the family were retained by a discourse of widow that presumed a foundational category called "woman" but did not give up either. Thus the plight of the widow, was addressed by many reformers who utilized it in the discourse of reform on the "condition of Indian womanhood" that had become a part of the language of many educated and literate Indians and incorporated into the literature written not only in English but also in the Indian languages. As a Marathi, Ramabai may have known about this literature and of the various reformers who were speaking about "the woman question." Jyotirao Phule was one well-known reformer who had led an anti-Brahmin struggle, opposed child marriage and polygamy, and spoke out for women's education and widow remarriage. He set up a school for girls in Pune around 1850. Another was Gopal Hari Deshmukh, who attacked practices such as the caste system, child marriage, and the treatment of widows, and advocated English studies for obtaining scientific knowledge.[72] D. K. Karve, too, worked on this issue, along with women such as Parvati Athavale.

Furthermore, literary productions presented such ideas and debates on the woman question in new contexts of modernization that were linked to travel and the comparative epistemology of colonial representational practices. In 1857 for instance, a Marathi novel entitled *Yamuna Paryatan* was published; it is the narrative of a young girl educated by Christians who feels caged in an orthodox Hindu family. She is married to a young man who is sympathetic to her wishes, unlike the rest of his family. The work is a string of episodes in which the couple travel across Maharashtra and in each place find a widow living in terrible conditions. The goal of the narrative is to argue for widow remarriage, one of the main issues concerning women articulated by the reform movement. Just a year before the publication of *Yamuna Paryatan*, Ishwarchandra Vidyasagar got a bill passed that made the remarriage of Hindu widows lawful.[73] The novel ends with Yamuna becoming a widow, then converting to Christianity and remarrying.

There was a considerable history of reform and change in Western India during the nineteenth century and with the advent of colonial education. Rosalind O'Hanlon argues that social reorganization involved two processes that were implicit in public debate and in colonial lawmaking. These were the "constitution of woman as the sign for a tradition" and the "simultaneous re-empowering of different groups of elite men as the transcendent social critics of that tradition."[74] Beginning with the 1820 Bombay Native School Book and School Society, which took as its goal the dissemination of "the benefits of intellectual and moral improvement to the natives," groups of elite men worked to change "native" society. Topics such as female education and infant marriage were debated in the Students' Literary and Scientific Society which was begun in June 1848 and which was comprised of college-educated men, most of them connected with the elite Elphinstone College. The nationalist leader Dadabahai Naraoji was part of this group. This society opened four Parsi and three Marathi girls' schools in 1849 and a school for Hindu Gujarati girls in 1851. The journal *Stri Bodh*, meant for women, was established by some of the same men in 1856,[75] the same year that the Hindu Widows' Remarriage Act was passed.

In 1865, Vishnushastri Pandit brought out a Marathi translation of Ishwarchandra Vidyasagar's *Remarriage of Hindu Widows* and in 1866 established a society for the promotion of widow remarriage. As historians have pointed out, such events did not mean that women's lives changed for the better, for the domination of Brahminical values on lower classes led to the adoption of such practices rather than their abolition.[76] Furthermore, Vishnushastri's society was debated by a conservative society, leading to many of Vishnushastri's group declaring they were in error.[77] Gopal Hari Deshmukh performed penance after one such important challenge and was readmitted to caste.[78]

The reform movement, however, reemerged with Behramji Malabari's attempts at abolition of child marriage in the 1880s and formed the background for Ramabai's efforts and agitations during the next two decades. The issue of widow remarriage was again taken up by D. K. Karve, Parvati Athavale's brother-in-law and mentor in the 1890s, who devoted his life to the education of women within a Hindu reformist framework.

Yet there were important differences between Ramabai's practices and those of the Indian reformers. For instance, O'Hanlon reveals that many reformers attacked each other or even women for following tradition. Malabari and his attackers all saw widows, for instance, as being morally vulnerable and easily susceptible to immorality and crime. Few, like Ramabai, attacked the men. Tarabai Shinde also did so, responding in her *Comparison Between Women and Men* to representations by both conservatives and reformers of women as power-less but also responsible for their problems through their moral weak-ness and passivity.[79] Ramabai blamed Hindu patriarchy and religion as well as colonial rule, arguing that women were "helpless victims of indolence and false timidity."[80]

Unlike Tarabai Shinde, or any of the male reformers, Ramabai saw British rule as responsible for the condition of Hindu women. Female infanticide, she charged, was ignored by the authorities even though the law in 1802 prohibited it. The fact that there were fewer women than men in India was not only because of female infanticide but because of "the imperfect treatment of the diseases of women in all parts of Hindustan, together with lack of proper hygienic care and medical attendance."[81] She believed such a situation came about be-cause colonial rule was careful not to upset Indian men so that it could extract its economic profits. Thus these profits came from sacrificing the concerns of Indian women.

The nationalists attacked her not only because of her conversion but also because she had pointed out the unholy alliance between the patriarchal local elites and the colonial rulers. In *The High-Caste Hindu Woman*, she states that "under the so-called Christian British rule, the woman is in no better condition than of old"[82] and that British rule with Hindu men have "conspired together to crush her [the Hindu woman] into nothingness."[83] By doing so British rule is "fulfilling its agreement made with the male population of India." Exposing colonial rule as being motivated by greed rather than be-nevolence, she says, "Should England serve God by protecting a helpless woman against the powers and principalities of ancient in-stitutions, Mammon would surely be displeased and British profit and rule in India might be endangered thereby."[84] The collaboration be-tween "native" and colonial patriarchies enables the success of the colonial enterprise, one that she says is "achieved at the sacrifice of the rights and comfort of over one hundred million women."[85]

Despite conflicts with nationalists, she was one of three women delegates to the National Congress in 1889, along with almost two thousand men. She argued against a loyalist position to British rule, saying, "I care more for the worship of the mother than for the worship of the queen. I see no point in worshipping the queen while ill-treating our mothers."[86] Her opposition to colonial rule came because she believed that change could bring some possibilities for women: "We will not ask what is revolutionary or reformist, only what is good for women."[87]

If certain reform movements had their influence on Ramabai, she herself also influenced the male reformers. Some found her inspirational and other learned from her how not to alienate conservative Hindu sentiment. One such person was D. K. Karve, who acknowledged her deep influence on his work. Married to Ramabai's first pupil, he both admired her and thought her problematic. As a man he was much more centrally located within the reformist discourse on the "woman question," even though, unlike some reformers, he practiced what he preached to the extent of marrying a widow and thus suffered the hostility of some section of the conservative Hindu opinion. He established a widows' home in Pune in 1899, at about the same time that Ramabai was creating a community at Kedgaon. He mentions that he was inspired to do so by Ramabai, whom he calls "that indefatigable . . . Brahmin lady," adding that "it was the success of Pandita Ramabai's Sadan that encouraged me to make a similar effort with due precautions in order to respect popular sentiment."[88] Because of such "due precautions," he would become the more acceptable reformer on the women's issue. Because he upheld the sanctity of the Hindu family, his work did not arouse the hostility that Ramabai's did. As a result, during the controversy over conversions at Sharada Sadan in Bombay, some of the widows removed by their families from Ramabai's care were sent to his widows' home.

Parvati Athavale also subscribed to Karve's reformist ideas on women, especially in the commitment to the Hindu family. Yet after her visit to the United States, her notions of the role of women in the domestic space and their connections with the public sphere were altered, though not radically. Such reformulations of reformist discourse mark the newly emerging idea of a positive version of female modernity, in opposition to the common caricatures of the modern woman pervasive at the time, in which "modern" women were seen as threatening. Athavale's ideas came from another site of enunciation than Ramabai's, reacting to Ramabai yet departing from the male reformers' ideas of the place of women in the nationalist telos.

Athavale in the United States

When Parvati Athavale was widowed at the age of twenty, her sister persuaded her to live with them and work at the widows' home that D. K. Karve had established. Athavale had gone through teacher's training and had started working at the widows' home despite considerable opposition from her family since she was a Brahmin widow.

In 1918, Parvati Athavale set off for America. Her aim was to learn English, to see the different institutions of the country, and to collect donations for the widows' home run by Karve, her brother-in-law, a home for which she had worked most of her adult life. Her experience of mobility is somewhat similar to Pandita Ramabai's since she too did not see movement as freedom. As Athavale did not have an English education, and came from a Brahmin family of modest means, the discourse of freedom is absent from the narrative of travel as it is recorded in her memoir *Hindu Widow*.[89] This narrative is a record of her life of service in the homes for widows started by Karve as well as of her trip to the United States.

European travel was not the paradigm through which Athavale experienced her visits to many parts of India, since she was not in search of pleasure or education but was seeking donations for the widows' home. This work started because Karve was injured when the oxcart in which he was traveling was overturned. Since there was no one else to do this work, Parvati Athavale undertook it. Like Ramabai's wanderings, Athavale's travels were undertaken with meager resources. On her first journey, she used a servant's ticket with one of the widows going home so that the home would not have to incur any expenses. In her recollections she does not go into her difficulties or the problems she might have faced as a woman traveling alone. She describes her trip simply: "Thus having started from Poona on a servant's ticket, and then having travelled all alone to distant places, and finally brought back five hundred rupees for the Home, my success gave Professor Karve great joy" (37).

Her search for funds in India took her as far north as Delhi and as far south as Mangalore. She estimates that she collected sixty or seventy thousand rupees for the home during these trips. While she speaks of the problem of finding audiences in the towns to which she travels for her speeches, she does not mention the hazards of travel that were being conceived in relation to a gendered colonial modernity. Since this is the early part of the twentieth century, some of the difficulties mentioned by Rokeya Hussain, for instance, may have become routine for many women and thus not worthy of mention. Train travel was the norm, and separate carriages for English, Indians, men, and women were part of this experience. From accounts of women who traveled in those days, it is clear that women still remained in fear of strangers that they would have to encounter, or of being stranded on their journeys. Yet there is no such account from Athavale, testifying to the amount of traveling she had to do as well as to her becoming so familiar with these difficulties that she does not see them as worthy of mention. Thus in a chapter translated as "Difficulties in Travelling," the difficulties alluded to are those of making connections to collect money from the people in the towns she visits. In comparison, much of the account of her visit to the United States mentions matters such as problems of obtaining food, not knowing the language, being cold, her shoes hurting her feet, and more.

Travel abroad, for Athavale, brings out problems in her ways of living that had never seemed problematic to her. It is clear here that arrangements for travel, in a Western context, become articulated in terms of a discrepancy between travel and women's lives in India. For instance, food becomes a major problem because the only foods Athavale can eat on her journey and in the United States are bread, butter, and fruits. This diet does not do much for her health; sometimes she is unable to even get these basic foods. Going barefoot is also difficult, so that she is forced to buy European shoes before she sets off and as a result has terrible blisters. For this she suggests: "any Indian woman, about to go to a foreign country, should practice at least three months the wearing of European shoes before going aboard the steamer" (73). She also does not have clothes adequate for cooler weather and much of the account mentions her rooms being either warm and comfortable or cold. Train travel within the United States, from California to New York, becomes a source of worry because there is no Indian person to accompany her and to translate for her. Changing trains and cars on the way is a "terrible trial" since, not knowing English, she has to depend on the kindness of strangers to direct her to the right car. Furthermore, when she is not met at the station, she has to rely on the railway station workers to take her to her destination and is afraid of being robbed. Though her narrative conveys these fears, what is obvious is also her determination and resourcefulness, which she never overtly mentions but disguises in a gendered way.

Whereas her intention had been to learn English through travel in the United States, she finds upon arriving in San Francisco that she is too ill to go on to Boston with the Indian family she had intended to live with, and that she has to live in the United States "like many a poor Indian student," working in menial jobs for room and board. She starts by living at the YWCA and cleaning the secretary's room; the secretary finds her a job at a home for the aged. One may have thought this would be ideal, since the superintendent of the home had been a missionary in West India, knew about Pandita Ramabai, and accepted Athavale by saying, "Just as formerly Jesus sent Ramabai to America for her education, so He has sent you. So may He save you" (80).

The home for aged missionaries in Oakland, California allowed her to cook her own food, which was important since her vegetarian diet often caused her to go hungry or be malnourished. However, since one way Athavale differed from Ramabai was that she remained a Hindu and objected to being saved, she disliked being the target of missionary endeavors to convert her while being made to perform vast amounts of work from morning to night. The work seemed to irk her only because it was accompanied by the aged missionaries' attempts at conversion. As she mentions, these missionaries who had worked in India but who were now "resting from their labors in this Home, spent their vacant moments in coming to me and preaching Christianity to me" (82). Cleverly she responded by saying, "Teach me English. I shall then be able to compare your religion with mine, and I shall surely accept the religion that is true" (82). They began to teach her from the Bible, but she says, "After being four or five days in this Missionary Home of Peace I found that I got no peace." Such an understatement is typical in her narrative, which resists indirectly without articulating a direct opposition that is, however, suggested quite clearly. She feared the methods of conversion used against her: "I determined, however, that whatever difficulties I might meet with, I would never leave my own religion" (83).

It is through the Indian nationalists that she is rescued from this home for colonial missionaries, in a gesture symbolic of Indian women's complex positioning between colonialists and nationalists, where all sides wish to construct her as an object for rescue. She had written to an acquaintance in Niagara Falls who passed on her letter to the New York office of the *Young India* periodical started by Lala Lajpat Rai. Lala Lajpat Rai organized groups to educate American public opinion on India and established the Home Rule League in the United States. His writings were published in the *New York Times* and the *New York Evening Post* and he used his influence against the deportation proceedings instituted against Indian revolutionists and nationalists.[90] The New York office therefore had become a center for Indian students and others who worked for Indian independence. Their struggle was not only against the British but also against British sympathizers in the United States, who had organized with racist sentiment against nonwhites in San Francisco to persecute and deport revolutionaries such as Ram Chandra, editor of the *Hindoostan Gadar*. The prevailing sentiment among the students and workers at the *Young India* office in New York was one of defending the independence movement against charges of conspiring with the Germans, fighting racist sentiment as well as sympathy for British colonialism.

It was within such a context that Parvati Athavale was put in touch with the *Young India* office in New York. The office contacted Indian students in San Francisco and Berkeley, and soon three Marathi-speaking students came to visit her and insisted she leave with them. She went to live with them, and since they were quite poor, she looked after them, cooking and cleaning. They insisted that she treat their home as hers and she states that "they treated me and honored me as if I were their aunt" (86). Yet she does not forget the purpose for which she is in the United States, worrying that "such a life would make impossible the purpose for which Professor Karve had sent me to America" (89). Though sorry for the poverty of the students, her domesticity soon becomes a prison: "Thus my unhappy life began to be intolerable and I kept wondering how I could escape from it. I received very little sympathy from these Indian students in regard to the purpose for which I had come to America. They used to say to me, 'Why did Professor Karve send one of your age to America?'" (89). It is clear that these young men had no sympathy for her needs nor for the widows on whose behalf she had to learn English. She begins to see their home as a prison, using the term *escape* to express her need to leave a place where she could not learn English, since the students only spoke Marathi at home and were seldom home to teach her the language. She says too that even though there were many Bengali and Sikhs who lived in the area, she could not contact them for she was not acquainted with them.

She "escapes" by contacting a Professor Gokhale, also Marathi-speaking, whom she has heard about in India and whose address, she says disingenuously, she "came upon" in an address book "one day in cleaning the cupboard of Keshav [one of the students]" (89). One may conclude that, being alone at home so many hours, she could have been actively seeking some means of escape, but she hesitates to present such an active agency in opposing those nationalist young men who had rescued her from the missionaries.

In New York, she worked as a maid in a succession of homes, where she came to know people and where she learned to speak English. She worked as a dishwasher in a hospital and fell ill because of the damp room she was given and the smell of meat coming from the kitchen next door. Washing dishes on which meat had been served was also nauseating to her, yet was not unacceptable. She made few claims about caste purity in her need to earn a living, be independent, and learn English. While travel to the West had been prohibited for caste Hindus just a few decades earlier because it would involve breaking caste practices, yet Athavale's narrative does not allude to such pro-hibitions nor does it present a conflicted or difficult negotiation with her situation in the United States. It is clear that she felt that her goals of learning English and helping widows in India justified the breaking of caste rules, and it was only in the conflicts with the nationalist young men who wished to rescue her that such difficulties are even mentioned.

Indian Nationalism and
the Reform Question in the United States

What Athavale describes as her greatest danger comes not from her work or from a life-threatening situation, but from a Bengali student who is appalled that a Brahmin widow could so demean and break her caste practices by working as a domestic in Christian homes. This student, whom Athavale describes as having "national pride," says to her, "Your life here makes us Indians extremely ashamed of you . . . to work in a foreigner's house, and wash his dishes brings a stain on Brahmanhood. You must go back to your own land" (105). While it is clear that she works with women in the homes rather than with men, this student sees as "foreigners" the men in whose house no Brahmin woman should work. This nationalist and masculinist view that suggests an identity that is not only nationalist but "Brahmin," "Hindu," as well as "Indian," comprehends Athavale as needing to be rescued from American white men. Indian women become embodiments of Indianness and cultural purity and repositories of nationalist values that create distinction from "foreigner," seen as essentially white, and American.

Athavale, against such essentialism, responds that she has "as much national pride" as the student and, like many male Indian students, accepts as honorable "the method of independence" of earning her own living. Clearly she understands and responds to the blatant sexism of his charge, refusing to become the symbolic object of masculinist nationalism. She goes on to deessentialize other subjects in this conflict by claiming that Mr. Baldwin, in whose house she worked, was not a Brahmin by birth, "yet by his true character and noble living, he was a Brahman" (106). Her attitude toward many whites she met in the United States, as with Mr. Baldwin and the housekeeper at the hospital who had nursed her, is rather to include them in a cosmology governed, to a certain extent, by functionalist explanations, turning one into a Brahmin and the other into the means through which she can learn English. While she locates herself within nationalist ideals, designating her desire to learn English as "selfishness" that she needs to overcome, she finds ways to create agency through a flexible teleology. Here the goals for women that she hopes to accomplish are never overtly claimed as being as significant or crucial as nationalist ones, yet they remain the chief motivators for her. Concerned for the struggle for independence, she hesitates to openly confront the student lest she present a "spectacle" of "enmity between a Maharashtra woman and the Bengali" as an "incompatibility and hostility" in the "sight of foreigners" (107). Thus she represents the student as behaving like "a son" who acted "without giving any consideration as to whether I wanted to return to India or not" (106). Such a revealing conceptualization of the relation between son and mother reveals that implicitly she acknowledges that family and nation are aligned and uncaring of the interests of women.

In a gesture typical of the gendered and masked agency that she employs, she seemingly gives up the battle: "I let this Bengali student pull the string that determined my life. It brought peace and comfort to him. . . . I accepted his opinion as my authority . . . I put my trust in God and waited to see what would happen." While suggesting the student is sincere, she also says that his actions emerge from "his own false patriotic sentiments" (106–107), within which he could believe that men and women should be governed by different rules. She refuses to accept such an inequality as nationalism, and in an attempt to accommodate reformist ideas within nationalist ones, argues that a "true" patriotic sentiment would be able to accommodate her goals as well.

Despite her dissatisfaction, she seemingly falls in with the student's arrangements for her return to India, believing that a refusal would have been seen as enmity "between a Maharashtra woman and the Bengali, and this in the sight of foreigners, and in a foreign land, a spectacle of incompatibility and hostility" (107). Within the context of New York, where Indian nationalists were struggling for sympathy in the midst of charges of sedition because of collaboration with Germany, her concern was valid. However, the difference between her formulation of nationalist concern and the student's is crucial. Whereas the student utilizes a patriarchal nationalist narrative of having "freed a Maratha woman from slavery in a non-Hindu home" (108), her narrative is one of the unity of equals. She conceptualizes nationalism as the gender-neutral unity of the various and different regions of India, while he sees it to be Indian men saving Indian women from white men.

To other students from the *Young India* group, she does not hesitate to express her unwillingness to be the object of this rescue. She argues that she needs the "opportunities of seeing American educational institutions" (108). One of the students supports her, saying that "if . . . sons of Brahmans on occasions work in the homes of non-Hindus, what objection is there if our sister follows our example?"

(109). The plan of the Bengali student (who is referred to throughout this narrative only by his language/ethnicity instead of by name, as are the other Bengali men who come to see her) is foiled. Even so, she is only freed from the student's plans when all the students refer to a higher authority, Professor Gokhale, who decrees that "Parvatibai is not a child. Do what she wishes" (110). This statement, from a higher male authority whose word is acceptable to all, disproves the equality she had argued for with the other students even as it leaves her believing that "the starkness of despair that surrounded me was pierced by a ray of hope, and my Bengali brother's castles in the air fell into ruins" (110). Nationalism's benevolent gesture toward women enables Athavale to reach her goal.

Indian Women and Irish Nationalism in the United States Context

It is only when Athavale came into contact with a Miss O'Reilly through the *Young India* office in New York that she felt that the reason she came to the United States was to be fulfilled. Miss O'Reilly, an Irishwoman dedicated to the Irish cause, was known to one of the *Young India* group, Dr. Hardikar, since she believed in the Indian cause for independence. The first action by O'Reilly was to suggest that Athavale attend the International Conference of Industrial Workers as a representative of Indian working women. We do not know what Athavale said at the conference or how she represented this new category, "Indian working women," but she did so to everyone's satisfaction. She only records in her memoir that there were many Indian women in the United States who belonged to the working class "along with their husbands" and that they faced many unjust and oppressive laws.

The consequence of attending the conference with O'Reilly was that Athavale began working in O'Reilly's home taking care of her mother. According to her narrative, all her goals are fulfilled by working in the O'Reilly home. She learned English as well as obtained knowledge about women's education in the United States, and came to admire the domestic arrangements that were "very neat and of a model kind, making it a delight to see them" (121). This admiration is visible in the attempts Athavale made on her return to the widows' home in India to create a similarly neat and orderly domestic realm, which she argued later was necessary for all women to establish.

She admired O'Reilly's devotion to social causes, which Athavale came to believe should be replicated by Indian women, especially widows:

In our country widows, whose husbands died when they were of a tender age, always look sad, and so do the guardians and relatives of those girls, who for some reason or another are unable to give them in marriage. But in America, when for any reason a girl does not marry, or if she is widowed, she does not give in to despondency and become helpless, as do the women and their relatives in India, but they face the situation, and take up duties as citizens of their country. This is a most valuable example for all of us to follow. (123)

This quite disingenuous argument ignores all the conditions in India that compelled women to see widowhood as a disaster, which it was in its material and social effects, while suggesting new roles for women in the public sphere and in the new nation-state of the future. Athavale came to believe that individually Indian women could overcome the social effects of widowhood in order to become like Miss O'Reilly, who, in Athavale's words, is the "example of a liberal mind and efficient womanhood" (123–124). O'Reilly's home is described by Athavale as a "pure and happy home" which provides her the oppor-tunity to speak before women's clubs and collect money and a car for Karve and the home. Here she also meets a wide network of Indian nationalists and benevolent and wealthy American women.

Athavale finds common cause with O'Reilly in the struggle against British rule. She provides information on the struggle in India, and her sharing Mahatma Gandhi's strategy to boycott British goods leads to O'Reilly's campaign of boycotting British tea and goods in New York. O'Reilly is able to collect money for the Irish cause through the profits from the many families in New York participating in the boycott.

On her return, Athavale travels through London and Paris, where she speaks on women's education for Indian groups and for those in the independence struggle. Her trip to Bombay is in company with Rabindranath Tagore and his daughter-in-law and about twenty-five students returning home. This part of the trip is a delight to her, for she says, "sometimes we spent hours in the bright moonlight listening to the nectar words of Rabindranath Tagore" (131).

Travel and Colonial Modernity:
The Comparative Method and the Reform Question

While Ramabai traveled in the United States as a spokeswoman and authority for the Hindu woman and Hindu widow, a comparison with Athavale's experiences reveals that Ramabai's position and authority were derived in part from the links with Christian missionary circles and with those involved in "Eastern" benevolence to less fortunate "sisters." Ramabai was able to collect much more money than Athavale, who was not, like Ramabai, feted and recognized wherever she went. Athavale learned English by working as a domestic in people's homes and it was through a chance encounter with an Irish nationalist, Miss O'Reilly, that she was able to come into contact with the wealthy and educated women who were interested in India and Indian women. Ramabai's conversion may have opened more doors for her than was possible for Athavale.

Athavale also had to concern herself in the United States both with Christian evangelism as well as with Indian nationalist constructs of women as they were expressed by Indians living or studying in the United States. For Ramabai, the United States was a relief from both these, since the former she had experienced in England and the latter in India. In 1918, Athavale was traveling in an era of powerful nationalist politics some two decades after Ramabai's initial visit to the United States, so that the context of Indian nationalist struggle in the United States is quite different from that of Ramabai's. Athavale's time in the United States includes the struggles against deportation of Indian revolutionaries and charges of German conspiracy and a heightened involvement in nationalist politics.

Obvious also in Athavale's ideas is the comparative epistemology that was central to nationalist constructions of culture and that was centrally linked to travel between "East" and "West" seen as essentialized, locational identities. In her memoir, Athavale claims her knowledge and authority emerge out of her travels in India and the

United States. Because she has seen the condition of widows and women in many parts of India and the United States, she can speak from that comparative knowledge. The scientific discourse of a systemic study of cultures no doubt is part of her knowledge base and is obvious when she can compare "social life" in its manifestations "here" and "there," as she terms them: "I have no book-knowledge as others have, and I have no university degrees. I feel therefore that I have not sufficient knowledge to write on this subject. Yet, as I have had to travel for many years . . . , I have observed many things connected with the social life of our people. On account of my visit to America and Europe, I feel able to make some comparisons between the social life here and the social life there" (133). In a trajectory similar to that of colonial modernity refracted through nationalism, Athavale compares not only "here" and "there" but also past and present to construct a better past and a more productive prehistory for nationalism: "In my home in the Konkan, where the old customs prevailed, there was no such disrespect shown" (135). In the present, children are disrespectful to parents and clever servants "dominate over their mistresses," whereas "fifty years ago we were taught in our homes tidy habits, but I see very little of that in our modern home" (135).

The comparative method is also merged with the anthropological framework that would later misrecognize the continuum between imperialism and nationalism and suggest them as oppositional. In Athavale's formulations—such as, "The world has before it two principles relating to the choice of a husband and wife. The Western, where mutual love determines the choice and the other, the Indian method, where the parent's choice predominates" (60)—two essentialisms are set up in terms of opposing cultural practices. Such a method refuses to deconstruct these essentialisms in the interest of maintaining different ideologies that vary by location. For Athavale's interest is liberal reform that includes a notion of "choice": "If parents can gain the approval of their children to their choice, our system will be free from fault" (61). Through such a negotiation, the individual can be reconciled with her role within the formulations of colonial modernity. Here then is the reformist mode that attempts to reconcile the "modern" Western notion of person as individual with the notion of person as one who performs a role in the family, a conflict that Meenakshi Mukherjee has suggested occurs within the novel in India.[91]

Even though, like Ramabai and other women who had been in many parts of India, Athavale's travels enabled her to see that the lives of Hindu widows were extremely difficult, her difference from Ramabai is that, like male reformers, she sees women as much to blame as the men for their oppression. Thus she writes that she visited the holy cities in order to see how widows were treated there: "Having accomplished my purpose in collecting funds, I devoted the remainder of the time to an investigation of the conditions of widows in those places" (44). Here she sees that widows are exploited but also argues that they spend their time idly. She makes such a claim even while revealing that women are sexually at the mercy of priests and other mendicants when they have to sleep in the temples, are not given enough clothes to cover their bodies, and have to go from place to place begging in search of food. Her solution is creating homes for widows rather than any changes in family or religious ideology that may render these homes unnecessary. Ramabai, on the other hand, had argued for both of these as necessary, even though her solution, that is, founding homes for women, was the same. When Athavale claims that widows have "neither worldly riches nor spiritual riches" (45), what is clear is that she blames a larger social structure for not providing for these but also blames the widows for not having "spiritual riches."

Such views mark her as much more conservative than Ramabai, who believed that the Hindu family was structurally flawed. These views also explain why Athavale could work with a male reformer such as Karve, when Ramabai could not. Whereas Ramabai thought the Hindu family could have a house and not a home, Athavale thought that the Hindu family was sacred and that the ideal for every woman was to be "the best sister, the best mother, and the best wife" (147). Her interest in women's education was not directed toward the goal of self-sufficiency as was Ramabai's, being aimed more at being a wife and mother. Such roles, according to Athavale, included an even greater responsibility to being involved in "home industry" or in nurturing roles of nurse, doctor, or teacher. On the other hand, she deplored the practice that led married women to drop education and participation in social activities and leave these to unmarried women, arguing that "if the married women would share in this work, it would be an encouragement for the men of the family to do the same and the result would be a happy one" (137).

Athavale's differences with those she terms "reformers" come because of her belief in the different education needed for men and for women. According to Athavale, the model was not ancient India of the golden past but contemporary Japan. The West could not be emulated because there, according to Athavale, evil had resulted out of turning marriage into a contractual arrangement. What is important to note here is that the male nationalist binaries, such as domestic/public that was homologous to that of spiritual/material, were not followed by women such as Athavale. For Athavale, the West can be followed in areas such as involvement of married women in the social welfare of the community, that is, "writing articles in newspapers, going to gatherings, giving lectures, working for child-welfare, developing conditions for healthy living in the cities, and planning for the removal of disabilities under which women may suffer" (137). What was also to be emulated from the West was the attraction of men for their homes (137), women's ability to make homes healthy and beautiful, and husbands' and wives' desire to please each other. Clearly, she aims at establishing a companionate nuclear arrangement within the Hindu joint family. Hygiene in U.S. homes was also appreciated, and she cites the lavatory as one place that requires cleaning in India. She personally cleaned the lavatories at the widows' home after her return from the United States, setting an example to the widows.

However, Athavale disapproved of "Western" educational goals for women, which she believed should be for the improvement of home rather than for employment. She did not approve of "love" as a basis for marriage, nor did she consider child marriages unacceptable. In a denial of women's sexuality, and with the emphasis on heterosexuality that she shared with many reformers including Pandita Ramabai, she felt that boys and girls should not stay unmarried for long after puberty because of its "resulting evils," and that "duty and self-renunciation must be the foundation of marriage if it is to remain permanent, and useful for our country and posterity":

European women have now received their freedom in material things but they are not yet entirely free from servitude. If freedom from servitude is meant freedom from men and a life of independence from them, then that freedom is unnatural, impossible, disastrous, and opposed to the laws of right living. . . . Our sisters in this country must learn a lesson from the sorrowful condition of European women who have obtained their material liberty. (146)

She saw "strife" between men and women in Europe and believed that women had become "strangers to the home, the sacred place for their duties" (147). Even though Athavale saw the home as a sacred realm, it is clear that this home was not uninfluenced by the West, since it was here that there needed to be changed marriage relations and changed notions of cleanliness and of different roles for women. Unlike Ramabai, who thought the Hindu custom as derived from religion would prevent the Hindu house from becoming a home, Athavale believed that women's education and modernization would make that happen. Therefore she applauded Karve's founding of a woman's university for the goal of making "Indian women . . . good mothers and home makers" (148), a goal that became pervasive within women's education in independent India. Difference was to be asserted from the West in keeping marriage central to a woman's life and for the larger good of the family. Even here, "Western" women had much to teach Indian women: "the Western women who have married and are carrying on their homes may well be copied by our women in the management of their homes" (147).

The comparative framework of colonial modernity is here utilized in a different version of a binary division that is not as clearly reducible to homologies of home / abroad, domestic / public, material / spiritual. Since Western women are represented as more involved in the public and social good, the West cannot stand simply for the material realm as it did in the cosmology of some Indian nationalists. Religion is not mentioned explicitly, even though it is clear that Athavale was a devout Hindu who broke down some social orthodoxies even as she upheld others. The inner / outer binary is also not applicable here because Athavale suggests that the "resolution" of West / India as outer / inner is extremely problematic because Indians do not imitate the inner "good points" of the West ("cleanliness, neatness, home teaching, dignity and the like" [136]), but the "outer fashions" only. Families living "half like Europeans and half like Hindus" (136) are seen as problematic because the kinds of modernities being adopted do not seem to be useful or necessary for reform.

The discourse of good and bad modernizations was part of the negotiations with modernity that were undertaken in India under colonization. The comparative method of travel and modernity, ignored by Ramabai's indigenous evangelism, comes to the fore in Athavale's negotiations with nationalism, because it enables feminist work to be carried out. Thus women's conceptualizations of comparative analysis were quite dissimilar to men's, revealing that in the understanding of gender relations in modern India, it is important to look at women's lives and beliefs. Such discursive practices were part of the colonial context in which feminism could find a space through opposition and accommodation with nationalism, articulating categories called "Indian women" and "Indian feminism" that performed their own erasures and silences. Yet the women's practices of resistance, recuperated by ever-emerging orthodoxies, present the possibilities and problematics of movements within geopolitical contexts. Ramabai, Athavale, and Toru Dutt can be called "pioneering" women, as nationalist historiography calls them, but the contexts of such pioneering practices require an engaged and feminist critical attention.

Afterword

In this book, I have examined how nationalism narrates gendered, classed, and racialized bodies. I have shown that feminist subjects are also produced within such narratives, so that the female body, both disciplined and undisciplined, can become part of the nation. I have implicitly relied on Homi K. Bhabha's conceptualization of the "double-time" of nationalist thought: its determination of the people as both subject and object. Yet rather than note the ambivalence of national cultures, I have emphasized also their coerciveness, the disciplinary imperative of creating the normative that is, of course, opposed and conflicted. The differential response to such normative nationalist subjects by men and women in both England and India, and the hegemonic formations produced by such processes, has also been my topic.

The narration of gender as a form of travel and the discourse of European travel within which such movements of ideas take shape have been my particular focus. The concept-metaphors of "home" and "harem" are articulated within such travel that traces its genealogy to European Romanticism and to class formations within England. Gender, class, and nation come together to create the home and harem both as spaces within which people belong to a heterogeneous nation or can be normalized within it by comparison to various racialized and gendered others. Home is the domestic space that is also a political entity invested with history and tradition represented through the female bodies located within it. Such a "home" is a site of resistance by the women living there, who wish to break the binary of home/outside, private/public on which nationalist culture grounds itself in India. Resistance is articulated by showing these to be infiltrated by each other rather than being inviolate and reveals that inviolate spaces are created by authoritarian and patriarchal forces so that women become not the subjects but the objects of the nation. Home is therefore cathected by a nationalist culture in both India and England, and travel, conceived as the movement out and back to home, provides a textual structure that creates the subjects and objects of the nation.

I have also examined the notion of "harem" as the Other of the nation, the cultural difference that is also constitutive of the nation within modern British culture. Within such a narrative, harem is the undifferentiated notion of female incarceration that is figured as inimical to the notion of citizenship which relies on an idea of freedom as the promise of the nation. Nationness in England, therefore, is also the knowledge of the possibilities and unfitness for citizenship of the subjects and objects of the nation, as well as that of the colonies. Incarceration and freedom form a binary whose functioning I examine in one particular context of colonialism, that of the British in India. Other contexts no doubt present vastly different strategies and other transnational contexts. The idea of the harem provides the national difference that, according to Geoffrey Bennington, forms the narrative that "attempts, interminably, to constitute identity against difference, inside against outside, and the superiority of inside over outside, prepares against invasion and for 'enlightened' colonialism."[1] The inside, the "home," is thus an object of some interest, as is the "outside," the version of home that is the harem.

Gender, race, sexuality, caste, class—these are the objects of interest for English and Indian nationalisms in the age of empire and colonialism. It is in the knowledge and construction of categories here that the nation grapples with its heterogeneity. British suffragists oppose patriarchy but find subject status as imperialists; Indian feminists negotiate with missionary discourse and with patriarchal reformist notions of the family. The British working classes become gendered consumers of the empire, recasting imperial culture into working-class culture.

And travel and its cultures provide colonial and anticolonial technologies for understandings of modernity and the particular comparative epistemology of British colonialism in terms of a modernizing project, as well as the Eurocentrism that justifies interventions into those categories that comprise the "native" and "indigenous." For those outside the cultures of travel, negotiations are formulated by alternate conceptions of "home," even though the power of travel infiltrates the knowledge of nation and its subjects and objects.

There is much that remains to be said in the histories of travel and mobility. I have focused on some instances of Victorian imperial culture and English nationalism that were of interest to me. Many other narratives of nation and empire within domestic culture in England need to be examined through sustained interrogations of the transnationalisms of discursive practices. Many other narratives of domestic culture, that is, culture within national boundaries, must also be located within a transnational frame that is not reduced to a narrative of center and periphery or of globalization.

There is much on the culture of travel that needs examination, particularly the various forms of precolonial and premodern travel in various parts of the world. Such accounts fracture and particularize the movements of European imperial travel and its dominant forms for vastly different possibilities and epistemologies, leading perhaps to new understandings of border crossings and nation-state formation that would be politically useful.[2] Particularly in the area of sexuality, more texts that attempt to decolonize cultural and national forms are necessary, creating narratives of the travel of sexualities that would, once again, fracture disciplinary practices that were part of European modernity and colonial modernities.

More recent imperatives within the contemporary conditions of postmodernity demand that we look outside the modern culture of travel to other classed, gendered, racialized movements, such as migration and immigration. Such mobilities and displacements may enable vastly different narratives in terms of multiple gendered, classed, racialized, and sexualized positions. It is this project that remains to be attempted within the methodologies enabled by cultural critiques and that would interrupt the legal and economic narratives so loved by policy- and lawmakers. In such contexts, texts of travel as articulated within European modernist narratives become problematic and reveal the limits of European travel.

Notes

Introduction

1. A good example of such writing is Pico Iyer's *Video Night in Kathmandu* (New York: Alfred Knopf, 1988). For critiques of such modes of travel see Caren Kaplan, *Questions of Travel* (Durham: Duke University Press, 1996) and Mary Louise Pratt's *Imperial Eyes: Travel Writing and Transculturation* (New York: Routledge, 1992). In Pratt see the analysis of Joan Didion's *Salvador*, 225–227.

2. Christopher Hibbert, *The Grand Tour* (New York: G. P. Putnam's Sons, 1969).

3. John Urry, *The Tourist Gaze: Leisure and Travel in Contemporary Societies* (London: Sage Publications, 1990), 4.

4. Edmund Swinglehurst, *The Romantic Journey* (New York: Harper & Row, 1974); for a critique of the tourist/traveler distinction see James Buzard, *The Beaten Track* (Oxford: The Clarendon Press, 1993).

5. An example of such work is Paul Fussell's *Abroad: British Literary Travelling Between the Wars* (Oxford: Oxford University Press, 1980).

6. Pratt, introduction, 1–11.

7. Two "lit crit" works that use such problematic stances are Percy G. Adams, *Travel Literature and the Evolution of the Novel* (Lexington: University Press of Kentucky, 1983), and Charles L. Batten Jr., *Pleasurable Instruction: Form and Convention in Eighteenth Century Travel Literature* (Berkeley: University of California Press, 1978). A less scholarly example of valorization of the traveler-hero is John Keay's *Eccentric Travelers* (Los Angeles: Jeremy P. Tarcher Inc., 1982).

8. See Caren Kaplan, "Deterritorializations: The Rewriting of Home and Exile in Western Feminist Discourse," in *The Nature and Context of Minority Discourse*, ed. Abdul R. JanMohamed and David Lloyd (New York: Oxford University Press, 1990), pp. 357–368. For a critique of the notion of exile, see Kaplan, *Questions of Travel*.

9. Out of many such texts I will cite a few: Hazel Carby's *Reconstructing*

Womanhood: The Emergence of the Afro-American Woman Novelist (New York: Oxford University Press, 1987); Angela Davis, *Woman, Race and Class* (New York: Random House, 1981); Paula Giddings, *Where and When I Enter* (New York: William Morrow and Co., 1984); Evelyn Nakano Glenn, *Issei, Nisei, War Bride* (Philadelphia: Temple University Press, 1986); Ron Takaki, *Strangers from a Different Shore* (New York: Little, Brown, 1989); Hector Calderon and Jose Saldivar, eds., *Criticism in the Borderlands* (Durham and London: Duke University Press, 1991).

10. Rozina Visram, *Ayahs, Lascars and Princes: The Story of Indians in Britain 1700–1947* (London: Pluto Press, 1986).

11. John Berger with Jean Mohr, *A Seventh Man* (London and New York: Writers and Readers, 1975); Homi K. Bhabha, "DissemiNation: Time, Narrative, and the Margins of the Modern Nation," in *Nation and Narration*, ed. Homi K. Bhabha (New York: Routledge, 1990); D. Emily Hicks, *Border Writing* (Minneapolis: University of Minnesota Press, 1991); Gloria Anzaldua, *Borderlands/La Frontera* (San Francisco: Spinsters/Aunt Lute, 1987).

12. In particular I would like to mention here the work of Chandra Mohanty, "Cartographies of Struggle: Third World Women and the Politics of Feminism," pp. 1–47, and "Under Western Eyes," pp. 51–80, in *Third World Women and the Politics of Feminism* (Bloomington: Indiana University Press, 1991); Cynthia Enloe, *Bananas, Beaches, and Bases* (Berkeley: University of California Press, 1989); Aihwa Ong's *Spirits of Resistance and Capitalist Discipline* (Albany: State University of New York Press, 1987); June Nash and Maria Patricia Fernandez-Kelly, *Women, Men and the International Division of Labor* (Albany: State University of New York Press, 1983); Inderpal Grewal and Caren Kaplan, eds., *Scattered Hegemonies: Postmodernity and Transnational Feminist Practices* (Minneapolis: University of Minnesota Press, 1994).

13. See for instance, Richard J. Barnet and John Cavanagh, *Global Dreams: Imperial Corporations and the New World Order* (New York: Simon and Schuster, 1994).

14. Pratt defines "contact zones" as "the space of colonial encounters, the space in which peoples geographically and historically separated come into contact with each other and establish ongoing relations, usually involving conditions of coercion, radical inequality, and intractable conflict," *Imperial Eyes*, 6.

15. Ali Behdad, *Belated Travelers* (Durham: Duke University Press, 1994); Edward Said, *Orientalism* (New York: Vintage Books, 1979); Malek Alloula, *The Colonial Harem* (Minneapolis: University of Minnesota Press, 1986); Ella Shohat, "Gender and the Culture of Empire: Towards a Feminist Ethnography of the Cinema, *Quarterly Review of Film and Video* 13: 1–3, 45–84; Mervat Hatem, "Through Each Other's Eyes," in *Western Women and Imperialism*, ed. Nupur Choudhury and Margaret Strobel (Bloomington: Indiana University Press, 1992), 35–38.

16. Gayatri Spivak, *In Other Worlds* (New York and London: Routledge, 1988), and *Outside in the Teaching Machine* (New York and London: Routledge, 1993); Nupur Choudhury and Margaret Strobel, *Western Women and Imperialism* (Bloomington: Indiana University Press, 1992); Tani Barlow, ed., *Gender Politics in Modern China: Writing and Feminism* (Durham: Duke University Press, 1993); Uma Chakravarty, "Whatever Happened to the Vedic Dasi?" in *Recasting Women*, ed. KumKum Sangari and Sudesh Vaid (New Delhi: Kali for Women, 1989).

17. Shohat, "Gender and Culture of Empire."

18. Alloula, *The Colonial Harem.*

19. Geoffrey Bennington, "Postal Politics and the Institution of the Nation," in *Nation and Narration*, ed. Homi K. Bhabha (New York: Routledge, 1990), 121–137.

20. James Clifford, "Notes on Travel and Theory," *Inscriptions* 5 (1989): 177–188.

21. Ibid.

22. Kaplan, *Questions of Travel.*

23. See their essays in KumKum Sangari and Sudesh Vaid, eds., *Recasting Women* (New Delhi: Kali for Women, 1989).

24. Lata Mani, "Contentious Traditions," in *Recasting Women*, ed. Sangari and Vaid (Delhi: Kali for Women, 1989).

25. Also in Sangari and Vaid, *Recasting Women.*

26. Partha Chatterjee, *The Nation and Its Fragments* (Princeton: Princeton University Press, 1993), 147.

27. For an important essay on the topic of "home" and community in contemporary U.S. culture see Biddy Martin and Chandra Mohanty, "Feminist Politics: What's Home Got to Do with It?" in *Feminist Studies / Critical Studies*, ed. Teresa de Lauretis (Bloomington: Indiana University Press, 1986), 191–212.

28. Pierre Bourdieu, *Outline of a Theory of Practice* (Cambridge: Cambridge University Press, 1977), 85.

29. David Lloyd, *Nationalism and Minor Literature* (Berkeley: University of California Press, 1987), introduction.

30. Matthew Arnold, *Culture and Anarchy* (Indianapolis: Bobbs-Merrill Educational Publishing, 1971).

31. In Gauri Viswanathan's *The Masks of Conquest* (New York: Columbia University Press, 1989), 158.

32. Philip Dodd, "Englishness and the National Culture," in *Englishness: Politics and Culture 1880–1920*, ed. Philip Dodd and Robert Colls (London: Croom Helm, 1986), 1–28.

33. Patrick Brantlinger, *Rule of Darkness* (Ithaca: Cornell University Press, 1988); Sara Suleri, *The Rhetoric of English India* (Chicago: University of Chicago Press, 1992); Viswanathan, *Masks of Conquest*; Lisa Lowe, *Critical Terrains*

(Ithaca: Cornell University Press, 1991); Jenny Sharpe, *Allegories of Empire* (Minneapolis: University of Minnesota Press, 1993).

34. Robert Young, *White Mythologies* (London and New York: Routledge, 1990), 174.

35. Svati Joshi, ed., *Rethinking English* (New Delhi: Trianka, 1991), 8.

36. Suleri, *Rhetoric*, 76. While her discussion of colonialism and postcolonialism is useful, Suleri's book sees the two in a dialogic relation rather than a continuum. However, the dialogic relation could be better addressed by looking at Indians writing during colonization as well, thus fracturing the canonicity of the "colonial literature" that she reinscribes, and problematizing the chronology of the postcolonial.

37. See Kamala Visweswaran, "Family Subjects: An Ethnography of the 'Woman Question' in Indian Nationalism" (Ph.D. thesis, Stanford University, 1990).

38. Margaret Strobel, *European Women in the Second British Empire* (Bloomington: Indiana University Press, 1991).

39. Helen Callaway, *Gender, Culture and Empire* (Urbana: University of Illinois Press, 1987); Dea Birkett, *Spinsters Abroad* (London: Basil Blackwell, 1989); Choudhuri and Strobel, *Western Women and Imperialism*; Margaret Strobel, *European Women and the Second British Empire* (Bloomington: Indiana University Press, 1991); Laura Donaldson, *Decolonizing Feminism: Race, Gender and Empire-Building* (Chapel Hill: University of North Carolina Press, 1992).

40. For a full discussion of "imperial" and "global" feminism, see the introduction to Grewal and Kaplan, eds., *Scattered Hegemonies*.

41. In the area of cultural studies an early collection with such critiques was published by the Birmingham school of cultural studies. Entitled *The Empire Strikes Back: Race and Racism in 70s Britain*, it contained ground-breaking essays by Hazel Carby, Pratibha Parmar, Valerie Amos, and Paul Gilroy (Center for Contemporary Cultural Studies [London: Routledge, 1992, 1982]).

42. An exception that attends to class differences between European women is Strobel's *European Women and the Second British Empire*.

43. A good example is Susan Blake's essay, "A Woman's Trek," in *Western Women and Imperialism*, ed. Nupur Choudhuri and Margaret Strobel (Bloomington: Indiana University Press, 1992), 19–34.

44. See Lowe, *Critical Terrains*, chapter 2, "Travel Narratives and Orientalism: Montagu and Mostesquiu," 30–74; Pratt, *Imperial Eyes*, 213–216. Another work that presents such a complex analysis is Caren Kaplan's "Getting to Know You: Travel, Gender, and the Politics of Postcolonial Representation in *Anna and the King of Siam* and *The King and I*," in *Late Imperial Culture*, ed. E. Ann Kaplan, Roman de la Campa, and Michael Sprinker (London: Verso, 1995), 33–52.

45. See Gayatri Spivak, "Three Women's Texts and a Critique of Imperialism," in *"Race," Writing and Difference*, ed. Henry Louis Gates (Chicago: Uni-

versity of Chicago Press, 1985); and Norma Alarcon, "The Theoretical Subject(s) of *This Bridge Called My Back* and Anglo-American Feminism," in *Making Face, Making Soul Haciendo Caras*, ed. Gloria Anzaldua (San Francisco: An Aunt Lute Foundation Book, 1990), 356–369.

46. While the feminist scholarship of the nineteenth century in England that leaves out imperialism and empire is too extensive to cite, the founding text in Anglo-American feminism is, of course, Sandra Gilbert and Susan Gubar's *Madwoman in the Attic: The Woman Writer and the Nineteenth-Century Literary Imagination* (New Haven: Yale University Press, 1980). Spivak's "Three Women's Texts and a Critique of Imperialism" was a major force in identifying this omission.

47. Papers delivered by Caren Kaplan and Inderpal Grewal, Society for Cinema Studies Conference, New York, March 2–5, 1995.

48. Akhil Gupta, "The Location of 'The Indigenous' in Critiques of Modernity" (paper delivered at the South Asia conference, Berkeley, Calif., 19 February 1993).

49. Mani, "Contentious Traditions," 88–126.

50. E. P. Thompson, *The Poverty of Theory and Other Essays* (New York: Monthly Review Press, 1978).

51. See Homi K. Bhabha's discussion on Foucault's ignoring colonialism in "Postcolonial Authority and Postmodern Guilt," in *Cultural Studies*, ed. Cary Nelson, Paula A. Treichler, and Lawrence Grossberg (New York: Routledge, 1992), 56–68.

52. Kaplan, *Questions of Travel*.

53. In particular I am thinking of the collection edited by Sangari and Vaid, *Recasting Women*, and the work of Dipesh Chakrabarty, "The Difference-Defferal of (A) Colonial Modernity: Public Debates on Domesticity in British Bengal," *History Workshop Journal* 36 (1993): 1–33.

54. Tani Barlow, editor's introduction, *positions* 1, no. 1 (Spring 1993): iv–vii.

55. Homi K. Bhabha, "Of Mimicry and Man: The Ambivalence of Colonial Discourse," *October* (Spring 1984): 125–133.

56. Lydia Liu, "Gender, Subjectivity and Discourse: The Female Tradition in Twentieth Century Literature," in *Scattered Hegemonies*, ed. Inderpal Grewal and Caren Kaplan (Minneapolis: University of Minnesota Press, 1994), 37–62.

57. Roberto Schwartz, *Misplaced Ideas* (London: Verso, 1992), 11.

58. Joshi, *Rethinking English*, 12.

59. Kamala Visweswaran, *Fictions of Feminist Ethnography* (Minneapolis: University of Minnesota Press, 1994).

60. Spivak, *In Other Worlds*.

61. For more explanation of this formation see Caren Kaplan and Inderpal Grewal, "Transnational Feminist Cultural Studies: Beyond the Marxism / Poststructuralism / Feminism Divides," *positions* (Fall 1994): 430–445.

62. On the contribution of Spivak to many fields of knowledge relating to women see Caren Kaplan and Inderpal Grewal, "Transnational Feminist Cultural Studies."

63. Edward Said, *The World, the Text, and the Critic* (Cambridge: Harvard University Press, 1983), 226–227.

64. Clifford, "Notes on Travel and Theory," 177–188. In looking at ways in which theories are culturally and historically located, he asks how "predicaments of theory have often presented themselves as issues of 'location.'" See preface.

65. A good example is Mary Layoun's work on the novel in Japan (*Travels of a Genre: Ideology and the Modern Novel* [Princeton, N.J.: Princeton University Press, 1990]), and Lydia Liu's forthcoming book on translingual practice and literary modernity in China. One essay of Liu's work, "Translingual Practice: The Discourse of Individualism between China and the West," appears in *positions* 1, no. 1 (Spring 1993): 160–193.

66. A well-known example is Partha Chatterjee's 1986 book, *Nationalist Thought and the Colonial World* (Minneapolis: University of Minnesota Press, 1993).

67. See the work of Chandra Mohanty, and Kumari Jayawardena's *Nationalism and Feminism in the Third World* (London: Zed Books, 1986).

68. Adrienne Rich, "Notes Toward a Politics of Location," in *Blood, Bread and Poetry* (New York: W. W. Norton, 1986).

69. Editor's comments, *Public Culture* 1, no. 1 (Fall 1988): 1–4.

70. Gayatri Spivak, "Scattered Speculations on the Question of Culture Studies," in *Outside in the Teaching Machine* (New York and London: Routledge, 1993), 255–284.

Chapter 1   Home and Harem:
Domesticity, Gender, and Nationalism

1. George Eliot, *Middlemarch* (1871) (Boston: Houghton, Mifflin, Riverside ed., 1968), 578.

2. Mary Louise Pratt, *Imperial Eyes* (New York and London: Routledge, 1992), 204–205.

3. Massooma R. Ali, "'The Lady of Shalott': a Feminist Reading," in *Woman/Image/Text*, ed. Lola Chatterji (New Delhi: Trianka, 1986), 61.

4. Pratt, *Imperial Eyes*, 213.

5. Rajeshwari Sunder Rajan, "Male Mentors and the Female Imagination: George Eliot's Intellectual Background," in *Women/Image/Text*, 116–132.

6. John Barrell, *The Dark Side of the Landscape* (Cambridge: Cambridge University Press, 1980), 14.

7. Michel Foucault, *Power/Knowledge: Selected Interviews and Other Writings*, ed. Colin Gordon (New York: Pantheon Books, 1980), 152–154.

8. Foucault, *Power/Knowledge*, 153.

9. For more discussion of the panopticon also see the chapter "The Eye of Power" in Foucault, *Power/Knowledge*.

10. Jean Starobinski, *The Invention of Liberty* (Geneva: Albert Skirra, 1964), 101.

11. Jeanne Fahnestock, "The Heroine of Irregular Features: Physiognomy and Conventions of Heroine Description," *Victorian Studies* 24, no. 3 (Spring 1981): 325–350.

12. Francoise Basch, *Relative Creatures* (New York: Schocken Books, 1974), 198.

13. William Acton, *Prostitution* (1857), 2nd ed., abridged and edited by Peter Fryer (London: MacGibbon & Kee, 1968); H. Mayhew, *London Labour and the London Poor* (1861) (New York: Dover Publications, 1968).

14. For more on the debates see my dissertation, "The Political Aesthetic of Victorian Travel," University of California, Berkeley, 1987.

15. Edmund Burke, *A Philosophical Enquiry into the Origin of Our Ideas of the Sublime and the Beautiful* (London: R. and J. Dodsley, 1764).

16. Edmund Burke, *Thoughts and Details on Scarcity*, vols. 1–3 (London: E. Moxon, 1848), 278.

17. Gertrude Himmelfarb, *The Idea of Poverty* (New York: Alfred A. Knopf, 1984), 67.

18. E. J. Hobsbawm, *The Age of Revolution* (New York and Toronto: New American Library, 1962), 284.

19. Burke, *A Philosophical Enquiry*, 14. Further references appear in the text.

20. In Sara Suleri's *The Rhetoric of English India* (Chicago: University of Chicago Press, 1992), on a chapter on "Burke and the Indian Sublime," Suleri argues that for Burke, India as a "catalog of the uncategorizable" embodies the Sublime, and the Sublime was what was "remote and obscure." Since Burke also describes the sublime as what was "great" and was the experience of fear in the face of the unknown and a fear that gave pleasure only if it was distanced, Suleri's view of India as the sublime because it is uncategorizable is problematic. In his definition of the beautiful, Burke sees the female body as deceitful, as a maze that makes the eye giddy; thus there is obscurity even in the beautiful. Such complexities and divergences testify to the attempt to categorize rather than to have an aesthetic that fits, as with India and the sublime. Thus my account examines Burke's conservative will to discipline through aesthetics, an attempt at ordering society that seems to be obscure and unclear at many levels.

21. For a connection between Burke and British cultural studies see Paul Gilroy, "Ethnic Absolutism and Cultural Studies," in *Cultural Studies*, ed. Lawrence Grossberg et al. (New York: Routledge, 1992), 187–198.

22. Suleri, *The Rhetoric*, 43.

23. Ibid., 47.

24. While Suleri's careful readings of Burke on India are much overdue, what is left out is Burke on England, and the connections between the *Reflections on the Revolution in France* and his writing on India. It is also necessary, however, to see how Burke's "anguish" of spectatorship translates into a concern for order, the hierarchy and the defense of the ancien régime. Class conflicts in England must be connected to much of Burke's thinking. Unfortunately, Suleri's "political use of sexuality" empties out the issue of gender and patriarchy by being wholly caught up in the uncertainties of Burke's conceptualizing.

25. Barrell, *The Dark Side*, 4.

26. William Wordsworth, *A Guide Through the District of the Lakes* (1846) (London: Rupert Hart-Davis, 1951). Further references appear in the text.

27. In her *Landscape and Ideology* (Berkeley: University of California Press, 1987), Ann Bermingham argues that the rural idylls which were part of the picturesque showed that the poverty of the poor was unrelated to the rule of the upper class and was caused by nature or fate.

28. Kurt Heinzelman, "The Cult of Domesticity," in *Romanticism and Feminism*, ed. Anne Mellor (Bloomington: Indiana University Press, 1988), 52–78.

29. Marlon Ross, "Romantic Quest and Conquest: Troping Masculine Power in the Crisis of Poetic Identity," in *Romanticism and Feminism*, ed. Anne Mellor (Bloomington: Indiana University Press, 1988), 26–51.

30. William Wordsworth, *The Prelude*, Norton Critical Edition, ed. Jonathan Wordsworth, M. H. Abrams, and Stephen Gill (New York: W. W. Norton, 1979). Book and line numbers appear in the text.

31. Raymond Williams, *The Country and the City* (New York: Oxford University Press, 1973), 151. Williams makes the claim that the change occurs in the 1850 version. However, many anthologies of Wordsworth's poetry show this change as appearing in book 8 of the 1805 *Prelude*.

32. John Barrell, *The Idea of the Landscape and the Sense of Place* (Cambridge: Cambridge University Press, 1972).

33. Andrew Wilton, ed., *Constable's "English Landscape Scenery"* (London: British Museum Prints and Drawings Series, 1979), 24.

34. Ibid.

35. Ibid., 23.

36. Martin Hardie, "Samuel Palmer," in *The Old Water-Colour Society's Club*, vol. 4, ed. Randall Davies (London: 5A Pall Mall, 1927), 36. It is important to note the kinds of interruption that Turner's work caused in this nationalist landscape school.

37. Quoted in Christopher Wood, *Victorian Panorama* (London: Faber, 1976), 222.

38. Besides being a prominent watercolorist, Redgrave was a curator at the

Victoria and Albert Museum as well as responsible for a number of years for the national system of art education.

39. Quoted in Graham Reynolds, *Victorian Painting* (London: The Herbert Press, 1987), 94.

40. John Ruskin, *Modern Painters* (London: Smith, Elder & Co., 1856–60), vol. 1, part 2, sec. 1, chap. 7. Vols. 1 and 2 published in 1843, vols. 3 and 4 in 1856, and vol. 5 in 1860.

41. Ibid.

42. Ibid., part 3, sec. 1, chap. 2.

43. Ibid., chap. 12.

44. Ibid.

45. Ibid., vol. 2, sec. 1, chap. 14.

46. Ibid., part 3, sec. 1, chap. 6.

47. Wilkie Collins, "The Woman in White," in *The Moonstone and The Woman in White* (New York: The Modern Library, 1937), 402.

48. Mrs Gaskell, *Mary Barton* (London: John Lehmann, 1947), 14.

49. Wanda Fraiken Neff, *Victorian Working Women* (New York: Columbia University Press, 1929).

50. Heidi Hartmann, "Capitalism, Patriarchy, and Job Segregation by Sex," in *Classes, Power, and Conflict*, ed. Anthony Giddens and David Held (Berkeley: University of California Press, 1982), 446–469.

51. Judith Walkowitz, *City of Dreadful Delight: Narratives of Sexual Danger in Late-Victorian London* (Chicago: University of Chicago Press, 1992), 19.

52. Ibid., 26–27.

53. Neff, *Victorian*, 13–15.

54. Hartmann, "Capitalism," 459.

55. Charles Dickens, *American Notes* (1842; rpt. Gloucester, Mass.: Peter Smith, 1968), 126.

56. Ibid., 130.

57. Susie Tharu, "Tracing Savitri's Pedigree," in *Recasting Women*, ed. KumKum Sangari and Sudesh Vaid (New Delhi: Kali for Women, 1989), 254–268.

58. Kenneth Ballhatchet, *Race, Sex and Class under the Raj: Imperial Attitudes and Policies and Their Critics, 1793–1905* (New York: St. Martin's Press, 1980).

59. Lata Mani, "Contentious Traditions: The Debate on Sati in Colonial India," in *Recasting Women*, ed. KumKum Sangari and Sudesh Vaid (New Delhi: Kali for Women, 1989), 88–126.

60. W. M. Thackeray, *Notes of a Journey from Cornhill to Grand Cairo*, in *Works*, vol. 11 (1845; rpt. Chicago and New York: Nathaniel Moore, 1910), 3081.

61. *Cook's Tourist's Handbook for Egypt, The Nile and The Desert* (London: Thomas Cook and Son, 1897), 167.

62. Harriet Martineau, *British Rule in India* (London: Smith, Elder & Co.; Bombay: Smith, Taylor & Co., 1857), 4–5.

63. Ibid., 11.

64. Ibid., 6.

65. Ibid., 11.

66. Ibid., 114–115.

67. Ibid., 152.

68. Harriet Martineau, *Eastern Life, Present and Past* (London: Edward Moxon, 1848), vol. 1, 9.

69. Ibid., 55.

70. The present poverty of a large section of the Egyptian population is an indication of the great transfer of wealth to England and the change from the period when Martineau visited Egypt.

71. Rana Kabbani, *Europe's Myths of Orient* (Bloomington: Indiana University Press, 1986), 67–85.

72. Rudyard Kipling, *From Sea to Sea* (1899) (Garden City: Doubleday, 1913), 206.

73. Ibid., 225–227.

74. Quoted in Hugh Ridley, *Images of Imperial Rule* (London: Croom Helm; New York: St. Martin's Press, 1983), 74.

75. Kipling, *From Sea to Sea*, 234.

76. Ibid., 267.

77. Ridley, *Images*, 93.

78. Ibid. See final chapter, "Colonial Theory and Domestic Practice," in which Ridley suggests that colonials such as Kipling returning to Europe brought with them a "particular combination of social radicalism, race-thinking and hostility to socialism," a combination that was a racialized nationalism. I see Kipling as a displaced nationalist who wanted to recreate in the United States what he could not have in England.

79. Kipling, *From Sea to Sea*, 156.

80. Ibid.

81. This homecoming to rural England has been recently recuperated by another writer who was born and grew up in a former colony of England. V. S. Naipaul's *The Enigma of Arrival*, a melancholy record of the end of a writer's journey through life, creates the English landscape as the refuge from the turmoil of a life spent in the awareness of difference between West and East, the civilized and the noncivilized regions of the world. This landscape once again offers harbor and refuge, for in viewing it, Naipaul, like many others before him, elides its socioeconomic reality in order to retain its mythic and idyllic beauty.

82. Barbara Harlow, introduction to Malek Alloula, *The Colonial Harem* (Minneapolis: University of Minnesota Press, 1986), ix–xxii.

83. Montesquieu, *Persian Letters* (1721) Trans. C. J. Betts. (New York: Penguin Books, 1973).

84. Lisa Lowe, *Critical Terrains* (Ithaca: Cornell University Press, 1991), 59.

85. Leila Ahmed, "Western Ethnocentrism and Perceptions of the Harem," *Feminist Studies* 8, no. 3 (1982): 521–534.

86. Alloula's *The Colonial Harem* fully describes such representations even though his nationalist take on the harem and on the female bodies that he represents is quite problematic.

87. Malavika Karlekar, *Voices from Within* (Delhi: Oxford University Press, 1991), 50.

88. Mary Frances Billington, *Women in India* (Delhi: Sri Satguru Publications, 1987). Quoted in Karlekar.

89. Karlekar, *Voices*, 50.

90. Ibid., 58.

91. Madhu Kishwar, "The Daughters of Aryavarta," in *Women in Colonial India*, ed. J. Krishnamurty (Delhi: Oxford University Press, 1989), 78–113.

92. Ester Boserup, *Women's Role in Economic Development* (London: George Allen and Unwin, 1970).

93. Hartmann, "Capitalism," 446.

94. Prem Choudhury, "Customs in a Peasant Economy," in *Recasting Women*, ed. KumKum Sangari and Sudesh Vaid (New Delhi: Kali for Women, 1989), 303–336.

95. K. Saradamoni, "Changing Land Relations and Women: A Case Study of Palghat District, Kerela," in *Women and Rural Transformation*, ed. Rekha Mehra and K. Saradamoni (New Delhi: Concept Pub. Co., 1983). Cited in Margot I. Duley and Mary Edwards, eds., *The Cross-Cultural Study of Women* (New York: The Feminist Press, 1986), 160.

96. Tapan Raychoudhuri, *Europe Reconsidered* (Delhi: Oxford University Press, 1988), 166.

97. Partha Chatterjee, "The Nationalist Resolution of the Women's Question," in *Recasting Women*, ed. KumKum Sangari and Sudesh Vaid (New Delhi: Kali for Women, 1989), 233–253.

98. Mani, "Contentious Traditions," 88–126.

99. Chatterjee, "The Nationalist Resolution," 247.

100. From *Londone Swami Vivekananda*, 3rd ed., 4th rpt., Calcutta, 1977. Quoted in Raychoudhuri, 302.

101. Karlekar, *Voices*, 58.

102. Uma Chakravarty, "Whatever Happened to the Vedic Dasi?" in *Recasting Women*, ed. KumKum Sangari and Sudesh Vaid (New Delhi: Kali for Women, 1989), 53.

103. Tharu, "Tracing Savitri's Pedigree," 254–268.

104. Sumanta Bannerjee, "Marginalization of Women's Popular Culture in Nineteenth Century Bengal," in *Recasting Women*, ed. KumKum Sangari and Sudesh Vaid (New Delhi: Kali for Women, 1989), 127–179.

Chapter 2   Empire and the Movement for
Women's Suffrage in Britain

1. Gayatri Spivak, "Political Economy of Women as Seen by a Literary Critic," in *Coming to Terms: Feminism, Theory, Politics*, ed. Elizabeth Weed (New York and London: Routledge, 1989), 219.

2. Flora Annie Steel, contribution to Marie Corelli and others in *The Modern Marriage Market* (London: Hutchinson, 1898), 95 / 132. Quoted in Hugh Ridley, *Images of Imperial Rule* (New York: St. Martin's Press, 1983), 97.

3. See Caren Kaplan, *Questions of Travel* (Durham: Duke University Press, 1996).

4. Lata Mani, "Multiple Mediations: Feminist Scholarship in the Age of Multinational Reception," *Inscriptions* 5 (1989): 1–24.

5. Josephine Butler, introduction, *Woman's Work and Woman's Culture* ed. Josephine Butler (London: Macmillan and Co., 1869), xxxiv.

6. Ibid., xxxv.

7. Ibid., x.

8. Ibid., xxv, xxviii.

9. Ibid., xix.

10. Ibid., xxi.

11. Antoinette Burton, "The White Woman's Burden," in *Western Women and Imperialism*, ed. Nupur Choudhury and Margaret Strobel (Bloomington: Indiana University Press, 1992), 137–157.

12. Jenny Sharpe, in *Allegories of Empire* (Minneapolis: University of Minnesota Press, 1993), lays out the broad terms of this debate in her chapter on *Jane Eyre*, "The Rise of Women in an Age of Progress," 27–55.

13. Charlotte Brontë, *Jane Eyre* (1847) (London: Penguin Books, 1966), 427, 431.

14. Ibid., 432–433.

15. Ibid.

16. Thanks to Kamala Visweswaran for her useful discussion on this topic.

17. Gayatri Spivak, "Three Women's Texts and a Critique of Imperialism," in *"Race," Writing and Difference*, ed. Henry Louis Gates Jr. (Chicago: University of Chicago Press, 1985).

18. Sharpe, *Allegories of Empire*.

19. Spivak, "Three Women's Texts."

20. John Boyd-Kinnear, "The Social Position of Women in the Present Age," in Butler, *Woman's Work and Woman's Culture*, 355.

21. See Lesley Blanch's *The Wilder Shores of Love* for a highly romanticized and valorized account of Jane Digby, Isabel Burton, Isabelle Eberhardt, and Aimee Dubucq de Rivery. The blurb on the cover says: " 'Seething.' The *New Yorker*."

22. See works by Edward Said, Thomas J. Asaad, Patrick Brantlinger, and Rana Kabbani for analyses of travelers such as Richard F. Burton, Charles Doughty, T. E. Lawrence, and other "explorers."

23. Arthur H. Nethercott, *The Last Four Lives of Annie Besant* (Chicago: University of Chicago Press, 1963), 400.

24. Kamala Visweswaran, "Family Subjects: An Ethnography of the 'Woman Question' in Indian Nationalism" (Ph.D. thesis, Stanford University, 1990).

25. Lucy Middleton, ed., *Women in the Labour Movement: The British Experience* (London: Croom Helm, 1987), 67.

26. Ibid., 76.

27. Constance Rover, *Women's Suffrage and Party Politics in Britain 1866–1914* (London: Routledge and Kegan Paul, 1967), 176.

28. Ibid., 46.

29. Nancy Fix Anderson, *Women against Women in Victorian England* (Bloomington: Indiana University Press, 1987), 192.

30. Ibid., 193.

31. Millicent Fawcett, "The Women's Suffrage Movement," in *The Woman Question in Europe*, ed. Theodore Stanton (London: G. P. Putnam's Sons, 1884), 1–29.

32. See essays in KumKum Sangari and Sudesh Vaid, eds., *Recasting Women* (New Delhi: Kali for Women, 1989).

33. John Stuart Mill, *Principles of Political Economy*, 1848.

34. Candida Ann Lacey, *Barbara Leigh Smith Bodichon and the Langham Place Group* (London and New York: Routledge and Kegan Paul, 1987), 295.

35. Ibid., 337.

36. For more on this topic see Joanna Trollope, *Britannia's Daughters* (London: Hutchinson, 1983).

37. Lacey, *Barbara Leigh Smith Bodichon*, 344.

38. Jessie Boucherett, "How to Provide for Superfluous Women," in Butler, *Woman's Work*, 27–48.

39. Ibid., 30.

40. Ibid., 31.

41. Ibid., 42.

42. Trollope, *Britannia's Daughters*, 124.

43. Ann Laura Stoler, "Rethinking Colonial Categories: European Communities and the Boundaries of Rule," *Comparative Studies in Society and History* 13, no. 1 (1989): 134–161.

44. A forthcoming history of Indian hill stations by Dane Kennedy deals with this imperial discourse.

45. Helen Callaway, *Gender, Culture and Empire: European Women in Colonial Nigeria* (London: Macmillan, 1987), 235–237.

46. Ibid., 240. Though medical work was no doubt of much help, the educational efforts of colonialists must be questioned. Callaway nowhere analyzed the *content* of what was being taught by the educationists and missionaries. Teaching English language and literature to the colonized has to be recognized as an important part of the imposition of colonial rule.

47. Ibid.

48. Boyd-Kinnear, "The Social Position of Women," 331–367.

49. Andrew Rosen, *Rise Up, Women!* (London and Boston: Routledge & Kegan Paul, 1974), 77.

50. Barbara Castle, *Sylvia and Christabel Pankhurst.* (Harmondsworth: Penguin Books Ltd., 1987), 44.

51. Ibid., 56.

52. Ibid., 134.

53. Ibid., 138.

54. Patricia W. Romero, *E. Sylvia Pankhurst* (New Haven: Yale University Press, 1987).

55. Castle, *Sylvia and Christabel Pankhurst*, 144.

56. E. Sylvia Pankhurst, *India and the Earthly Paradise* (1926) (Delhi: B. R. Publishing Corporation, 1985). Further references appear in text.

57. Dea Birkett, *Spinsters Abroad* (London: Basil Blackwell, 1989), 218.

58. Callaway, *Gender*, 167.

59. Birkett, *Spinsters*, 19.

60. It is important to remember that solitude meant being the only European, since these travelers were often accompanied by numbers of native guides and servants. For more on this issue see Mary Louise Pratt, *Imperial Eyes* (New York: Routledge, 1992).

61. Alexander Kinglake, *Eothen* (1844) (Philadelphia: J. B. Lippincott Company, 1912), 86.

62. Birkett, *Spinsters*, 86.

63. Mary Kingsley, *West African Studies* (London: Frank Cass & Co. Ltd., 1964), 310–334.

64. Malek Alloula, *The Colonial Harem* (Minneapolis: University of Minnesota Press, 1986).

65. Revealing the persistence of orientalist tropes of harem life in our time, Joanna Trollope, the author of *Britannia's Daughters*, includes this quote to indicate the "dreary and tawdry reality of harem life." Trollope seems to have internalized the words of Flora Shaw, the subject of her analysis; Trollope, 136.

66. Birkett, *Spinsters*, 167.

67. Dierdre David, *Intellectual Women and Victorian Patriarchy* (London: Macmillan, 1987), 53.

68. Montesquieu's *Persian Letters* is another example of such worlding. There the women in the harem are shown to be rebellious and lying slaves precisely

because the master is a despot and will not give them any freedoms. What is suggested is that the rule of love and freedom will not foster such rebellion, whereas despotism will cause it. Montesquieu is, of course, not talking about women but about the French people.

69. Lacey, *Barbara Leigh Smith Bodichon*.

70. Harriet Martineau, *British Rule in India* (London: Smith, Elder & Co., 1857); *Eastern Life: Present and Past* (London: Edward Moxon, 1848); *Suggestions Toward the Future Government of India* (London: Smith, Elder, 1858).

71. John Lawrence and Audrey Woodiwiss, eds., *The Journals of Honoria Lawrence* (London: Hodder and Stoughton, 1980).

72. Martineau, *Eastern Life: Present and Past*, 284.

73. Ibid., 285.

Chapter 3   The Guidebook and the Museum

1. Homi K. Bhabha, "DissemiNation: Time, Narrative, and the Margins of the Modern Nation," in *Nation and Narration*, ed. Homi K. Bhabha (London and New York: Routledge, 1990), pp. 291–322.

2. See the work of John Barrell on class, ideology, and aesthetics, *The Political Theory of Painting from Reynolds to Hazlitt* (London and New Haven: Yale University Press, 1986).

3. While Pierre Bourdieu's *Distinction* has been central to this project, I am not suggesting upper-class aesthetics to be the dominant form that imposes itself without resistance to it.

4. John Mackenzie, ed., *Imperialism and Popular Culture* (Manchester: Manchester University Press, 1986), 9; *Propaganda and Empire* (Manchester: Manchester University Press, 1984).

5. Harriet Martineau, *British Rule in India* (London: Smith, Elder & Co., 1857), 4–5, in the year of the Indian Mutiny, desires the British public to learn about Anglo-India in order to participate in its government. All of Richard F. Burton's writings contain the same plea. Many travelogues were written with this intention and their popularity indicates that the aim may have been successful. Much recent historiography has focused on this issue of imperialism and its study of "native" cultures. Two works on this broad topic that I have cited in earlier chapters are Edward Said's *Orientalism* and Lata Mani's "Contentious Traditions" in *Recasting Women*. Two other works are Bernard Cohn's essays on British in India in *The Anthropologist among the Historians* (Delhi: Oxford University Press, 1987), and Javed Majeed's *Ungoverned Imaginings* (Oxford: Clarendon Press, 1992).

6. Pierre Bourdieu, *Distinction* (Cambridge, Mass.: Harvard University Press, 1984), 7.

7. Pierre Bourdieu, *Outline of a Theory of Practice* (Cambridge: Cambridge University Press, 1977).

8. Thomas Richards, *The Commodity Culture of Victorian England: Advertising and Spectacle, 1851–1914* (Stanford: Stanford University Press, 1990), 40.

9. Timothy Mitchell, "Orientalism and the Exhibitory Order," in *Colonialism and Culture*, ed. Nicholas B. Dirks (Ann Arbor: University of Michigan Press, 1992), 289–318.

10. Matthew Arnold, *On the Study of Celtic Literature and Other Essays* (New York: Dutton, 1976).

11. Matthew Arnold, *Culture and Anarchy*, ed. Ian Gregor (Indianapolis: Bobbs-Merrill Educational Publishing, 1971).

12. Ibid., 170.

13. Arnold, *Celtic Literature*, 187.

14. Benedict Anderson, *Imagined Communities*, rev. ed. (New York: Verso, 1991); section on "The Museum," 178–185.

15. Mitchell, "Orientalism and the Exhibitory Order," 299.

16. For a greater description of sexual practices at "home" and in the "raj" see Ronald Hyam, *Empire and Sexuality: The British Experience* (Manchester and New York: Manchester University Press, 1990).

17. I have addressed the issue of disguise and costume in my dissertation, "The Political Aesthetic of Victorian Travel." Also see Marjorie Garber's work on cross-dressing, *Vested Interests: Cross-Dressing and Cultural Anxiety* (New York: Routledge, 1992).

18. In contrast with this demarcation of women and "native," Marianna Torgovnik comments that Margaret Mead left behind many photographs of herself in "native" garb, while no photos of Malinowski show him without Western clothes (*Gone Primitive* [Chicago: University of Chicago Press, 1990], 228). Torgovnik makes the point that "going primitive" as "getting physical" was not possible for European men within the conceptions of "controlled individualism and masculinity" (229).

19. See Lisa Bloom, *Gender on Ice* (Minneapolis: University of Minnesota Press, 1993), for an excellent analysis of connection between masculinity and exploration.

20. Richard Francis Burton, *Personal Narrative of a Pilgrimage to Al-Madinah and Mecca*. Reprint of 1893 Memorial Ed. in 2 vols. (New York: Dover Publications Inc.), 1964.

21. For more on this aspect of travel see Edward Said's *Orientalism*; Thomas J. Asaad, *Three Victorian Travellers* (London: Routledge and Kegan Paul, 1964); Robin Bidwell, *Travellers in Arabia* (London: Hamlyn, 1976).

22. Alfred Bates Richard and St. Clare Baddeley, *A Sketch of the Career of Richard F. Burton* (London: Waterlow & Sons Ltd., 1886), 4.

23. See F. M. Brodie, *The Devil Drives: A Life of Richard F. Burton* (New York: W. W. Norton, 1967, 1971).

24. Ali Behdad, *Belated Travelers* (Durham and London: Duke University Press, 1994).

25. Harriet Martineau, *Eastern Life: Present and Past* (London: Edward Moxon, 1848), vol. I, 55.

26. John Murray, *A Handbook for Travellers in Egypt* (London: John Murray, 1858), 7.

27. *Cook's Tourist's Handbook for Egypt* (London: Thomas Cook and Son, 1897), 4.

28. John Murray, *The Imperial Guide to India* (London: John Murray, 1904), 5.

29. For a detailed explanation of this problematic distinction see Caren Kaplan's *Questions of Travel* (Durham: Duke University Press, 1996).

30. Susan Stewart suggests this metonymic value as an important aspect of the museum collection in *On Longing* (Baltimore: Johns Hopkins University Press, 1984), 162–165.

31. Edward Said, *Orientalism* (New York: Vintage Books, 1979).

32. Ali Behdad also mentions this point in *Belated Travelers*, 36.

33. W. A. B. Coolidge, *Swiss Travel and Swiss Guide-Books* (London: Longmans, Green & Co., 1889), 76.

34. Behdad, *Belated Travelers*; see chapter 2, "From Travelogue to Tourist Guide: The Orientalist as Sightseer."

35. For more on the contemporary manifestation of this Romantic search in the United States as it pertains to gender issues, see James Clifford, *The Predicament of Culture* (Cambridge: Harvard University Press, 1988), and Torgovnik's *Gone Primitive*.

36. Mary Louise Pratt, in *Imperial Eyes* (New York: Routledge, 1992), points out that Romantic impulses could also have emerged from shifts in relations between Europe and the Americas, and the contacts with various peoples emerging from travels and "contact zones" such that Romanticism cannot be seen as a movement that Europeans "invent from within" (137). Pratt's point is well taken; however, even as I see that picturesque as a means to come to terms with, that is, domesticate, what seems alien, Romanticism is a movement entwined in nineteenth-century England not only with, for instance, orientalist studies, but also with the class conflict within England.

37. On the topic of the picturesque see W. J. Hipple, *The Beautiful, the Sublime and the Picturesque in Eighteenth Century British Aesthetic Theory* (Carbondale: University of Illinois Press, 1957), and Christopher Hussey, *The Picturesque: Studies in a Point of View* (London: Putnam, 1927).

38. Uvedale Price, *An Essay on the Picturesque as Compared with the Sublime and the Beautiful* (London: J. Robson, 1842); Richard Payne Knight, *The Landscape, a Didactic Poem in Three Books Addressed to Uvedale Price* (London:

W. Bulmer & Co., 1794); William Gilpin, *Three Essays: On Picturesque Beauty; On Picturesque Travel; and on Sketching Landscape* (London: Printed for R. Blamire, 1803); Humphrey Repton, *An Enquiry into the Changes of Taste in Landscape Gardening* (London: J. Taylor, 1806).

39. The connections between this notion of variety and contemporary ideas of multiculturalism are interesting to consider.

40. For more discussion on this use of the picturesque, see my Ph.D. dissertation, "The Political Aesthetic of Victorian Travel." For more on the political nature of aesthetics see Barrell, *The Political Theory of Painting*. For more discussions on the picturesque and India see Partha Mitter, *Much-Maligned Monsters* (Oxford: Clarendon Press, 1977); Sara Suleri, *The Rhetoric of English India* (Chicago: University of Chicago Press, 1992), chapter 2, "The Feminine Picturesque," 75–110; and Bernard Cohn, "The Past in the Present: India as Museum of Mankind," unpublished paper.

41. Barrell, *Political Theory*, 13.

42. Stephen Copley, ed., *Literature and the Social Order* (London: Croom Helm, 1984), 6–7.

43. Gilpin, *Three Essays*, 13.

44. Price, *An Essay*, 19.

45. William Wordsworth, *A Guide Through the District of the Lakes* (1846) (London: Rupert Hart-Davis, 1951), 55.

46. Ibid.

47. Ibid.

48. Other guidebooks to the Lake District were written following the great success of Wordsworth's. One such was written by Harriet Martineau. This guidebook, called simply *The English Lakes*, went through three editions; it described views, as had Wordsworth's, and mapped the Lake District with the tourist geography of tours and walks. In addition, it catered to the Victorian interest in the scientific study of nature with an appendix containing meteorological, botanical, and geological details of the area. Interestingly, Martineau's Lake District is a middle-class idyll (27) of economic potential; she erases the poor and the rural folk, whom Wordsworth sees as picturesque. Thus she says, "There can hardly be a safer or more profitable investment than cottage building here, for a good dwelling is as convertible a property as a banknote." With the building of railway lines into the region, people from a "more enlightened region" (27) could improve the area. Harriet Martineau, *A Complete Guide to the English Lakes* (Windermere: J. Garnett; London: Whittaker, 1855).

49. John Murdoch, *The Discovery of the Lake District* (Grasmere: Trustees of Dove Cottage, 1982), 25.

50. Ibid., 28.

51. For a detailed development of this trope see Clifford, *The Predicament of Culture*; also see Torgovnik, *Gone Primitive*.

52. For more on Wordsworth's politics see Roger Sales, *English Literature in History 1780–1830* (New York: St. Martin's Press, 1983), esp. the chapter entitled "William Wordsworth and the Real Estate," 52–68.

53. T. D. Fosbroke, *The Tourist's Grammar* (London: John Nichols & Son, 1826).

54. Ibid., iii.

55. Bernard Cohn, "The Past in the Present: India as Museum of Mankind," 19.

56. Quoted in Judith Walkowitz, *City of Dreadful Delight: Narratives of Sexual Danger in Late-Victorian London* (Chicago: University of Chicago Press, 1992), 26–27.

57. John Barrell, *The Dark Side of the Landscape* (Cambridge: Cambridge University Press, 1980), 5.

58. Walkowitz, *City of Dreadful Delight*, 27.

59. Ann Bermingham, *Landscape and Ideology* (Berkeley: University of California Press, 1987).

60. Thomas Wright, *Some Habits and Customs of the Working Classes, By a Journeyman Engineer* (London: Tinsley Brothers, 1867), 110–111.

61. Samuel Smiles, *A Publisher and his Friends* (London: J. Murray, 1891), vol. 2, 151.

62. Ibid., 459.

63. Jon Klancher, *The Making of English Reading Audiences* (Madison: University of Wisconsin Press, 1987).

64. John Murray IV, *John Murray III, 1808–1892, A Brief Memoir* (London: J. Murray, 1919), 42.

65. M. M. Bakhtin, *The Dialogic Imagination*, trans. Caryl Emerson and Michael Holquist (Austin: University of Texas Press, 1981).

66. Ali Behdad, *Belated Travelers*, 40–41.

67. Murray, *A Brief Memoir*, 42.

68. Stewart, *On Longing*, 164.

69. *A Guide to the Beauties of the British Museum* (London: Thomas and George Underwood, 1826); further references to this work, cited as 1826, appear in the text.

70. Richard Altick, *The English Common Reader* (Chicago: University of Chicago Press, 1957), 266.

71. Ed Cohen, *Talk on the Wilde Side* (New York: Routledge, 1993), 20.

72. Stewart, *On Longing*, 164–166.

73. It is still taken to be value-free. There are very few readings of the guidebooks in current scholarship. Susan Stewart's *On Longing*, which is so useful on the collection, has very little to say about the catalogue or the museum guide. Barthes's very brief piece on "The Blue Guide" in *Mythologies* is an exception.

74. Stewart, *On Longing*, 158.

75. See Martin Bernal, *Black Athena* (New Brunswick, N.J.: Rutgers University Press, 1987).

76. It is important to consider how new ways of objectifying bodies, especially female ones, emerge with the aesthetic of the fragments of these statues.

77. Sculpture in the Greek style was also popular and replicated the gendered and racial aesthetic; Hiram Powers's *The Slave Girl*, which was exhibited in the Great Exhibition of 1851, was the statue of a naked Greek girl with chained wrists, which suggested that she was being sold into a Turkish harem. Elizabeth Barrett Browning wrote a sonnet praising its "passionless perfection." For more on the Greek heritage also see Fani Maria Tsigakou, *The Rediscovery of Greece* (London: Thames and Hudson, 1981).

78. Said, *Orientalism*.

79. Bernal, *Black Athena*, vol. 1.

80. Joseph Mordaunt Crook, *The British Museum* (London: Lane, 1972).

81. Charles Knight, *The Old Printer and the Modern Press* (London: J. Murray, 1854), 307.

82. Peter Bailey, *Leisure and Class in Victorian England: Rational Recreation and the Contest for Control, 1830–1885* (London: Routledge, 1978).

83. J. A. Mangan, " 'The Grit of our Forefathers': Invented Tradition, Propaganda and Imperialism," in *Imperialism and Popular Culture*, ed. John Mackenzie (Manchester: Manchester University Press, 1986), 113–139; Penny Summerfield, "Patriotism and Empire: Music-Hall Entertainment," in *Imperialism and Popular Culture*, 17–48.

84. Thomas Hodgskin, *Mechanics Magazine*, 11 October, 1823. In Patricia Hollis, *Class and Conflict in Nineteenth-Century England, 1815–1850* (London and Boston: Routledge and Kegan Paul, 1973).

85. Richard Johnson, "Really Useful Knowledge: Radical Education and Working-Class Culture," in *Working-Class Culture*, ed. J. Clarke, C. Critchen, and Richard Johnson (New York: St. Martin's Press, 1979), 76–88.

86. Altick, *The English Common Reader*, 190.

87. J. M. Golby and A. W. Purdue, *The Civilization of the Crowd* (London: Batsford Academic and Educational, 1984), 93.

88. Marjorie Caygill, *The Story of the British Museum* (London: British Museum Publications, 1981), 25.

89. W. H. Boulton, *The Romance of the British Museum* (London: Low, Marston, 1931), 12.

90. B. Harrison, "Teetotal Chartism," *History* 58 (1973): 197.

91. Kenneth Hudson, *A Social History of Museums* (London: Macmillan, 1975), 10.

92. *Minutes of Evidence Taken before the Select Committee on the Condition, Management and Affairs of the British Museum* (1835), 99.

93. Ibid., 100.

94. Ibid., 81.

95. Altick, *The English Common Reader*, 192.

96. G. Long, *The British Museum: Egyptian Antiquities*, The Library of Entertaining Knowledge (London: Charles Knight, 1832), vol. 1, 5; further references to this work, cited as 1832, will appear in the text.

97. Bernard Cohn, "The Transformation of Objects into Artifacts, Antiquities and Art in 19th Century India," unpublished ms.

98. Though I include the explorers with the collectors, the latter were still the patrons of the former. For instance, Giovanni Belzoni, who was responsible for the excavations of the pyramids at Giza, was funded by Sir Henry Salt, the English consul-general in Egypt, who then became the owner of the artifacts that Belzoni discovered. Many of the collectors were men of rank who, like Sir William Hamilton, were in influential government positions abroad where they could obtain local artifacts and had enough money to make their own classical collections.

99. Henry Ellis, *Elgin & Phigaleian Marbles of Classical Ages*, The Library of Entertaining Knowledge (London: Charles Knight, 1846); *The Townley Marbles*, The Library of Entertaining Knowledge (London: Charles Knight, 1848). All further references to these works will be cited in the text as 1846 and 1848.

100. This idea of ideology from Marx's *The German Ideology* is described by Juliet Mitchell in *Women's Estate* (New York: Random House-Vintage, 1973).

101. Crook, *The British Museum*, 90–91.

102. From the *Minutes of Evidence Taken before the Select Committee on the Condition, Management and Affairs of the British Museum*, 1835.

103. Richards, *The Commodity Culture*, 3–5.

104. Robert Rydell, *All the World's a Fair: Visions of Empire at American International Expositions, 1876–1916* (Chicago: University of Chicago Press, 1984).

105. See Edmund Swinglehurst, *The Romantic Journey* (New York: Harper & Row, 1974). Swinglehurst comments that this tour fulfilled James Cook's best ambitions: "to bring travel to people, to stimulate desire for learning and to make them aware of the glorious future which the Great Exhibition presaged" (35).

106. Crook, *The British Museum*, 196.

107. Ibid., 90.

108. Johnson, "Really Useful Knowledge," 95.

109. Hudson, *A Social History*, 42.

110. Richards, *The Commodity Culture*, 54.

111. Ibid., 108–109.

112. Ibid., 134.

113. Walkowitz, *City*, 45.

114. *The British Museum in Four Sections or, How to View the Whole at Once*,

The New Library of Useful Knowledge (London: Cradock & Co., 1852); further references to this book appear in the text as 1852.

115. The 1985 BBC series (also an exhibition at the National Gallery) called *The Treasure Houses of Britain* does exactly the reverse. It reeducates the British public about the glories of the English aristocracy by taking the viewers back into the houses of the wealthy and showing them the art and artifacts within.

116. Richards, *The Commodity Culture*, 19.

117. Walkowitz, *City*, 69.

118. Stewart, *On Longing*, 156.

119. Walkowitz, *City*, 47.

120. Comment by a John Wade, recorded in E. P. Thompson's *The Making of the English Working Class* (New York: Vintage Books, 1963), 416.

121. Walkowitz, *City*, 46.

122. Walkowitz, *City*, 48.

123. Nupur Choudhury, "Shawls, Jewelry, Curry, and Rice in Victorian Britain," in *Western Women and Imperialism*, ed. Nupur Choudhury and Margaret Strobel (Bloomington: Indiana University Press, 1992), 231–246.

124. Walkowitz, *City*, 53.

125. William Morris, *News from Nowhere and Selected Writings and Designs* (Hammondsworth: Penguin, 1984), 143.

126. Ibid., 123.

127. Ibid., 96.

128. Charles Hercules Read and Ormonde Maddock Dalton, *Antiquities from the City of Benin* (London: British Museum, 1899), 4.

129. Ibid.

130. E. Maude Thompson, *A Guide to the British Museum* (London: Trustees of the British Museum, 1890), xi.

131. John Russell, chief art critic of the *New York Times*, writes in the *New York Times Magazine* of June 2, 1985, that "art is everywhere in India, if we know how to look." Rejecting any Indian idea of art or beauty, Russell appreciates India in moments of epiphany when he can see "a private India, a confidential India and an alternative India." Proving that he still thinks he can turn dust to gold, Russell writes that art "is just there [in India], in the air, on the ground, all over the place, for the taking, and no name attached to it."

132. The Victoria and Albert Museum even at the present time vividly brings back England's imperial past.

133. The British Museum is now a journey into the past of all the cultures of the world. As one popular guidebook (*Let's Go: The Budget Guide to Britain and Ireland*, ed. Teresa Twivey [New York: St. Martin's Press, 1985], 115) says: "it is the closest thing this planet has to a complete record of its civilizations." The British Museum is popularly considered the historian of the world.

134. Ibid., 64.

*Chapter 4 The Culture of Travel and the Gendering
of Colonial Modernity in Nineteenth-Century India*

1. Roberto Schwartz, *Misplaced Ideas* (London: Verso, 1992), 16.

2. Sudipta Kaviraj, *The Imaginary Institution of India* (New Delhi: Teen Murti Publications, Nehru Memorial Museum and Library, 1991; 2d series, no. 42, August), subsequently reprinted in *Subaltern Studies 7*; and *On the Construction of Colonial Power: Structure, Discourse, Hegemony* (New Delhi: Teen Murti Publications, 2d series, no. 35, February 1991).

3. Kaviraj, *The Imaginary Institution of India*. Subsequent quotes from Kaviraj are from this essay.

4. An initial work on this topic is Ghulam Murshid's *Reluctant Debutante* (Rajshahi: Rajshahi University, 1983). Critiques of this approach are found in Sumit Sarkar's "The Woman Question in Nineteenth-Century Bengal," in *Women and Culture*, ed. KumKum Sangari and Sudesh Vaid (Bombay: SNDT Women's University, 1985), and Partha Chatterjee, "The Nationalist Resolution of the Women's Question," in *Recasting Women*, ed. KumKum Sangari and Sudesh Vaid (New Delhi: Kali for Women, 1989), 233–253.

5. Kaviraj, *On the Construction of Colonial Power*, 66.

6. Tani Barlow, editor's introduction, *positions* 1, no. 1 (Spring 1993): vi.

7. Dipesh Chakrabarty, "The Difference-Defferal of (A) Colonial Modernity: Public Debates on Domesticity in British Bengal," *History Workshop Journal* 36 (1993).

8. Lisa Lowe, *Critical Terrains* (Ithaca: Cornell University Press, 1991), 60n.

9. The Romantic connection with exploration and empire has been mentioned quite often, for instance by Edward Said in *Orientalism*. I developed this connection at length in my dissertation, "The Political Aesthetic of Victorian Travel," Berkeley, 1987. Works that connect travel and the English Romantics (but do not mention politics or empire) are Charles Norton Coe, *Wordsworth and the Literature of Travel* (New York: Bookman Associates, 1953); John Livingston Lowes, *The Road to Xanadu* (Boston and New York: Houghton, Mifflin, 1927); James M. Osborn, "Travel Literature and the Rise of Neo-Hellenism in England," in *Literature as a Mode of Travel*, ed. Paul Fussel Jr. (New York: New York Public Library, 1963).

10. John Clubbe and Earnest J. Lovell Jr., *English Romanticism* (Dekalb: Northern Illinois University Press, 1983).

11. Schwartz, *Misplaced Ideas*, see chapter 1, 1–18.

12. Gayatri Chakravorty Spivak, *The Post-Colonial Critic*, ed. Sarah Harasym (New York and London: Routledge, 1990), 126.

13. See for instance, KumKum Sangari and Sudesh Vaid, eds., *Recasting Women* (New Delhi: Kali for Women, 1989).

14. Pramatha Nath Bose, *History of Hindu Civilization during British Rule*, 105.

15. Bose, *History*, 106.

16. Rozina Visram, *Ayahs, Lascars and Princes: The Story of Indians in Britain 1700–1947* (London: Pluto Press, 1986).

17. For instance see Amitav Ghosh, *In an Antique Land* (New York: Vintage Books, 1992), who attempts to trace the movements of a slave, Bomma, from Mangalore to Egypt.

18. See *Ibn Battuta: Travels in Asia and Africa*, trans. and selected by H. A. R. Gibb (New Delhi: Saeed International, rpt. 1990); Edward Sachau, ed., *Alberuni's India* (New Delhi: Atlantic Publishers, rpt. 1989).

19. C. A. Bayly, *Rulers, Townsmen and Bazaars* (Cambridge: Cambridge University Press, 1983).

20. Himani Bannerji, "The Mirror of Class," *Economic and Political Weekly* (May 13, 1989): 1041–1051.

21. Pradip Sinha, *Nineteenth-Century Bengal* (Calcutta: Firma K. L. Mukhopadhyay, 1965), 5.

22. Ibid., Appendix C, 158.

23. Visram, *Ayahs, Lascars and Princes*.

24. For careful examination of the classes and castes affected by English education in Bengal see Sinha, *Nineteenth-Century Bengal*, especially the chapter entitled "English Education—A Study in Rural Response."

25. Gauri Viswanathan, *Masks of Conquest* (New York: Columbia University Press, 1989), 134.

26. Kaviraj, *The Imaginary Institution of India*, 103.

27. Harish Trivedi, in "Reading English, Writing Hindi: English Literature and Indian Creative Writing," in *Rethinking English*, ed. Svati Joshi (New Delhi: Trianka, 1991), 181–205, argues that Viswanathan, influenced by Said, focuses more on "the orientalizing notions and mental constructs of some assorted British administrators than on the reality on the ground, on not what in fact happened (to Indians) but instead on what was proposed or sought to be done (by the British)." While his point that focus on the British is not enough is certainly well taken, it is important not to see British discourse as unreal in comparison with an Indian "reality on the ground" that is subversive or contestatory. Such a dichotomy does not deal with the notion of hegemony in the colonial context.

28. Meenakshi Mukherjee, *Realism and Reality* (Delhi: Oxford University Press, 1985), 46.

29. Ibid.

30. Behramji Malabari, *The Indian Eye on English Life* (London: A. Constable, 1893); *Gujarat and the Gujaratis*, 3d ed. (1889; rpt. New Delhi: Mittal Publications, 1983); Bholanath Chandra, *The Travels of a Hindoo to Various Parts of Bengal and Upper India* (London: N. Trubner & Co., 1869); Devendra N. Das, *Sketches of Hindoo Life* (London: Chapman and Hall, 1887). For analysis of

nationalism and colonialism see Partha Chatterjee, *Nationalist Thought and the Colonial World* (Tokyo, 1986; rpt. Minneapolis: University of Minnesota Press, 1993).

31. Harish Trivedi, "Reading English, Writing Hindi: English Literature and Indian Creative Writing," in *Rethinking English*, ed. Svati Joshi (New Delhi: Trianka, 1991), 181–205.

32. Homi K. Bhabha, "Of Mimicry and Man: The Ambivalence of Colonial Discourse," *October* 28 (Spring 1984): 125–133.

33. Schwartz, *Misplaced Ideas.*

34. Partha Chatterjee, *The Nation and Its Fragments* (Princeton: Princeton University Press, 1993).

35. Meera Kosambi, "Girl-Brides and Socio-Legal Change," *Economic and Political Weekly* (August 3–10, 1991): 1857–1868.

36. John B. Alphonse-Karkala, *Indo-English Literature in the Nineteenth Century* (Mysore: The Literary Half-Yearly, University of Mysore, 1970), 56–57.

37. Quoted in Kosambi, "Girl-Brides," 1858.

38. Ibid.

39. Behramji Malabari, cited in Dayaram Gidumal, *Behramji M. Malabari: A Biographical Sketch* (London: T. Fisher Unwin, 1892), 198.

40. Ibid.

41. In Dayaram Gidumal, *Behramji M. Malabari*, 250–251.

42. Malabari, *The Indian Eye on English Life*, 7.

43. Behramji Malabari, speech delivered at Jaipur on May 5, 1882, cited in Gidumal, *Behramji M. Malabari*, 160–161.

44. Ibid., 198.

45. Kosambi, "Girl-Brides," 1858.

46. My thanks to Ambra Pirri for clearing up the issue of whether Nightingale had even been to India.

47. Gidumal, *Behramji M. Malabari*, i.

48. Ibid., vii.

49. Uma Chakravarty, "Whatever Happened to the Vedic Dasi?" in *Recasting Women*, ed. KumKum Sangari and Sudesh Vaid (New Delhi: Kali for Women, 1989), 27–87.

50. Viswanathan, *Masks of Conquest.*

51. Malabari, *Indian Eye*, 1.

52. Malabari, in *Indian Spectator* (July 1, 1988): 411. Quoted in Gidumal, *Behramji M. Malabari*, 149.

53. Renato Rosaldo, *Culture and Truth* (Boston: Beacon Press, 1989), 68–87.

54. Dean MacCannell, *The Tourist* (New York: Schocken Books, 1976), 30–31.

55. Malabari, *Indian Eye*, 1–2.

56. Malabari, in *Indian Spectator*, quoted in Gidumal, *Behramji M. Malabari.*

57. Ibid.

58. Ibid.

59. In a letter to Malabari, Muller writes that one of his goals is to correct the ideas of "your half-Europeanized youths" who despise their own religions. Letter to Malabari quoted in Gidumal, *Behramji M. Malabari*, 159.

60. Ibid.

61. Bankimchandra Chatterji, "Letters on Hinduism," in *Bankim Racanabali*, ed. Hogesh Chandra Bagal (Calcutta: Sahitya Sansad, 1969), 230.

62. Chatterjee, *The Nation and Its Fragments*, 136. What is surprising in this work is Chatterjee's aesthetic judgments on Bankim's work, in disregard of the connections between canons and ideology, calling him "the most brilliant rationalist essayist of the time." The centrality given to Bankim's work in much recent historiography of India that is published in the United States no doubt comes from postcolonial critiques of communalism and nationalism, but the emphasis on writers such as Bankim and on the history of the Bengali upper class leaves much to be desired in terms of understanding the politics of nationalism as its "DissemiNation" (in Homi Bhabha's understanding of this phenomenon).

63. Chandra, *Travels of a Hindoo* (London: N. Trübner & Co., 1869), dedication.

64. Ibid., 165.

65. Ibid., 4.

66. Ibid., 164.

67. Ibid., 108.

68. MacCannell, *The Tourist*, 3.

69. J. Talboys Wheeler, introduction, *Travels of a Hindoo*, by Bholanath Chandra, xi.

70. For more on this issue see Marianna Torgovnik, *Gone Primitive* (Chicago: University of Chicago Press, 1990). For a discussion of travel and "native" dress, see my dissertation, "The Political Aesthetic of Victorian Travel," University of California, Berkeley, 1987. Also on native dress and cross-dressing see Marjorie Garber, *Vested Interests: Cross-Dressing and Cultural Anxiety* (New York: Routledge, 1992), 304–352.

71. Chatterjee, "The Nationalist Resolution."

72. Meredith Borthwick, *The Changing Role of Women in Bengal 1849–1905* (Princeton: Princeton University Press, 1984), 239.

73. Murshid, *Reluctant Debutante*, 82–88.

74. Borthwick, *The Changing Role*, 231.

75. Ibid., 232.

76. Surendra Bhana, *Indentured Indian Emigrants to Natal* (New Delhi: Promilla & Co., 1991).

77. Brij V. Lal, "Kunti's Cry: Indentured Women on Fiji Plantations," in

Women in Colonial India, ed. J. Krishnamurty (Delhi: Oxford University Press, 1989), 163–179.

78. Rokeya Sakhawat Hossain, *Inside Seclusion: The Avarodhbasini of Rokeya Sakhawat Hossain*, ed. and trans. Roshan Jahan (Dacca: Women for Women, 1981).

79. In fact, my mother repeated this narrative to me in telling me of her fears of traveling alone in the 1930s and 1940s.

80. My thanks to Parama Roy for bringing up this point.

81. Uma Chakravarty, "Cultural Identity, Notions of Womanhood and Feminist Consciousness in a Postcolonial Society," unpublished paper cited in Amrita Chhachhi, "Forced Identities: The State, Communalism, Fundamentalism and Women in India," in *Women, Islam and the State*, ed. Deniz Kandiyoti (Philadelphia: Temple University Press, 1991), 155.

82. Borthwick, *The Changing Role*, 236.

83. Ibid., 235.

84. Usha Chakraborty, *Condition of Bengali Women around the 2nd Half of the 19th Century* (Calcutta: n.p., 1963).

85. Ibid. Universities in India opened their degrees to women earlier than in England. Madras University had women candidates in 1876, Calcutta University in 1878, and the University of London in 1879.

86. Sumanta Banerjee, "Marginalization of Women's Popular Culture in Nineteenth Century Bengal," in *Recasting Women*, ed. KumKum Sangari and Sudesh Vaid (New Delhi: Kali for Women, 1989), 160.

87. Such attitudes persist. Charles Skilton, in a preface to a collection of her poems, says, "That a young girl should have so well mastered English, and even more especially French, as so mellifluously to translate into two languages neither of which was her native tongue, is little short of miraculous" (preface, *A Slender Sheaf Gleaned in French and English Fields* by Toru Dutt [Edinburgh: The Fortune Press, 1977]).

88. Quoted in Skilton's preface.

89. Toru Dutt, "Bianca, or The Young Spanish Maid," *The Indian Field* (Calcutta) (January–April 1878); *Le Journal de Mademoiselle d'Arvers*, ed. Clarisse Bader (Paris: Didier, Library Academique, 1879).

90. Harihar Das, *Life and Letters of Toru Dutt* (London: Oxford University Press, 1921), 222. All further citations appear in the text.

91. Badri Raina, "A Note on Language and the Politics of English in India," in *Rethinking English*, ed. Svati Joshi (New Delhi: Trianka, 1991), 264–279.

92. Chatterjee, *Nationalist Thought and the Colonial World*.

93. Susie Tharu, "Tracing Savitri's Pedigree," in *Recasting Women*, ed. KumKum Sangari and Sudesh Vaid (New Delhi: Kali for Women, 1989), 254–268.

94. James Mill, *The History of British India*, ed. John Clive (Chicago: University of Chicago Press, 1975).

95. Chakravarty, "Whatever Happened to the Vedic Dasi?" 60.

96. Tharu, "Tracing Savitri's Pedigree," 260.

97. Ibid.

98. Krishnabhabini Das, "Englande Banga Mahila." Quoted in Murshid, *Reluctant Debutante*, 85–86.

99. Borthwick, *The Changing Role*, 45.

100. Padmini Sengupta, *Pioneer Women of India* (Bombay: Thacker, 1944).

101. A recent work that focuses on the "peripatetic" in England, especially in regard to Romantic ideology, is Anne D. Wallace, *Walking Literature and English Culture* (Oxford: Clarendon Press, 1993).

102. John Elder, *Imagining the Earth: Poetry and the Vision of Nature* (Urbana and Chicago: University of Illinois Press, 1985), 93, 97.

103. Wallace, *Walking*, 12.

104. My thanks to Parama Roy for this last point and for her discussion on this divide.

105. Borthwick, *The Changing Role*, 238.

106. Toru Dutt, "Our Casuarina Tree," *A Slender Sheaf Gleaned in French and Indian Fields* (1876), ed. Charles Skilton (Rpt. Edinburgh: The Fortune Press, 1977).

107. Quoted in Sengupta, *Pioneer Women*, 27.

108. Viswanathan, 140.

Chapter 5 Pandita Ramabai and Parvati Athavale: Homes for Women, Feminism, and Nationalism

1. Rachel Bodley, introduction, *The High-Caste Hindu Woman*, by Pandita Ramabai Saraswati (Philadelphia: n.p., 1888).

2. Rosalind O'Hanlon, "Issues of Widowhood: Gender and Resistance in Colonial Western India," in *Contesting Power*, ed. Douglas Haynes and Gyan Prakash (Delhi: Oxford University Press, 1991), 62–108.

3. Tarabai Shinde, *A Comparison Between Women and Men*, trans. and ed. Rosalind O'Hanlon, in *A Comparison Between Women and Men: Tarabai Shinde and the Critique of Gender Relation in Colonial India* (Madras: Oxford University Press, 1994).

4. Ibid.

5. Joanna Liddle and Rama Joshi, *Daughters of Independence: Gender, Class and Caste in India* (Delhi: Kali for Women, 1986), 40.

6. Partha Chatterjee, "The Nationalist Resolution of the Women's Question," in *Recasting Women*, ed. KumKum Sangari and Sudesh Vaid (New Delhi: Kali for Women, 1989), 233–253.

7. Uma Chakravarty, "The Myth of 'Patriots' and 'Traitors': Pandita Ramabai, Brahmanical Patriarchy, and Militant Hindu Nationalism," in *Gender, Class, and Nation: The Life and Times of Pandita Ramabai* (New Delhi: Kali for Women Press, forthcoming).

8. Accounts of this early part of her life are available in her own words in *A Testimony* (Kedgaon: Mukti Mission, 1917). Additional accounts, most of them based on her book, are available in Padmini Sengupta's *Pandita Ramabai Saraswati: Her Life and Work* (London: Asia Publishing House, 1970); Helen Dyer, *Pandita Ramabai: The Story of Her Life* (London: Morgan and Scott, 1900); Nicol Macnicol, *Pandita Ramabai* (Calcutta: Association Press, 1926).

9. Uma Chakravarty, "Whatever Happened to the Vedic Dasi?" in *Recasting Women*, 67.

10. Ramabai, 5, 6.

11. Sengupta, 69.

12. Uma Chakravarty, "Whatever Happened to the Vedic Dasi?" in *Recasting Women*, 66. Ramabai's subsequent participation in women's culture is relevant here.

13. Macnicol, *Pandita Ramabai*, 57.

14. Meera Kosambi, "Women, Emancipation and Equality," *Economic and Political Weekly* (October 29, 1988): WS38–WS49.

15. Macnicol, *Pandita Ramabai*, 58.

16. Bodley, introduction, xiii.

17. For an extended discussion of this concept formulated by Sudipta Kaviraj, see the previous chapter.

18. Tani Barlow has written about this emergence of the category "woman" in China in "Theorizing Woman: Funu, Guojia, Jiating (Chinese Women, Chinese State, Chinese Family)" in *Scattered Hegemonies: Postmodernity and Transnational Feminist Practices*, ed. Inderpal Grewal and Caren Kaplan (Minneapolis: University of Minnesota Press, 1994), 173–196. I have discussed this issue in my essay, "Autobiographic Subjects and Diasporic Locations: *Meatless Days* and *Borderlands*," in the collection cited above.

19. Pandita Ramabai, *The Letters and Correspondence of Pandita Ramabai*, ed. A. B. Shah (Bombay: Maharashtra State Board for Literature and Culture, 1977), 17.

20. Dyer, *Pandita Ramabai*, 17.

21. Macnicol, *Pandita Ramabai*, 12.

22. Ibid., 13.

23. John Urry, *The Tourist Gaze: Leisure and Travel in Contemporary Societies* (London: Sage Publications, 1990), 4.

24. Chakravarty, "The Myth."

25. Ramabai, *Letters*, 7.

26. Ibid., 17.

27. Madhu Kishwar, introduction, *Women Bhakta Poets* (New Delhi: Manushi Trust, 1989), 3–8.

28. KumKum Sangari, "Mirabai and the Spiritual Economy of Bhakti," *Economic and Political Weekly* (July 7, 1990): 1464–1552.

29. Ruth Vanita, "Three Women Saints of Maharashtra," *Women Bhakta Poets* (New Delhi: Manushi Trust, 1989), 45–61.

30. Macnicol, *Pandita Ramabai*, 5.

31. Quoted in Rajas Krishnarao Dongre and Josephine Patterson, *Pandita Ramabai: A Life of Faith and Prayer* (Madras: Christian Literature Society, 1963), 12.

32. Ramabai, *Letters*, 25. Further references are given in the text.

33. Ibid.

34. Sengupta, *Pandita Ramabai*, 65.

35. Pandita Ramabai, *A Testimony* (Mukti Mission, 1917), quoted in Sengupta, *Pandita Ramabai*, 124.

36. Catherine Hall, in "Missionary Stories: Gender and Ethnicity in England in the 1830s and 1840s," in *Cultural Studies*, ed. Laurence Grossberg, Cary Nelson, and Paula Trichler (New York: Routledge, 1992), 240–276, remarks on the "ambivalence" of the Baptist missionary enterprise that combined belief in brotherhood with racism. I'm not sure that this "ambivalence" is one that can acknowledge the tremendous power differentials in the colonial missionary enterprise. Hall's essay, however, is extremely useful in delineating the location of the "mission family" and its gender relations.

37. E. F. Chapman, *Sketches of Some Distinguished Indian Women* (London, Calcutta: W. H. Allen & Co., Ltd., 1891).

38. Ibid., 39.

39. From Gardner's *Life of Nehemiah Goreh*, cited in Macnicol, *Pandita Ramabai*, 63.

40. Chapman, *Sketches*, 31.

41. Manoramabai, *Pandita Ramabai, The Widows' Friend* (Melbourne: George Robertson & Co., 1903), cited in Sengupta, *Pandita Ramabai*, 157.

42. The following information on the contents of the book come from Padmini Sengupta's description in *Pandita Ramabai*, 195–201.

43. This poem by a Lucy Larcom is also printed in *Letters*, 1.

44. Lata Mani, "Contentious Traditions," in *Recasting Women*, ed. KumKum Sangari and Sudesh Vaid (New Delhi: Kali for Women, 1989), 88–126.

45. For a good analysis of U.S. discourses of missionary benevolence in this century, see Caren Kaplan, "'Getting to Know You': Travel, Gender and the Politics of Postcolonial Representation in *Anna and the King of Siam* and *The King and I*," in *Postmodern Occasions*, ed. E. Ann Kaplan, Roman de la Campa, and Michael Sprinker (London: Verso, forthcoming).

46. While official accounts suggest that the famine years were 1876–1877, Ramabai states in her narrative that it had begun three years before that and had claimed her parents and sister.

47. Bodley, introduction, xiv.

48. Dyer, *Pandita Ramabai*, 23.

49. Ramabai, *Letters*, 256.

50. Rosalind O'Hanlon, *Caste, Conflict and Ideology* (Cambridge: Cambridge University Press, 1985), 83.

51. Ibid., 116.

52. Meenakshi Mukherjee, *Realism and Reality* (Delhi: Oxford University Press, 1985), 32.

53. J. C. Masselos, *Towards Nationalism* (Bombay: Popular Prakashan, 1974), 33–34.

54. O'Hanlon, *Caste, Conflict and Ideology*, 52.

55. Ibid., 96.

56. Quoted in Sengupta, *Pandita Ramabai*, 67.

57. In Macnicol, *Pandita Ramabai*, 82.

58. Chakravarty, "The Myth."

59. N. C. Kelkar, *Life and Times of Lokmanya Tilak* (1923; rpt. Delhi: Anupama Publications, 1987), 220.

60. Kelkar, *Life*, 223.

61. Chakravarty, "Whatever Happened to the Vedic Dasi?"

62. Partha Chatterjee discusses Indian historiography's relation between reformist and nationalist movements in "The Nationalist Resolution of the Women's Question." His point about the containment of the women's question in the home / outside binary, however, looks only at the male writers on women. My interest here is to see whether women were utilizing this binary as well.

63. Quoted in Dyer, *Pandita Ramabai*, 26.

64. Chakravarty, "Whatever Happened to the Vedic Dasi?"

65. Ram Bapat, *Pandita Ramabai* (unpublished ms., 1990), quoted in Rosalind O'Hanlon, *A Comparison between Men and Women: Tarabai Shinde and the Critique of Gender Relations in Colonial India* (Madras: Oxford University Press, 1994), 17.

66. Ibid., 44.

67. Ibid., 48.

68. Sornamma Appasamy, "Ramabai as I Knew Her," in *Pandita Ramabai*, ed. R. K. Dongre and Josephine Patterson (Madras: Christian Literature Society, 1963), 87–93.

69. For later repercussions of this figure see Geeta Patel, "Homely Housewives Run Amok: Lesbians in Marital Fixes," paper presented at the American Anthropology Association meeting, Atlanta, December 2, 1994.

70. Quoted in Dyer, *Pandita Ramabai*, 42.

71. Ramabai, *Testimony*, 73.

72. Kumari Jayawardena, *Feminism and Nationalism in the Third World* (London: Zed Books, 1986), 84–85.

73. Mukherjee, *Realism and Reality*, 28–29.

74. O'Hanlon, "Issues of Widowhood," 62–108.

75. Masselos, *Towards Nationalism*, 30–32.

76. See O'Hanlon, "Issues of Widowhood," 67, and Masselos, *Towards Nationalism*, 37.

77. O'Hanlon, "Issues of Widowhood," 67.

78. Masselos, *Towards Nationalism*, 92.

79. O'Hanlon, "Issues of Widowhood," 92.

80. Ramabai, *The High-Caste Hindu Woman*, 101.

81. Ibid., 28.

82. Ibid., 62.

83. Ibid., 67.

84. Ibid., 68.

85. Ibid.

86. "Pandita Ramabai," *Manushi* (May–June 1980): 25.

87. Ibid.

88. From Ramabai Ranade's *Himself*, trans. Katherine Gates, included in appendix 2 in *Pandita Ramabai*, ed. Dongre and Patterson, 112.

89. Parvati Athavale, *Hindu Widow*, trans. Rev. Justin E. Abbott (1928; rpt. New Delhi: Reliance Publishing House, 1986). Further references to this work appear in the text.

90. Kalyan Kumar Bannerjee, *Indian Freedom Movement Revolutionaries in America* (Calcutta: Jijnasa, 1969), 15.

91. Mukherjee, *Realism and Reality*.

Afterword

1. Geoffrey Bennington, "Postal Politics and the Institution of the Nation," in *Nation and Narration*, ed. Homi K. Bhabha (New York and London: Routledge, 1990), 121–137.

2. For instance, see Ella Shohat's essay, "Columbus, Palestine, and Arab-Jews: Towards a Relational Approach to Community Identity," in *Reflections on the Work of Edward Said: Cultural Identity and the Gravity of History*, ed. Keith Ansell-Pearson et al. (London: Lawrence and Wishart, forthcoming).

Bibliography

Acton, William. *Prostitution* (1857). Ed. Peter Fryer. London: MacGibbon & Kee, 1968.

Adams, Percy G. *Travel Literature and the Evolution of the Novel*. Lexington: University of Kentucky Press, 1983.

Ahmed, Leila. "Western Ethnocentrism and Perceptions of the Harem." *Feminist Studies* 8, no. 3 (1982): 521–534.

Alarcón, Norma. "The Theoretical Subject(s) of *This Bridge Called My Back* and Anglo-American Feminism." In *Making Face, Making Soul Haciendo Caras*. Ed. Gloria Anzaldua. San Francisco: An Aunt Lute Foundation Book, 1990: 356–369.

Ali, Masooma R. " 'The Lady of Shalott': A Feminist Reading." In *Woman, Image, Text*. Ed. Lola Chatterji. New Delhi: Trianka, 1986: 61–65.

Alloula, Malek. *The Colonial Harem*. Minneapolis: University of Minnesota Press, 1986.

Alphonse-Karkala, John B. *Indo-English Literature in the Nineteenth Century*. Mysore: The Literary Half-Yearly, University of Mysore, 1970.

Altick, Richard. *The English Common Reader*. Chicago: University of Chicago Press, 1957.

Anderson, Benedict. *Imagined Communities*. Rev. Ed. New York: Verso, 1991.

Anderson, Nancy Fix. *Woman against Women in Victorian England*. Bloomington: Indiana University Press, 1987.

Anzaldua, Gloria. *Borderlands/La Frontera*. San Francisco: Spinsters/Aunt Lute, 1987.

Appadurai, Arjun. Editor's comments. *Public Culture* 1, no. 1 (Fall 1988): 1–4.

Appasamy, Sornamma. "Ramabai as I Knew Her." In *Pandita Ramabai*. Ed. R. K. Dongre and Josephine Patterson. Madras: Christian Literature Society, 1963: 87–93.

Arnold, Matthew. *Culture and Anarchy*. Ed. Ian Gregor. Indianapolis: Bobbs-Merrill Educational Publishing, 1971.

——. *On the Study of Celtic Literature and Other Essays.* New York: Dutton, 1976.

Asaad, Thomas J. *Three Victorian Travellers.* London: Routledge and Kegan Paul, 1964.

Athavale, Parvati. *Hindu Widow.* Trans. Rev. Justin E. Abbott. 1928. Rpt. New Delhi: Reliance Publishing House, 1986.

Bailey, Peter. *Leisure and Class in Victorian England: Rational Recreation and the Context for Control, 1830–1885.* London: Routledge, 1978.

Ballhatchet, Kenneth. *Race, Sex and Class under the Raj: Imperial Attitudes and Policies and Their Critics, 1793–1905.* New York: St. Martin's Press, 1980.

Bannerjee, Sumanta. "Marginalization of Women's Popular Culture in Nineteenth Century Bengal." In *Recasting Women.* Ed. KumKum Sangari and Sudesh Vaid. New Delhi: Kali for Women, 1989: 127–179.

Bannerjee, Kalyan Kumar. *Indian Freedom Movement Revolutionaries in America.* Calcutta: Jijnasa, 1969.

Bannerji, Himani. "The Mirror of Class." *Economic and Political Weekly* (May 13, 1989): 1041–1051.

Barlow, Tani. Editor's introduction. *positions* 1, no. 1 (Spring 1993): v–vii.

——, ed. *Gender Politics in Modern China: Writing and Feminism.* Durham: Duke University Press, 1993.

——. "Theorizing Woman: Funu, Guojia, Jiating (Chinese Women, Chinese State, Chinese Family)." In *Scattered Hegemonies: Postmodernity and Transnational Feminist Practices.* Ed. Inderpal Grewal and Caren Kaplan. Minneapolis: University of Minnesota Press, 1994: 173–196.

Barnet, Richard J., and John Cavanagh. *Global Dreams: Imperial Corporations and the New World Order.* New York: Simon and Schuster, 1994.

Barrell, John. *The Idea of the Landscape and the Sense of Place.* Cambridge: Cambridge University Press, 1972.

——. *The Dark Side of the Landscape.* Cambridge: Cambridge University Press, 1980.

——. *The Political Theory of Painting from Reynolds to Hazlitt.* New Haven and London: Yale University Press, 1986.

Basch, Françoise. *Relative Creatures.* New York: Schocken Books.

Batten, Charles L., Jr. *Pleasurable Instruction: Form and Convention in Eighteenth Century Travel.* Berkeley: University of California Press, 1978.

Bayly, C. A. *Rulers, Townsmen and Bazaars.* Cambridge: Cambridge University Press, 1983.

Behdad, Ali. *Belated Travelers.* Durham and London: Duke University Press, 1994.

Bennington, Geoffrey. "Postal Politics and the Institution of the Nation." In *Nation and Narration.* Ed. Homi K. Bhabha. New York and London: Routledge, 1990: 121–137.

Berger, John with Jean Mohr. *A Seventh Man*. London and New York: Writers and Readers, 1975.

Bermingham, Ann. *Landscape and Ideology*. Berkeley: University of California Press, 1987.

Bernal, Martin. *Black Athena*. New Brunswick, N.J.: Rutgers University Press, 1987.

Bhabha, Homi. K. "Of Mimicry and Man: The Ambivalence of Colonial Discourse." *October* (Spring 1984): 125–133.

———. "DissemiNation: Time, Narrative, and the Margins of the Modern Nation." In *Nation and Narration*. Ed. Homi K. Bhabha. New York: Routledge, 1990: 291–322.

———. "Postcolonial Authority and Postmodern Guilt." In *Cultural Studies*. Ed. Cary Nelson, Paula A. Treichler, and Lawrence Grossberg. New York: Routledge, 1992: 56–65.

Bhana, Surendra. *Indentured Indian Emigrants to Natal*. New Delhi: Promilla & Co., 1991.

Bidwell, Robin. *Travellers in Arabia*. London: Hamlyn, 1976.

Birkett, Dea. *Spinsters Abroad*. London: Basil Blackwell, 1989.

Blake, Susan. "A Woman's Trek." In *Western Women and Imperialism*. Ed. Nupur Choudhuri and Margaret Strobel. Bloomington: Indiana University Press, 1992: 19–34.

Blanch, Lesley. *The Wilder Shores of Love*. 1954. New York: Carroll & Graf Publishers, Inc., 1982.

Bloom, Lisa. *Gender on Ice*. Minneapolis: University of Minnesota Press, 1993.

Bodley, Rachel. Introduction to *The High-Caste Hindu Woman*, by Pandita Ramabai Saraswati. Philadelphia: n.p., 1988.

Borthwick, Meredith. *The Changing Role of Women in Bengal 1849–1905*. Princeton: Princeton University Press, 1984.

Boserup, Ester. *Women's Role in Economic Development*. London: Allen and Unwin, 1970.

Boucherett, Jessie. "How to Provide for Superfluous Women." In *Woman's Work and Woman's Culture*. Ed. Josephine Butler. London: Macmillan and Co., 1869: 27–48.

Bourdieu, Pierre. *Outline of a Theory of Practice*. Cambridge: Cambridge University Press, 1977.

———. *Distinction*. Cambridge, Mass.: Harvard University Press, 1984.

Boyd-Kinnear, John. "The Social Position of Women in the Present Age." In *Woman's Work and Woman's Culture*. Ed. Josephine Butler. London: Macmillan, 1869: 331–367.

Brantlinger, Patrick. *Rule of Darkness*. Ithaca: Cornell University Press, 1988.

Brodie, F. M. *The Devil Drives: A Life of Richard F. Burton*. New York: W. W. Norton, 1967, 1971.

Brontë, Charlotte. *Jane Eyre.* 1847. London: Penguin Books, 1966.

Butler, Josephine, ed. *Woman's Work and Woman's Culture.* London: Macmillan and Co., 1869.

Burke, Edmund. *A Philosophical Enquiry into the Origin of Our Ideas of the Sublime and the Beautiful.* London: R. and J. Dodsley, 1764.

———. *Thoughts and Details on Scarcity.* London: E. Moxon, 1848.

Burton, Antoinette. "The White Woman's Burden." In *Western Women and Imperialism.* Ed. Nupur Choudhury and Margaret Strobel. Bloomington: Indiana University Press, 1992: 137–157.

Burton, Richard Francis. *Personal Narrative of a Pilgrimage to Al-Madinah and Mecca.* Reprint of 1893 Memorial Ed. in 2 vols. New York: Dover Publications Inc., 1964.

Buzard, James. *The Beaten Track.* Oxford: The Clarendon Press, 1993.

Calderón, Héctor, and José David Saldívar, eds. *Criticism in the Borderlands: Studies in Chicano Literature, Culture, and Ideology.* Durham: Duke University Press, 1991.

Callaway, Helen. *Gender, Culture and Empire: European Women in Colonial Nigeria.* Urbana: University of Illinois Press, 1987.

Carby, Hazel. *Reconstructing Womanhood: The Emergence of the Afro-American Woman Novelist.* New York: Oxford University Press, 1987.

Castle, Barbara. *Sylvia and Christabel Pankhurst.* Hammondsworth: Penguin Books Ltd., 1987.

Caygill, Marjorie. *The Story of the British Museum.* London: British Museum Publications, 1981.

Center for Contemporary Cultural Studies. *The Empire Strikes Back: Race and Racism in 70's Britain.* London: Routledge, 1992, 1982.

Chakrabarty, Dipesh. "The Difference-Defferal of (A) Colonial Modernity: Public Debates on Domesticity in British Bengal." *History Workshop Journal* 36 (1993): 1–33.

Chakraborty, Usha. *Condition of Bengali Women around the 2nd Half of the 19th Century.* Calcutta, 1963.

Chakravarty, Uma. "Whatever Happened to the Vedic Dasi?" In *Recasting Women.* Ed. KumKum Sangari and Sudesh Vaid. New Delhi: Kali for Women, 1989: 27–87.

———. "Cultural Identity, Notions of Womanhood and Feminist Consciousness in a Postcolonial Society." Unpublished paper cited in Amrita Chhachhi, "Forced Identities: The State, Communalism, Fundamentalism and Women in India." In *Women, Islam and the State.* Ed. Deniz Kandiyoti. Philadelphia: Temple University Press, 1991: 155.

———. "The Myth of 'Patriots' and 'Traitors': Pandita Ramabai, Brahmanical Patriarchy, and Militant Hindu Nationalism." In *Gender, Class, and Nation:*

The Life and Times of Pandita Ramabai. New Delhi: Kali for Women, forthcoming.

Chandra, Bholanath. *The Travels of a Hindoo to Various Parts of Bengal and Upper India.* London: N. Trubner & Co., 1869.

Chapman, E. F. *Sketches of Some Distinguished Indian Women.* London, Calcutta: W. H. Allen & Co., Ltd., 1891.

Chatterjee, Partha. "The Nationalist Resolution of the Women's Question." In *Recasting Women.* Ed. KumKum Sangari and Sudesh Vaid. New Delhi: Kali for Women, 1989: 233–253.

——. *Nationalist Thought and the Colonial World.* Tokyo, 1986; rpt. Minneapolis: University of Minnesota Press, 1993.

——. *The Nation and Its Fragments.* Princeton: Princeton University Press, 1993.

Chatterji, Bankimchandra. "Letters on Hinduism." In *Bankim Racanabali.* Ed. Hogesh Chandra Bagal. Calcutta: Sahitya Sansad, 1969.

Choudhury, Nupur, and Margaret Strobel, eds. *Western Women and Imperialism.* Bloomington: Indiana University Press, 1992.

Choudhury, Nupur. "Shawls, Jewelry, Curry, and Rice in Victorian Britain." In *Western Women and Imperialism.* Ed. Nupur Choudhury and Margaret Strobel. Bloomington: Indiana University Press, 1992: 231–246.

Choudhury, Prem. "Customs in a Peasant Economy." In *Recasting Women.* Ed. KumKum Sangari and Sudesh Vaid. New Delhi: Kali for Women, 1989: 303–336.

Clifford, James. *The Predicament of Culture.* Cambridge: Harvard University Press, 1988.

——. "Notes on Travel and Theory." *Inscriptions* 5 (1989): 177–188.

Clubbe, John, and Earnest J. Lovell, Jr. *English Romanticism.* Dekalb: Northern Illinois University Press, 1983.

Coe, Charles Norton. *Wordsworth and the Literature of Travel.* New York: Bookman Associates, 1953.

Cohen, Ed. *Talk on the Wilde Side.* New York: Routledge, 1993.

Cohn, Bernard. *The Anthropologist among the Historians.* Delhi: Oxford University Press, 1987.

——. "The Past in the Present: India as Museum of Mankind." Unpublished ms., n.d.

——. "The Transformation of Objects into Artifacts, Antiquities and Art in 19th Century India." Unpublished ms., n.d.

Collins, Wilkie. *The Woman in White.* In *The Moonstone and The Woman in White.* New York: The Modern Library, 1937.

Cook's Tourist's Handbook for Egypt, The Nile and The Desert. London: Thomas Cook and Son, 1897.

Coolidge, W. A. B. *Swiss Travel and Swiss Guide-Books*. London: Longmans, Green & Co., 1889.

Crook, Joseph Mordaunt. *The British Museum*. London: Lane, 1972.

Copley, Stephen, ed. *Literature and the Social Order*. London and Dover, N.H.: Croom Helm, 1984.

Das, Devendra N. *Sketches of Hindoo Life*. London: Chapman and Hall, 1887.

Das, Harihar. *Life and Letters of Toru Dutt*. London: Oxford University Press, 1921.

David, Dierdre. *Intellectual Women and Victorian Patriarchy*. London: Macmillan, 1987.

Davis, Angela. *Women, Race and Class*. New York: Random House, 1981.

Dickens, Charles. *American Notes*. 1842. Rpt. Gloucester, Mass.: Peter Smith, 1968.

Dodd, Philip. "Englishness and the National Culture." In *Englishness: Politics and Culture 1880–1920*. Ed. Philip Dodd and Robert Colls. London: Croom Helm, 1986: 1–28.

Donaldson, Laura. *Decolonizing Feminism: Race, Gender and Empire-Building*. Chapel Hill: University of North Carolina Press, 1992.

Dongre, R. K., and Josephine Patterson, eds. *Pandita Ramabai: A Life of Faith and Prayer*. Madras: Christian Literature Society, 1963.

Dutt, Toru. "Our Casuarina Tree." In *A Slender Sheaf Gleaned in French and Indian Fields*. 1876. Ed. Charles Skilton. Rpt. Edinburgh: The Fortune Press, 1977.

———. "Bianca, or The Young Spanish Maid." In *The Indian Field* (Calcutta) (January–April 1878).

———. *Le Journal de Mademoiselle d'Arvers*. Ed. Clarisse Bader. Paris: Didier, Library Academique, 1879.

Dyer, Helen S. *Pandita Ramabai: The Story of Her Life*. London: Morgan and Scott, 1900.

Elder, John. *Imagining the Earth: Poetry and the Vision of Nature*. Urbana and Chicago: University of Illinois Press, 1985.

Eliot, George. *Middlemarch*. 1871. Boston: Houghton, Mifflin, Riverside edition, 1968.

Ellis, Henry. *Elgin and Phigaleian Marbles of Classical Ages*. London: Charles Knight, 1846.

———. *The Towneley Marbles*. London: Charles Knight, 1848.

Enloe, Cynthia. *Bananas, Beaches and Bases*. Berkeley: University of California Press, 1989.

Fahnestock, Jeanne. "The Heroine of Irregular Features: Physiognomy and Conventions of Heroine Description." *Victorian Studies* 24, no. 3 (1981): 325–350.

Fawcett, Millicent. "The Women's Suffrage Movement." In *The Woman Question in Europe*. Ed. Theodore Stanton. London: G. P. Putnam's Sons, 1884: 1–29.

Foucault, Michel. *Power/Knowledge: Selected Interviews and Other Writings*. Ed. Colin Gordon. New York: Pantheon Books, 1980.

Fussell, Paul. *Abroad: British Literary Travelling Between the Wars*. Oxford: Oxford University Press, 1980.

Garber, Marjorie. *Vested Interests: Cross-Dressing and Cultural Anxiety*. New York: Routledge, 1992.

Gaskell, Mrs. *Mary Barton*. London: John Lehmann, 1947.

Ghosh, Amitav. *In an Antique Land*. New York: Vintage Books, 1992.

Giddings, Paula. *Where and When I Enter*. New York: William Morrow and Co., 1984.

Gidumal, Dayaram. *Behramji M. Malabari: A Biographical Sketch*. London: T. Fisher Unwin, 1892.

Gilbert, Sandra, and Susan Gubar. *Madwoman in the Attic: The Woman Writer and the Nineteenth-Century Literary Imagination*. New Haven: Yale University Press, 1980.

Gilpin, William. *Three Essays on Picturesque Beauty; On Picturesque Travel; and on Sketching Landscape*. London: R. Blamire, 1803.

Gilroy, Paul. "Ethnic Absolutism and Cultural Studies." In *Cultural Studies*. Ed. Lawrence Grossberg et al. New York: Routledge, 1992: 187–198.

Glenn, Evelyn Nakano. *Issei, Nisei, War Bride*. Philadelphia: Temple University Press, 1986.

Golby, J. M., and A. W. Purdue. *The Civilization of the Crowd*. London: Batsford Academic and Educational, 1984.

Grewal, Inderpal. "The Political Aesthetic of Victorian Travel." Ph.D. diss., University of California, Berkeley, 1987.

——, and Caren Kaplan, eds. *Scattered Hegemonies: Postmodernity and Transnational Feminist Practices*. Minneapolis: University of Minnesota Press, 1994.

——. "Autobiographic Subjects and Diasporic Locations: *Meatless Days* and *Borderlands*." In *Scattered Hegemonies: Postmodernity and Transnational Feminist Practices*. Ed. Inderpal Grewal and Caren Kaplan. Minneapolis: University of Minnesota Press, 1994: 231–254.

Guide to the Beauties of the British Museum, A. London: Thomas and George Underwood, 1826.

Gupta, Akhil. "The Location of 'The Indigenous' in Critiques of Modernity." Paper delivered at the South Asia conference, Berkeley, Calif., 19 February 1993.

Hall, Catherine. "Missionary Stories: Gender and Ethnicity in England in the 1830s and 1840s." In *Cultural Studies*. Ed. Laurence Grossberg, Cary Nelson, and Paula Trichler. New York: Routledge, 1992: 240–276.

Hardie, Martin. "Samuel Palmer." In *The Old Water-Colour Society's Club*, vol. 4. Ed. Randall Davies. London: 5A Pall Mall, 1927: 36.

Harrison, B. "Teetotal Chartism." *History* 58 (1973): 197.

Hartmann, Heidi. "Capitalism, Patriarchy, and Job Segregation by Sex." In *Classes, Power, and Conflict*. Ed. Anthony Giddens and David Held. Berkeley: University of California Press, 1982: 446–469.

Hatem, Mervat. "Through Each Other's Eyes." In *Western Women and Imperialism*. Ed. Nupur Choudhury and Margaret Strobel. Bloomington: Indiana University Press, 1992: 35–58.

Heinzelman, Kurt. "The Cult of Domesticity." In *Romanticism and Feminism*. Ed. Anne Mellor. Bloomington: Indiana University Press, 1988: 52–78.

Hibbert, Christopher. *The Grand Tour*. New York: G. P. Putnam's Sons, 1969.

Hicks, D. Emily. *Border Writing*. Minneapolis: University of Minnesota Press, 1991.

Himmelfarb, Gertrude. *The Idea of Poverty*. New York: Alfred A. Knopf, 1984.

Hipple, W. J. *The Beautiful, the Sublime and the Picturesque in Eighteenth Century British Aesthetic Theory*. Carbondale: University of Illinois Press, 1957.

Hobsbawn, E. J. *The Age of Revolution*. New York and Toronto: New American Library, 1962.

Hollis, Patricia. *Class and Conflict in Nineteenth-Century English, 1815–1850*. London and Boston: Routledge & Kegan Paul, 1973.

Hossain, Rokeya Sakhawat. *Inside Seclusion: The Avarodhbasini of Rokeya Sakhawat Hossain*. Ed. and trans. Roshan Jahan. Dacca: Women for Women, 1981.

Hudson, Kenneth. *A Social History of Museums*. London: Macmillan, 1975.

Hussey, Christopher. *The Picturesque: Studies in a Point of View*. London: Putnam, 1927.

Hyam, Ronald. *Empire and Sexuality: The British Experience*. Manchester and New York: Manchester University Press, 1990.

Ibn Battuta: Travels in Asia and Africa. Trans. and selected by H. A. R. Gibb. New Delhi: Saeed International, rpt. 1990.

Iyer, Pico. *Video Night in Kathmandu*. New York: Alfred Knopf, 1988.

Jayawardena, Kumari. *Feminism and Nationalism in the Third World*. London: Zed Books, 1986.

Johnson, Richard. "Really Useful Knowledge: Radical Education and Working-Class Culture." In *Working-Class Culture*. Ed. J. Clarke, C. Critchen, and Richard Johnson. New York: St. Martin's Press, 1979.

Joshi, Svati, ed. *Rethinking English*. New Delhi: Trianka, 1991.

Kabbani, Rana. *Europe's Myths of Orient*. Bloomington: Indiana University Press, 1986.

——. " 'Getting to Know You': Travel, Gender and the Politics of Postcolonial Representation in *Anna and the King of Siam* and *The King and I*." In *Late*

Imperial Culture. Ed. E. Ann Kaplan, Roman de la Campa, and Michael Sprinker. London: Verso, 1995: 33–52.

———. *Questions of Travel: Postmodern Discourses of Displacement.* Durham: Duke University Press, 1996.

———. "Deterritorializations: The Rewriting of Home and Exile in Western Feminist Discourse." In *The Nature and Context of Minority Discourse.* Ed. Abdul R. JanMohammed and David Lloyd. New York: Oxford University Press, 1990: 357–368.

———, and Inderpal Grewal. "Transnational Feminist Cultural Studies: Beyond the Marxism / Poststructuralism / Feminism Divides," *positions* 2, no. 2 (Fall 1994): 430–445.

Karlekar, Malavika. *Voices from Within.* Delhi: Oxford University Press, 1991.

Kaviraj, Sudipta. "The Imaginary Institution of India." New Delhi: Teen Murti Publications, Nehru Memorial Museum and Library, 1991. 2nd series, no. 42.

———. "On the Construction of Colonial Power: Structure, Discourse, Hegemony." New Delhi: Teen Murti Publications, 1991. 2nd series, no. 35.

Keay, John. *Eccentric Travelers.* Los Angeles: Jeremy P. Tarcher Inc., 1982.

Kelkar, N. C. *Life and Times of Lokmanya Tilak.* 1923. Rpt. Delhi: Anupama Publications, 1987.

Kinglake, Alexander. *Eothen.* 1844. Philadelphia: J. B. Lippincott Company, 1912.

Kingsley, Mary. *West African Studies.* London: Frank Cass & Co. Ltd., 1964.

Kipling, Rudyard. *From Sea to Sea.* 1899. Garden City: Doubleday, 1913.

Kishwar, Madhu. Introduction to *Women Bhakta Poets.* New Delhi: Manushi Trust, 1989.

———. "The Daughters of Aryavarta." In *Women in Colonial India.* Ed. J. Krishnamurty. Delhi: Oxford University Press, 1989: 78–114.

Knight, Charles. *The Old Printer and the Modern Press.* London: J. Murray, 1854.

Knight, Richard Payne. *The Landscape, a Didactic Poem in Three Books Addressed to Uvedale Price.* London: W. Bulmer & Co., 1794.

Kosambi, Meera. "Women, Emancipation and Equality." *Economic and Political Weekly* (October 29, 1988): WS38–WS49.

———. "Girl-Brides and Socio-Legal Change." *Economic and Political Weekly* (August 3, 1991): 1857–1868.

Lacey, Candida Ann. *Barbara Leigh Smith Bodichon and the Langham Place Group.* London and New York: Routledge and Kegan Paul, 1987.

Lal, Brij V. "Kunti's Cry: Indentured Women on Fiji Plantations." In *Women in Colonial India.* Ed. J. Krishnamurty. Delhi: Oxford University Press, 1989: 163–179.

Larcom, Lucy. "Ramabai," in *Letters*, i.

Lawrence, John, and Audrey Woodiwiss, eds. *The Journals of Honoria Lawrence.* London: Hodder and Stoughton, 1980.

Layoun, Mary. *Travels of a Genre: Ideology and the Modern Novel.* Princeton, N.J.: Princeton University Press, 1990.

Liddle, Joanna, and Rama Joshi. *Daughters of Independence: Gender, Class and Caste in India.* Delhi: Kali for Women, 1986.

Liu, Lydia. "Translingual Practice: The Discourse of Individualism between China and the West." *positions* 1, no. 1 (Spring 1993): 160–193.

——. "Gender, Subjectivity and Discourse: The Female Tradition in Twentieth Century Literature." In *Scattered Hegemonies.* Ed. Inderpal Grewal and Caren Kaplan. Minneapolis: University of Minnesota Press, 1994: 37–62.

Lloyd, David. *Nationalism and Minor Literature.* Berkeley: University of California Press, 1987.

Long, G. *The British Museum: Egyptian Antiquities.* The Library of Entertaining Knowledge. London: Charles Knight, 1832.

Lowe, Lisa. *Critical Terrains.* Ithaca: Cornell University Press, 1991.

Lowes, John Livingston. *The Road to Xanadu.* Boston and New York: Houghton, Mifflin, 1927.

MacCannell, Dean. *The Tourist: A New Theory of the Leisure Class.* New York: Schocken Books, 1976.

Mackenzie, John, ed. *Imperialism and Popular Culture.* Manchester: Manchester University Press, 1986.

——. *Propaganda and Empire.* Manchester: Manchester University Press, 1984.

Macnicol, Nicol. *Pandita Ramabai.* Calcutta: Association Press, 1926.

Malabari, Behramji. *Gujarat and the Gujaratis.* 3d ed. 1889. Rpt. New Delhi: Mittal Publications, 1983.

——. *The Indian Eye on English Life.* London: A. Constable, 1893.

Mangan, J. A. " 'The Grit of Our Forefathers': Invented Traditions, Propaganda and Imperialism." In *Imperialism and Popular Culture.* Ed. John Mackenzie. Manchester: Manchester University Press, 1986: 113–139.

Mani, Lata. "Contentious Traditions: The Debate on Sati in Colonial India." In *Recasting Women.* Ed. KumKum Sangari and Sudesh Vaid. New Delhi: Kali for Women, 1989: 88–126.

——. "Multiple Mediations: Feminist Scholarship in the Age of Multinational Reception." *Inscriptions* 5 (1989): 1–24.

Martin, Biddy, and Chandra Mohanty. "Feminist Politics: What's Home Got to Do with It?" In *Feminist Studies/Critical Studies.* Ed. Teresa de Lauretis. Bloomington: Indiana University Press, 1986: 191–212.

Martineau, Harriet. *Eastern Life, Present and Past.* London: Edward Moxon, 1848.

——. *A Complete Guide to the English Lakes.* Windermere: J. Garnett; London: Whittaker, 1855.

——. *British Rule in India.* London: Smith, Elder & Co.; Bombay: Smith, Taylor & Co., 1857.

————. *Suggestions Towards the Future Government of India*. London: Smith, Elder, & Co., 1858.

Masjeed, Javed. *Ungoverned Imaginings*. Oxford: Clarendon Press, 1992.

Masselos, J. C. *Towards Nationalism*. Bombay: Popular Prakashan, 1974.

Mayhew, Henry. *London Labour and the London Poor*. 1861. New York: Dover Publications, 1968.

Middleton, Lucy, ed. *Women in the Labour Movement: The British Experience*. London: Croom Helm, 1987.

Mill, James. *The History of British India*. Ed. John Clive. Chicago: University of Chicago Press, 1975.

Mill, John Stuart. *Principles of Political Economy*. 1848.

Mitchell, Juliet. *Women's Estate*. New York: Random House-Vintage, 1973.

Mitchell, Timothy. "Orientalism and the Exhibitory Order." In *Colonialism and Culture*. Ed. Nicholas B. Dirks. Ann Arbor: University of Michigan Press, 1992: 289–318.

Mitter, Partha. *Much Maligned Monsters*. Oxford: Clarendon Press, 1977.

Mohanty, Chandra Talpade. "Cartographies of Struggle: Third World Women and the Politics of Feminism." In *Third World Women and the Politics of Feminism*. Ed. Chandra Talpade Mohanty et al. Bloomington: Indiana University Press, 1991: 1–47.

————. "Under Western Eyes." In *Third World Women and the Politics of Feminism*. Ed. Chandra Talpade Mohanty et al. Bloomington: Indiana University Press, 1991: 51–80.

Montesquieu. *Persian Letters*. 1721. Trans. C. J. Betts. New York: Penguin Books, 1973.

Morris, William. *News From Nowhere and Selected Writings and Designs*. Hammondsworth: Penguin, 1984.

Mukherjee, Meenakshi. *Realism and Reality*. Delhi: Oxford University Press, 1985.

Murdoch, John. *The Discovery of the Lake District*. Grasmere: Trustees of Dove Cottage, 1982.

Murray, John. *Handbook for Travellers in Egypt*. London: John Murray, 1858.

————. *The Imperial Guide to India*. London: John Murray, 1904.

Murray, John, IV. *John Murray III, 1808–1892: A Brief Memoir*. London: J. Murray, 1919.

Murshid, Ghulam. *Reluctant Debutante: Response of Bengali Women to Modernization, 1849–1905*. Rajshahi: Rajshahi University, 1983.

Nash, June and Maria Patricia Fernandez-Kelly, eds. *Women, Men and the International Division of Labor*. Albany: State University of New York Press, 1983.

Neff, Wanda Fraiken. *Victorian Working Women*. New York: Columbia University Press, 1929.

Nethercott, Arthur H. *The Last Four Lives of Annie Besant*. Chicago: University of Chicago Press, 1963.

New Library of Useful Knowledge. *The British Museum in Four Sections, or, How to View the Whole at Once*. London: Cradock & Co., 1852.

O'Hanlon, Rosalind. *Caste, Conflict and Ideology*. Cambridge: Cambridge University Press, 1985.

——. "Issues of Widowhood: Gender and Resistance in Colonial Western India." In *Contesting Power: Resistance and Everyday Social Relations in South Asia*. Ed. Douglas Haynes and Gyan Prakash. Delhi: Oxford University Press, 1991: 62–108.

——. *A Comparison Between Men and Women: Tarabai Shinde and the Critique of Gender Relations in Colonial India*. Madras: Oxford University Press, 1994.

Ong, Aihwa. *Spirits of Resistance and Capitalist Discipline*. Albany: State University of New York Press, 1987.

Osborn, James M. "Travel Literature and the Rise of Neo-Hellenism in England." In *Literature as a Mode of Travel*. Ed. Paul Fussel Jr. New York: New York Public Library, 1963.

"Pandita Ramabai." *Manushi* (May–June 1980): 25.

Pankhurst, E. Sylvia. *India and the Earthly Paradise*. 1926. Delhi: B. R. Publishing Corporation, 1985.

Pratt, Mary Louise. *Imperial Eyes*. New York and London: Routledge, 1992.

Price, Uvedale. *An Essay on the Picturesque as Compared with the Sublime and the Beautiful*. London: J. Robson, 1842.

Raina, Badri. "A Note on Language and the Politics of English in India." In *Rethinking English*. Ed. Svati Joshi. New Delhi: Trianka, 1991: 264–279.

Rajan, Rajeswari Sunder. "Male Mentors and the Female Imagination: George Eliot's Intellectual Background." In *Woman, Image, Text*. Ed. Lola Chatterji. New Delhi: Trianka, 1986: 116–132.

Ramabai, Pandita. *The High-Caste Hindu Woman*. Philadelphia, 1888.

——. *A Testimony*. Kedgaon: Mukti Mission, 1917.

——. *The Letters and Correspondence of Pandita Ramabai*. Comp. Sister Geraldine. Ed. A. B. Shah. Bombay: Maharashtra State Board for Literature and Culture, 1977.

Raychoudhuri, Tapan. *Europe Reconsidered*. Delhi: Oxford University Press, 1988.

Read, Charles Hercules, and Ormonde Maddock Dalton. *Antiquities from the City of Benin*. London: British Museum, 1899.

Repton, Humphrey. *An Enquiry into the Changes of Taste in Landscape Gardening*. London: J. Taylor, 1806.

Rich, Adrienne. "Notes Toward a Politics of Location." *Blood, Bread and Poetry: Selected Prose, 1979–1985*. New York: W. W. Norton, 1986: 210–231.

Richard, Alfred Bates, and St. Clare Baddeley. *A Sketch of the Career of Richard F. Burton*. London: Waterlow & Sons Ltd., 1886.

Richards, Thomas. *The Commodity Culture of Victorian England: Advertising and Spectacle, 1851–1914.* Stanford: Stanford University Press, 1990.

Ridley, Hugh. *Images of Imperial Rule.* London: Croom Helm; New York: St. Martin's Press, 1983.

Romero, Patricia W. *E. Sylvia Pankhurst.* New Haven: Yale University Press, 1987.

Rosaldo, Renato. *Culture and Truth.* Boston: Beacon Press, 1989.

Rosen, Andrew. *Rise Up, Women!* London and Boston: Routledge & Kegan Paul, 1974.

Ross, Marlon. "Romantic Quest and Conquest: Troping Masculine Power in the Crisis of Poetic Identity." In *Romanticism and Feminism.* Ed. Anne Mellor. Bloomington: Indiana University Press, 1988: 26–51.

Rover, Constance. *Women's Suffrage and Party Politics in Britain 1866–1914.* London: Routledge and Kegan Paul, 1967.

Ruskin, John. *Modern Painters.* London: Smith, Elder & Co., 1856–60.

Rydell, Robert. *All the World's a Fair: Visions of Empire at American International Expositions, 1876–1916.* Chicago: University of Chicago Press, 1984.

Sachau, Edward, ed. *Alberuni's India.* New Delhi: Atlantic Publishers, 1989.

Said, Edward. *Orientalism.* New York: Vintage Books, 1979.

———. *The World, the Text, and the Critic.* Cambridge: Harvard University Press, 1983.

Sales, Roger. *English Literature in History 1780–1830.* New York: St. Martin's Press, 1983.

Sangari, KumKum. "Mirabai and the Spiritual Economy of Bhakti." *Economic and Political Weekly* (July 7, 1990): 1464–1552.

———, and Sudesh Vaid, eds. *Recasting Women.* New Delhi: Kali for Women, 1989.

Saradamoni, K. "Changing Land Relations and Women: A Case Study of Palghat District, Kerala." In *Women and Rural Transformation.* Ed. Rekha Mehta and K. Saradamoni. New Delhi: Concept Publishing Co., 1983.

Sarkar, Sumit. "The Woman Question in Nineteenth-Century Bengal." In *Women and Culture.* Ed. KumKum Sangari and Sudesh Vaid. Bombay: SNDT Women's University, 1985: 157–172.

Schwartz, Roberto. *Misplaced Ideas.* London: Verso, 1992.

Sengupta, Padmini. *Pioneer Women of India.* Bombay: Thacker, 1944.

———. *Pandita Ramabai Saraswati: Her Life and Work.* London: Asia Publishing House, 1970.

Sharpe, Jenny. *Allegories of Empire.* Minneapolis: University of Minnesota Press, 1993.

Shinde, Tarabai. *A Comparison Between Women and Men.* Trans. Rosalind O'Hanlon. In *A Comparison Between Women and Men: Tarabai Shinde and the*

Critique of Gender Relations in Colonial India. Madras: Oxford University Press, 1994.

Shohat, Ella. "Gender and the Culture of Empire: Towards a Feminist Ethnography of the Cinema." *Quarterly Review of Film and Video* 13, nos. 1–3: 45–84.

———. "Columbus, Palestine, and Arab-Jews: Towards a Relational Approach to Community Identity." In *Reflections on the Work of Edward Said: Cultural Identity and the Gravity of History.* Ed. Keith Ansell-Pearson et al. London: Lawrence and Wishart, forthcoming.

Sinha, Pradip. *Nineteenth-Century Bengal.* Calcutta: Firma K.L. Mukhopadhyay, 1965.

Skilton, Charles. Preface, *A Slender Sheaf Gleaned in French and English Fields* by Toru Dutt. Edinburgh: The Fortune Press, 1977.

Smiles, Samuel. *A Publisher and his Friends.* London: J. Murray, 1911.

Spivak, Gayatri. "Three Women's Texts and a Critique of Imperialism." In *"Race," Writing and Difference.* Ed. Henry Louis Gates. Chicago: University of Chicago Press, 1985: 262–280.

———. *In Other Worlds.* New York and London: Routledge, 1988.

———. "Political Economy of Women as Seen by a Literary Critic." In *Coming to Terms: Feminism, Theory, Politics.* Ed. Elizabeth Weed. New York and London: Routledge, 1989: 219.

———. *The Post-Colonial Critic.* Ed. Sarah Harasym. New York and London: Routledge, 1990.

———. "Scattered Speculations on the Question of Culture Studies." In *Outside in the Teaching Machine.* New York and London: Routledge, 1993: 255–284.

———. *Outside in the Teaching Machine.* New York and London: Routledge, 1993.

Starobinski, Jean. *The Invention of Liberty.* Geneva: Albert Skirra, 1964.

Stewart, Susan. *On Longing.* Baltimore: Johns Hopkins University Press, 1984.

Stoler, Ann Laura. "Rethinking Colonial Categories: European Communities and the Boundaries of Rule." *Comparative Studies in Society and History* 13, no. 1 (1989): 134–161.

Strobel, Margaret. *European Women and the Second British Empire.* Bloomington: Indiana University Press, 1991.

Suleri, Sara. *The Rhetoric of English India.* Chicago: University of Chicago Press, 1992.

Summerfield, Penny. "Patriotism and Empire: Music-Hall Entertainment, 1870–1914." In *Imperialism and Popular Culture.* Ed. John Mackenzie. Manchester: Manchester University Press, 1986: 17–48.

Swinglehurst, Edmund. *The Romantic Journey.* New York: Harper & Row, 1974.

Takaki, Ron. *Strangers from a Different Shore.* New York: Little, Brown, 1989.

Thackeray, W. M. *Notes of a Journey from Cornhill to Grand Cairo,* in *Works,* vol. 11. 1845. Rpt. Chicago and New York: Nathaniel Moore, 1910.

Tharu, Susie. "Tracing Savitri's Pedigree." In *Recasting Women*. Ed. KumKum Sangari and Sudesh Vaid. New Delhi: Kali for Women, 1989: 254–268.

Thompson, E. Maude. *A Guide to the British Museum*. London: British Museum Trustees, 1890.

Thompson, E. P. *The Making of the English Working Class*. New York: Vintage Books, 1963.

———. *The Poverty of Theory and Other Essays*. New York: Monthly Review Press, 1978.

Torgovnik, Marianna. *Gone Primitive*. Chicago: University of Chicago Press, 1990.

Trivedi, Harish. "Reading English, Writing Hindi: English Literature and Indian Creative Writing." In *Rethinking English*. Ed. Svati Joshi. New Delhi: Trianka, 1991: 181–205.

Trollope, Joanna. *Britannia's Daughters*. London: Hutchinson, 1983.

Urry, John. *The Tourist Gaze: Leisure and Travel in Contemporary Societies*. London: Sage Publications, 1990.

Vanita, Ruth. "Three Women Saints of Maharashtra." *Women Bhakta Poets*. New Delhi: Manushi Trust, 1989: 45–61.

Visram, Rozina. *Ayahs, Lascars and Princes: The Story of Indians in Britain 1700–1947*. London: Pluto Press, 1986.

Viswanathan, Gauri. *The Masks of Conquest*. New York: Columbia University Press, 1989.

Visweswaran, Kamala. *Fictions of Feminist Ethnography*. Minneapolis: University of Minnesota Press, 1994.

———. "Family Subjects: An Ethnography of the 'Woman Question' in Indian Nationalism." Ph.D. Thesis, Stanford University, 1990.

Walkowitz, Judith. *City of Dreadful Delight: Narratives of Sexual Danger in Late-Victorian London*. Chicago: University of Chicago Press, 1992.

Wallace, Anne D. *Walking Literature and English Culture*. Oxford: Clarendon Press, 1993.

Williams, Raymond. *The Country and the City*. New York: Oxford University Press, 1973.

Wilton, Andrew, ed. *Constable's "English Landscape Scenery."* London: British Museum Prints and Drawings Series, 1979.

Wood, Christopher. *Victorian Panorama*. London: Faber, 1976.

Wordsworth, William. *A Guide Through the District of the Lakes*. 1846. London: Rupert Hart-Davis, 1951.

———. *The Prelude*. Norton Critical Ed. Ed. Jonathan Wordsworth, M. H. Abrams, and Stephen Gill. New York: W. W. Norton, 1979.

Young, Robert. *White Mythologies*. London and New York: Routledge, 1990.

Index

About the Author

Inderpal Grewal is associate professor of women's studies at
San Francisco State University. She is coeditor (with Caren Kaplan)
of *Scattered Hegemonies: Postmodernity and Transnational
Feminist Practices.*